21 世纪高职高专规划教材·机电系列

现代机电专业英语
（第 2 版）

杨承先　杨璐维　张　琦　编著

清华大学出版社
北京交通大学出版社
·北京·

内 容 简 介

本书是为现代机电技术专业编写的专业英语教材,全书共分为4篇12章:第1篇是基础篇,全面讲述了该学科专业英语阅读和翻译所必需的基础知识;第2篇是阅读篇,系统地阐述了专业英语阅读的方法和技巧;第3篇是翻译篇,总结了专业英语翻译的基本方法与技巧;第4篇是应用篇,根据现代机电设备的专业特点及所涉及的相关内容,分6个专题,精选相关课文36篇,其中精读24篇、泛读12篇,作为学习现代机电专业英语的范文。每章均附有课文注释、阅读文章和练习,供学习训练之用。全书最后给出了课文的参考译文和练习的参考答案。

本书可作为大专院校现代机电专业(包括机电技术、机电一体化、数控技术等)专业英语教材,也可作为相关技术人员学习现代机电技术专业英语的自学教材或参考书。

本书封面贴有清华大学出版社防伪标签,无标签者不得销售。
版权所有,侵权必究。侵权举报电话:010-62782989　13501256678　13801310933

图书在版编目(CIP)数据

现代机电专业英语/杨承先,杨璐维,张琦编著. —2版. —北京:北京交通大学出版社,2012.6 (2018.4重印)
 21世纪高职高专规划教材·机电系列
 ISBN 978-7-5121-1073-1

Ⅰ. ①现… Ⅱ. ①杨… ②杨… ③张… Ⅲ. ①机电工业-英语-高等职业教育-教材 Ⅳ. ①H31

中国版本图书馆 CIP 数据核字(2012)第154555号

责任编辑:高振宇
出版发行:清 华 大 学 出 版 社　邮编:100084　电话:010-62776969
　　　　　北京交通大学出版社　邮编:100044　电话:010-51686414
印　刷　者:北京时代华都印刷有限公司
经　　　销:全国新华书店
开　　　本:185×260　印张:15.25　字数:236千字
版　　　次:2005年4月第1版　2012年8月第2版　2018年4月第3次印刷
书　　　号:ISBN 978-7-5121-1073-1/H·270
印　　　数:5 801~7 300册　定价:29.00元

本书如有质量问题,请向北京交通大学出版社质监组反映。对您的意见和批评,我们表示欢迎和感谢。
投诉电话:010-51686043,51686008;传真:010-62225406;E-mail:press@bjtu.edu.cn。

21世纪高职高专规划教材·机电系列
编审委员会成员名单

主任委员	李兰友	边奠英			
副主任委员	周学毛	崔世钢	王学彬	丁桂芝	赵 伟
	韩瑞功	汪志达			
委　　员	（按姓名笔画排序）				
	马 辉	万志平	万振凯	王永平	王建明
	尤晓昕	丰继林	左文忠	叶 华	叶 伟
	付晓光	付慧生	冯平安	江 中	佟立本
	刘 炜	刘建民	刘 晶	曲建民	孙培民
	邢素萍	华铨平	吕新平	陈小东	陈月波
	李长明	李 可	李志奎	李 琳	李源生
	李群明	李静东	邱希春	沈才梁	宋维堂
	汪 繁	张文明	张权范	张宝忠	张家超
	张 琦	金忠伟	林长春	林文信	罗春红
	苗长云	竺士蒙	周智仁	孟德欣	柏万里
	宫国顺	柳 炜	钮 静	胡敬佩	姚 策
	赵英杰	高福成	贾建军	徐建俊	殷兆麟
	唐 健	黄 斌	章春军	曹豫莪	程 琪
	韩广峰	韩其睿	韩 劼	裘旭光	童爱红
	谢 婷	曾瑶辉	管致锦	熊锡义	潘玫玫
	薛永三	操静涛	鞠洪尧		

出版说明

高职高专教育是我国高等教育的重要组成部分，它的根本任务是培养生产、建设、管理和服务第一线需要的德、智、体、美全面发展的高等技术应用型专门人才，所培养的学生在掌握必要的基础理论和专业知识的基础上，应重点掌握从事本专业领域实际工作的基本知识和职业技能，因而与其对应的教材也必须有自己的体系和特色。

为了适应我国高职高专教育发展及其对教学改革和教材建设的需要，在教育部的指导下，我们在全国范围内组织并成立了"21世纪高职高专教育教材研究与编审委员会"（以下简称"教材研究与编审委员会"）。"教材研究与编审委员会"的成员单位皆为教学改革成效较大、办学特色鲜明、办学实力强的高等专科学校、高等职业学校、成人高等学校及高等院校主办的二级职业技术学院，其中一些学校是国家重点建设的示范性职业技术学院。

为了保证规划教材的出版质量，"教材研究与编审委员会"在全国范围内选聘"21世纪高职高专规划教材编审委员会"（以下简称"教材编审委员会"）成员和征集教材，并要求"教材编审委员会"成员和规划教材的编著者必须是从事高职高专教学第一线的优秀教师或生产第一线的专家。"教材编审委员会"组织各专业的专家、教授对所征集的教材进行评选，对列选教材进行审定。

目前，"教材研究与编审委员会"计划用2~3年的时间出版各类高职高专教材200种，范围覆盖计算机应用、电子电气、财会与管理、商务英语等专业的主要课程。此次规划教材全部按教育部制定的"高职高专教育基础课程教学基本要求"编写，其中部分教材是教育部《新世纪高职高专教育人才培养模式和教学内容体系改革与建设项目计划》的研究成果。此次规划教材编写按照突出应用性、实践性和针对性的原则编写并重组系列课程教材结构，力求反映高职高专课程和教学内容体系改革方向；反映当前教学的新内容，突出基础理论知识的应用和实践技能的培养；适应"实践的要求和岗位的需要"，不依照"学科"体系，即贴近岗位，淡化学科；在兼顾理论和实践内容的同时，避免"全"而"深"的面面俱到，基础理论以应用为目的，以必要、够用为度；尽量体现新知识、新技术、新工艺、新方法，以利于学生综合素质的形成和科学思维方式与创新能力的培养。

此外，为了使规划教材更具广泛性、科学性、先进性和代表性，我们希望全国从事高职高专教育的院校能够积极加入到"教材研究与编审委员会"中来，推荐"教材编审委员会"成员和有特色、有创新的教材。同时，希望将教学实践中的意见与建议及时反馈给我们，以便对已出版的教材不断修订、完善，不断提高教材质量，完善教材体系，为社会奉献更多更新的与高职高专教育配套的高质量教材。

此次所有规划教材由全国重点大学出版社——清华大学出版社与北京交通大学出版社联合出版。适合于各类高等专科学校、高等职业学校、成人高等学校及高等院校主办的二级职业技术学院使用。

21世纪高职高专教育教材研究与编审委员会
2012年8月

前　言

随着现代机电技术的发展，人类已经进入"信息时代"。世界似乎在悄悄地变小，特别是中国加入WTO，各种经济、文化、科技交往日趋频繁，而这一切均以语言为载体。英语是目前国际上最通用的语种，在世界文化交流中具有重要地位。因此，为了掌握最新的现代机电技术，了解现代机电技术的最新发展动态，必须具备较高的机电专业英语水平。

由于现代机电设备涉及的知识面广，包括机械、电子、计算机、信息处理、材料科学等多个领域知识，目前关于现代机电专业英语方面的教材和参考书尚较少，学校教学中大都以相关专业英语教材代替，如机械工程英语、计算机英语等，学生在专业英语方面难以得到比较全面的训练。

为此，本书以现代机电技术为背景，在选材中充分体现专业特色，尽可能兼顾机电专业的各个技术侧面，使读者能得到较为全面的现代机电设备专业英语方面的阅读和翻译技能训练。

本书根据科技英语的系统化教学方法安排内容，兼顾科技英语的词法、句法和文章阅读；在夯实基础的同时，扩展专业词汇量；在课文和阅读材料的选取上充分考虑现代机电设备的各个技术侧面，以使学生能得到较为全面的现代机电技术专业英语方面的阅读和翻译技能训练。

本书每一章形成一个技术侧面，完成专业英语学习的一个主题，使专业词汇、科技语法、专业知识融合为一体，形成互动互惠的学习机制。具体编写上注重实际阅读能力的训练，做到词汇由少到多，内容由浅入深，理解由易渐难。

本书共分为4篇11章：第1篇全面讲述了该学科专业英语阅读和翻译所必需的基础知识；第2篇系统地阐述了专业英语阅读的方法和技巧；第3篇总结了专业英语翻译的基本方法与技巧；第4篇根据现代机电设备的专业特点及所涉及的相关内容，分5个专题，精选相关课文，作为学习现代机电专业英语的范文。每章均附有课文注释、阅读文章和练习，供学习训练之用。全书最后给出了课文的参考译文和练习的参考答案。

本书可作为大专院校现代机电专业（包括机电技术、机电一体化等）专业英语教材，也可作为相关技术人员学习现代机电技术专业英语的自学教材或参考书。

本书由杨承先、张琦策划，第1章至第9章由杨承先、张琦编写，第10、11、12章由杨璐维（北京工业大学生计算机学院）编写，由崔秀娟审稿。

在本书的编写过程中，广泛参阅了国内多种相关专业英语教材和参考书，在此谨向有关作者表示衷心感谢！

由于编者水平及知识所限，加之现代机电技术发展迅速，涉及的知识面广，书中错误和不足之处在所难免，敬请同行和读者批评指正。

编　者
2012年8月

目 录

第1篇 基础篇 ··· 1

第1章 机电专业英语基础知识 ····································· 3
1.1 机电专业英语文体结构和特点 ···························· 3
- 1.1.1 一般结构 ··· 3
- 1.1.2 语言特征 ··· 3
- 1.1.3 机电专业英语的词汇特征 ························· 6
- 1.1.4 句型特点 ··· 9
- 1.1.5 逻辑关系 ··· 19

1.2 机电专业英语表达方式 ····································· 20
- 1.2.1 动词的常用表达 ···································· 20
- 1.2.2 时态、语态特点 ···································· 23
- 1.2.3 句型表达 ··· 25

第2章 机电专业英语词法基础 ····································· 31
2.1 专业英语词法特点 ·· 31
2.2 构词法 ··· 31
- 2.2.1 派生词 ·· 31
- 2.2.2 合成词 ·· 37
- 2.2.3 转化法 ·· 39
- 2.2.4 缩略词 ·· 40
- 2.2.5 拼缀法 ·· 40

2.3 词义的引申 ·· 40
2.4 词性变化 ··· 41
2.5 词义的差异 ·· 42
2.6 词的搭配 ··· 43

第2篇 阅读篇 ··· 45

第3章 机电专业英语阅读概论 ····································· 47
3.1 机电专业英语的阅读要求 ································· 47
3.2 掌握正确的阅读方法 ······································· 47

第4章 机电专业英语阅读技巧 ····································· 49
4.1 获取主题思想 ··· 49
4.2 获取细节 ··· 53
4.3 领悟词义 ··· 53
4.4 弄清文中的指代关系 ······································· 54
4.5 把握文中的对比逻辑关系 ································· 55
4.6 把握文中描述的位置关系 ································· 56

4.7　两种快速阅读方法 ·· 56

第3篇　翻译篇 ·· 59

第5章　专业英语翻译的标准与过程 ·· 61
5.1　翻译的标准 ·· 61
5.2　翻译的过程 ·· 61

第6章　翻译的方法与技巧 ·· 64
6.1　词的增减翻译法 ·· 64
　6.1.1　增词译法 ··· 64
　6.1.2　减词译法 ··· 64
6.2　词性的转译 ·· 65
6.3　句子成分转译 ·· 66
6.4　被动语态的翻译 ·· 69
6.5　It 结构的翻译 ·· 73
6.6　专业术语的翻译 ·· 75
　6.6.1　意译 ·· 75
　6.6.2　音译 ·· 75
　6.6.3　形译 ·· 76
6.7　从句的翻译 ·· 76
　6.7.1　定语从句的翻译 ··· 76
　6.7.2　同位语从句的翻译 ··· 79
　6.7.3　状语从句的翻译 ··· 80
6.8　长句的翻译 ·· 83
6.9　否定结构的翻译 ·· 85

第4篇　应用篇 ·· 89

第7章　Mechatronics Technology ·· 91
7.1　Intensive Reading ·· 91
　Lesson 1　Mechatronics ··· 91
　Lesson 2　Mechanization and Automation ·· 94
　Lesson 3　Numerical Control and Automatic Machines ···················· 97
　Lesson 4　Computer-Integrated Manufacturing System（CIMS）···· 100
7.2　Extensive Reading ·· 102
　Lesson 1　Flexible Manufacturing System（FMS）························· 102
　Lesson 2　Robot ··· 104

第8章　Mechanical Technology ·· 107
8.1　Intensive Reading ·· 107
　Lesson 1　Mechanisms ··· 107
　Lesson 2　Machine Elements ··· 110
　Lesson 3　Power Steering System ·· 112
　Lesson 4　Brake System ··· 116
8.2　Extensive Reading ·· 119

Lesson 1	Hydraulic Power Transmission	119
Lesson 2	Diesel Engine	121

第9章 Manufacture Technology for Machinery …… 124

9.1 Intensive Reading …… 124
- Lesson 1　Tolerances and Fits …… 124
- Lesson 2　Heat Treatment of Steel …… 126
- Lesson 3　Welding …… 129
- Lesson 4　Machine Tools …… 131

9.2 Extensive Reading …… 134
- Lesson 1　Material Properties …… 134
- Lesson 2　Iron and Steel …… 136

第10章 Control Technology …… 140

10.1 Intensive Reading …… 140
- Lesson 1　Introduction to Control Engineering …… 140
- Lesson 2　Applications of Automatic Control …… 143
- Lesson 3　Programmable Controllers …… 147
- Lesson 4　Adaptive Control Systems …… 150

10.2 Extensive Reading …… 153
- Lesson 1　Closed-loop Control System …… 153
- Lesson 2　Digital Control Systems …… 154

第11章 Computer Technologies for the Design and Manufacture of Machinery …… 157

11.1 Intensive Reading …… 157
- Lesson 1　CAD (Computer-aided Design) Technology …… 157
- Lesson 2　CAPP (Computer Aided Process Planning) Technology …… 160
- Lesson 3　Dynamic Simulation Technique for the Design of Machine …… 164
- Lesson 4　Virtual Reality …… 168

11.2 Extensive Reading …… 171
- Lesson 1　The Five Phases of Software Development …… 171
- Lesson 2　Database Technologies …… 173

第12章 Information and Network Technology …… 177

12.1 Intensive Reading …… 177
- Lesson 1　GPS …… 177
- Lesson 2　Electronic Mail …… 179
- Lesson 3　Network Security Problems …… 182
- Lesson 4　Digital Television and Flat Television …… 186

12.2 Extensive Reading …… 189
- Lesson 1　The Application of Data Bus Technology …… 189
- Lesson 2　Multimedia Technology …… 191

参考译文及参考答案 …… 193

参考文献 …… 232

第1篇 基 础 篇

第1章 机电专业英语基础知识

1.1 机电专业英语文体结构和特点

1.1.1 一般结构

在阅读一篇完整的机电专业英语时，只要仔细分析一下这类文章的篇章结构，不难发现机电专业英语文章的一般结构由以下几部分组成：

标题　　Title
目录　　Contents
摘要　　Abstract（包含 Key words）
引言　　Introduction，Preface
正文　　Body
结论与建议　Conclusions，Suggestions
总结　　Summary
致谢　　Acknowledgement
注释　　Notes
参考文献　References
附录　　Appendix

但对于一般的机电科技文章来说，不一定需要上述齐全的文体结构，可以进行取舍，一般机电科技文章的文体结构如下：

标题　　Title
摘要　　Abstract（包含 Key words）
引言　　（概述） Introduction，General Description
正文　　Body
结论与建议　Results，Conclusions，Suggestions
参考文献　References

1.1.2 语言特征

1. 标题

科技文章的标题往往是文章的中心主旨，文章的标题反映了作者所研究的主要内容或作者所描述的科学真理和事实或作者要说明的科学实验过程和产品使用说明等，其语言特征如下。

（1）关于……的研究、探讨、调查、介绍、分析、描述、说明等，其表达方式如下：
research/study/probe...on...
introduction/brief introduction to...

investigation/survey/analysis/description of...

（2）说明一个科学真理和事实、实验过程、产品说明等，一般采用名词性词组、现在分词的形式，如 The Miracle Chip, Machine Tools, Computer in the Future, Robots for Tomorrow, Digital Age, Information Highway, The Jet Engine, Operating System, Cloning Technology, Prototyping。

2. 摘要

摘要反映了一篇科技文章论述的主要内容、思想方法、重要的观点和结论等，一般摘要的长度为 150~200 words，主要由 3 部分组成，即主题句、支持句和结论句，其主要语言特征如下。

（1）主题句常用句型如下：

The purpose of this paper is...

The primary goal of this research is...

The overall objective of this study is...

In this paper, we aim at...

Our goal has been to provide...

The chief aim of the present work is to investigate the facts that...

The main objective of our study has been to obtain some results...

The emphasis of the research lies in...

The author intends to build a model/a framework of...

Experiment on... is made in order to measure the amount of...

（2）支持句常用的句型如下：

The method used in our study is known as...

The technique we applied is referred to as...

The procedure they followed can be briefly described as...

The approach adopted extensively is called...

Detailed information has been acquired by the authors using...

The research has recorded valuable data using the newly-developed method.

This is a working theory which is based on the idea that...

The fundamental feature of this theory is as follows.

The theory is characterized by...

The experiment consisted of three steps, which are described in...

The test equipment that was used consisted of...

The winch is composed of the following main parts...

We have carried out several sets of experiments to test the validity of...

They undertook many experiments to support the hypothesis which...

Recent experiments in this area suggested that...

A number of experiments were performed to check...

Examples with actual experiment demonstrate...

Special mention is given here to...

This formula is verified by...
We also supply...

（3）结论句句型如下：

In conclusion, we state that...
In summing up it may be stated that...
It is concluded that...
The results of the experiment indicate that...
The studies we have performed showed that...
The pioneer studies that the authors attempted have indicated in...
We carried out several studies that have demonstrated that...
The research we have done suggests that...
The investigation carried out by... has revealed that...
Laboratory studies of... did not furnish any information about...
All our preliminary results throw light on the nature of...
As a result of our experiments, we concluded that...
From our experiment, the authors came to realize that...
This fruitful work gives explanation of...
The author's pioneer work has contributed to our present understanding of...
The research work has brought about a discovery of...
These findings of the research have led the author to the conclusion that...
The data obtained appear to be very similar to those reported earlier by...
Our work involving studies of... prove to be encouraging.
The author has satisfactorily come to the conclusion that...
Finally, a summary is given of...

3. 引言

引言是对全文的综合和概述，包括研究的背景及目的意义，向读者介绍文章的思想和内容，常用的句型如下：

Over the past several decades...
Somebody reported...
The previous work on... has indicated that...
Recent experiments by... have suggested...
Several researchers have theoretically investigated...
In most studies of... has been emphasized with attention being given to...
Industrial use of... is becoming increasingly common.
There have been a few studies highlighting...
It is well known that...

4. 正文

正文是科技文章的主体，是科学分析和试验论证的过程反映，经常使用各种图表、公式论证作者的观点。各种图表一般翻译如下：

表—Table；

图—Figure/Diagram/Graph/view/Flow Diagram/Chart/Frame Figure，and so on；

公式、算式、方程式—Formula/Equation；

如图 X 所示，如表 Y 所示—As it is shown in Fig. X, as it is shown in Table Y.

5. 结论

结论是对全文的总结，经过科学的分析、研究而得出的结论，其语言特征如下：

The following conclusions can be drawn from...

It can be concluded that...

We may conclude that...

We come to the conclusion that...

It is generally accepted (believed, held, acknowledged) that...

We think (consider, believe, feel) that...

It is advantageous to do...

It should be realized (emphasized, stressed, noted, pointed out) that...

It is suggested (proposed, recommended, desirable) that...

It would be better (helpful, advisable) that...

6. 致谢

致谢是作者在完成论文之后，为了表达对曾经帮助自己的人的感谢，常用的句型如下：

I am thankful to sb. for sth.

I am grateful to sb. for sth.

I am deeply indebted to sb. for sth.

I would like to thank sb. for sth.

Thanks are due to sb. for sth.

The author wishes to express his sincere appreciation to sb. for sth.

The author wishes to acknowledge sb.

The author wishes to express his gratitude for sth.

7. 参考文献

在论文最后应将参考的主要文献一一列出，表示对别人成果的尊重及作者的写作依据。

1.1.3 机电专业英语的词汇特征

1. 机电专业英语词汇的特征

机电专业英语词汇来源如下。

（1）来自英语中的普通词汇，但在机电专业中被赋予了新的词义。例如：Work is the transfer of energy expressed as the product of a force and the distance through. Which its point of application moves in the direction of the force. 在这句话中，"work"、"energy"、"product"、"force" 都是从普通词汇中借来的物理学术语。"work" 的意思不是"工作"，而是"功"；"energy" 的意思不是"活力"，而是"能"；"product" 的意思不是"产品"，而是"乘积"；"force" 的意思不是"力量"，而是"力"。

（2）来自希腊或拉丁语等语言。

例如：therm—热（希腊语），thesis—论文（希腊语），parameter—参数（拉丁语），radius—半径（拉丁语）。

这些来源于希腊语和拉丁语的词的复数形式有些仍按原来的形式，如 thesis 的复数形式是 theses，stratus 的复数形式是 strati；但由于在英语里使用时间较长，不少词除保留了原来的复数形式外，又采用了英语的复数形式，例如：formula（公式，拉丁语）的复数形式可以是 formulae，也可以是 formulas，stratum 的复数形式（层，拉丁语）可以是 strata，也可以是 stratums。特别有意思的是，datum（数据，拉丁语）的复数形式是 data，但是由于这个词经常用复数，所以有些外国人甚至误把它当成单数，又造出了一个所谓的复数形式 datas。

（3）新出现的词汇。每当出现新的科学技术现象时，人们都要通过词汇把它表示出来，这就需要构造新的词汇。构造新词主要有以下几种方法。

① **转化**：通过词类转化构成新词。英语中名词、形容词、副词、介词可以转化成动词，动词、形容词、副词、介词可以转化成名词；但最活跃的是名词转化成动词和动词转化成名词。例如，名词 island（小岛）转化成动词 island（隔离），动词 coordinate（协调）转化成名词 coordinate（坐标）。

② **合成**：由两个独立的词合成为一个词。例如：air + craft—aircraft（飞机），air + port—airport（机场），metal + work—metalwork（金属制品），power + plant—powerplant（发电站）。

有的合成词的两个成分之间要有连字符，例如，cast-iron（铸铁），conveyer-belt（传送带），machine-made（机制的）。英语中有很多专业术语由两个或更多的词组成，叫做复合术语。它们的构成成分虽然看起来是独立的，但实际上合起来构成一个完整的概念；因此应该把它们看成是一个术语。

例如：liquid crystal—液晶，water jacket—水套，computer language—计算机语言，machine building—机器制造，linear measure—长度单位，civil engineering—土木工程。

③ **派生**：这种方法也叫缀合。派生词是由词根加上前缀或后缀构成的。构成新词，只改变词义，不改变词性。例如：

  decontrol（取消控制） *v.*—de + control（control 是动词）；
  ultrasonic（超声的） *a.*—ultra + sonic（sonic 是形容词）；
  subsystem（分系统） *n.*—sub + system（system 是名词）。

有些加前缀的派生词在前缀和词根之间有连字符，例如，hydro-electric（发电），extra-terrestrial（行星际的）。英语的前缀是有固定意义的，记住其中的一些常用前缀对于记忆生词和猜测词义有帮助。这里只举一些表示否定的前缀来说明问题，例如：anti-表示"反对"，antibody（抗体）；counter-表示"反对，相反"，counterbalance（反平衡）；contra-表示"反对，相反"，contradiction（矛盾）；de-表示"减少，降低，否定，去除"，decrease（减少），devalue（贬值），decode（解码）；dis-表示"否定，除去"，discharge（放电），disassemble（拆卸）；in，il（单词首字母为 l）表示"不"，inaccurate（不准确的）；im-（在字母 m、b、p 前）表示"不"，imbalance（不平衡的），impure（不纯的）；mis-表示"错误"，mislead（误导）；non-表示"不，非"，non-ferrous（有色金属的）；un-表示

"不，未，丧失"，unaccountable（说明不了的），unknown（未知的），unbar（清除障碍）。

加后缀构成新词可能改变也可能不改变词义，但一般改变词性。例如：

electricity　n.　—electric + ity（electric 是形容词）；
liquidize（液化）　v.　—liquid + ize（liquid 是名词）；
conductor　n.　—conduct + or（conduct 是动词）；
invention　n.　—invent + ion（invent 是动词）。

有的派生词加后缀的时候，语音或拼写可能发生变化。例如：

simplicity（单纯）—simple + icity；
maintenance（维修）—maintain + ance；
propeller（推进器）—propel + l + er。

英语后缀的作用和前缀有所不同，它们主要用来改变词性。从一个词的后缀可识别它的词类，这是它的语法意义。它们的词汇意义往往并不明显，下面是一些常见的形容词后缀。例如：

-able，-ible，-uble 表示"可……的"，avoidable（可以避免的），audible（听得见的），soluble（可溶的）；

-al，-ant，ent，表示属性、性质，译为"……的"，fundamental（基本的），abundant（富饶的），apparent（显然的）；

-ed，表示"有……的"，cultured（有文化的）；

-ful，表示"充满……的，有……倾向的"，useful（有用的）；

-ic，ical，形容词尾，basic（基本的），economical（经济的）；

-less，表示"没有"，useless（无用的）；

-ous，形容词尾，numerous（众多的）；

-let，表示"小的"，booklet（小册子），wavelet（小波）。

④ 缩略：把词省略或简化，然后组合成新词。现在的趋势是缩略词的数目不断增大，使用面不断扩大。例如：

laboratory 截短成 lab（实验室）；
Unidentified flying object 缩合成 UFO（不明飞行物）；
Radio detection and ranging 缩减成 radar（雷达）；
transistor 和 receiver 各取一部分，组合成 transceiver（收发机）；
motor + hotel→motel（汽车旅店）；
mechanics + electronics→mechatronics（机电一体化）；
Telecommunications satellite 缩略为 Telesat（通信卫星）。

(4) 英语科技文体中有很多词汇并不是专业术语，且在日常口语中用得不是很多，它们多见于书面语中，叫做文语词。掌握这类词对阅读科技文献或写科技论文十分重要。这类词用得很广，它们不仅出现在各专业的科技文体中，也出现在政治、经济、法律、语言等社会科学的文体中，例如：

accordance（按照），imply（隐含），acknowledge（承认），inclusion（包括），alter（改变），incur（招致），alternative（交替的），indicate（指示），amend（修正），induce

（归纳），application（应用），initial（初始的），appropriate（恰当的），modification（修改），attain（达到），nevertheless（然而），circumstance（情况），nonetheless（然而），compensation（补偿），obtain（获得），confirm（证实），occur（发生），consequence（后果），omission（省略），considering（鉴于），providing（假设），consist（组成），reduce（减少），constitute（构成），replacement（代替），consume（消耗），specifically（具体地说），deduce（推理），distinction（差别），valid（有效的），function（功能），verify（验证），illustrate（说明）。

2. 缩短（略）词的大量采用

采用的缩短词有以下几种。

（1）缩略词的首部（front clipping），如 telephone = phone，university = varsity，helicopter = copter，etc.

（2）缩略词的尾部（back clipping），如 advertisement = ad，debutante = deb，modern = mod，professional = pro，exposition = expo，memorandum = memo，etc.

（3）缩略词的首尾部，如 influenza = flu，detective = tec，refrigerator = fridge，etc.

（4）首字母缩略词，如 V. O. A. = Voice of America，IOC = International Olympic Committee，WTO = World Trade Organization，CAD = Computer Aided Design，NATO = North Atlantic Treaty Organization，CAE = Computer Aided Engineering，CAM = Computer Aided Manufacture，etc.

3. 约定的专业术语

在机电专业英语中大量出现专业术语，专业术语语义较固定，翻译也是固定表达方式，如 TCP/IP（Transmission Control Protocol/Internet Protocol，传输控制协议/国际网协议），relay（继电器），interface（计算机通信接口），point-to-point（点对点），topology（拓扑学），HTML（Hypertext Markup Language，超文本标识语言），HTTP（Hypertext Transfer Protocol，超文本传输协议），LAN（Local Area Network，局域网），Modem（调制解调器），aerodynamics（空气动力学），cybernetics（控制论），precision（精度），vector（向量或矢量），matrix（矩阵），prototype（原型，样机），state-of-the-art（工艺水平），detect（探测，检测），fault（故障），hydraulic system（液压系统），NC（Numerical Control，数控），milling（铣，磨），feed（进给量），machine tool（机床），feedback（反馈），hardness（硬度），coolant（冷却液），roughness（粗糙度），sensor（传感器），integration（集成，综合），pulse train（脉冲序列），patent（专利），poly-phase（多相的），transformer（变压器），integrate circuit（集成电路）。

1.1.4 句型特点

英语的句子不论多长，多么复杂，解剖到最后，总是由一些简单句即句子的主干所组成。就其主要成分（即不包括定语、宾语、状语）而言，有以下几种基本句型。

1. 基本句型结构

1）主语 + 动词 + 直接宾语

（1）They have already finished the work.

他们已经完成了那项工作。

(2) He often does that.

他经常这样做。

2) 主语+动词+动词不定式

(1) He promised to help me.

他答应帮助我。

(2) That company agreed to pay for it.

那家公司同意支付它的费用。

(3) They decided not to sell their software.

他们决定不卖掉他们的软件。

3) 主语+动词+名词或代词+动词不定式

(1) The professor asked them to look carefully.

教授请他们仔细观察。

(2) I warned him not to smoke here.

我警告他不要在此吸烟。

(3) I'd like Tom to do it.

我愿意让汤姆做这件事。

4) 主语+动词+名词或代词+(to be)+补足语

(1) We consider him (to be) honest.

我们认为他很诚实。

(2) They believe this printer (to be) the best.

他们相信这台打印机是最好的。

(3) We proved this idea (to be) wrong.

我们证明了这个观点是错误的。

5) 主语+动词+名词或代词+不带to的不定式

(1) We saw him go out.

我们看见他出去的。

(2) The guard wouldn't let him go in.

卫兵不让他进去。

(3) The father had the boy work harder.

父亲让男孩工作更努力些。

6) 主语+动词+名词或代词+现在分词

(1) They kept us waiting for a long time.

他们让我们等了好长时间。

(2) We found her working at her desk.

我们看见她在伏案工作。

(3) The boy saw his father coming this way.

男孩看见他父亲朝这边走来。

7) 主语+动词+宾语+形容词

(1) What he said made her uneasy.

他的话使她不安。

(2) When he came back, he found the room empty.

他回来时发现房间是空的。

(3) Don't get your hands dirty.

不要把手弄脏。

8) 主语+动词+宾语+名词

(1) We elected him monitor.

我们选他为班长。

(2) They all call him Fred.

他们都叫他弗雷德。

(3) They made him President of the Royal Society.

他们选他为皇家学会主席。

9) 主语+动词+宾语+过去分词

(1) Where do you often have your printer repaired?

你经常在什么地方修理打印机?

(2) Are you going to have your hair cut tomorrow?

你打算明天去理发吗?

(3) He couldn't make himself understood.

他不能让别人理解。

10) 主语+动词+宾语+副词或副词短语

(1) Please put your books here.

请把你们的书放在这。

(2) He took his cap off.

他脱去帽子。

(3) Later he showed me to the door.

后来他把我送到门口。

(4) We employed him as a computer engineer.

我们雇他当计算机工程师。

11) 主语+动词+that 从句（有时 that 省略）

(1) I hope that everything is all right.

我希望一切都很好。

(2) He suggested that we should do it at once.

他建议我们马上做这件事。

(3) I think his design is the best.

我认为他的设计最好。

12) 主语+动词+名词或代词+that 从句

(1) I told her that she was wrong.

我告诉她她错了。

(2) Please remind me that there is a meeting at six.

请提醒我六点开会。

（3）Mother often warns him that he mustn't smoke.

妈妈经常告诫他不应该吸烟。

13）主语+动词+连接词+不定式

（1）She was wondering which to buy.

她正踌躇不知该买哪一个。

（2）I really don't know what to do.

我真不知道该怎么办。

（3）You must learn how to look after yourself.

你必须学会如何照顾自己。

（4）Do you know when to start?

你知道什么时候开始吗？

14）主语+动词+名词或代词+连接词+不定式

（1）Please show me how to operate this printer.

请给我示范一下如何操作这台打印机。

（2）That old engineer told her what to do next.

那位老工程师告诉她下一步该做什么。

（3）Could you advise me which to buy?

你能建议我买哪一个吗？

15）主语+动词+连接词+从句

（1）Nobody knows who he is.

没人知道他是谁。

（2）You needn't care what he said.

你不必介意他说的话。

（3）I wonder whether he will come.

我不知道他会不会来。

16）主语+动词+名词或代词+连接词+从句

（1）Could you tell me when he will be back?

你能告诉我他什么时候回来吗？

（2）He asked her where she bought the scanner.

他问她在哪儿买的这台扫描仪。

（3）Did he tell you what he was doing?

他告诉你他在干什么了吗？

17）主语+动词+动名词

（1）He enjoys reading books.

他喜欢读书。

（2）The professor went on talking.

教授继续谈下去。

（3）Your bike needs repairing.

你的自行车需要修理。(repairing 这里表被动含义)

(4) It began raining.

天开始下雨了。

18) 主语+动词+直接宾语+介词+间接宾语

(1) She gave the money to me.

她把钱给我了。

(2) His father bought a bike for him.

父亲给他买了一辆自行车。

(3) Thank you for your help.

谢谢你的帮助。

(4) The heavy rain prevented him from coming.

那场大雨使他不能来。

19) 主语+动词+间接宾语+直接宾语

(1) He showed me his design.

他给我看了他的设计。

(2) Would you do me a favour?

你愿意给我帮个忙吗?

20) 主语+动词+双宾语

(1) That will save us a lot of trouble.

那将省去我们许多麻烦。

(2) He struck the man a heavy blow.

他重重地给了那个男人一下。

21) 主语+动词+状语

(1) He waited for two hours.

他等了两个小时。

(2) They walked three miles.

他们步行了三英里。

(3) This house costs 200 000 yuan.

这座房子值二十万元。

22) 主语+动词

(1) The sun is shining.

阳光照耀着。

(2) Everybody breathes, eats and drinks.

人人都呼吸、饮食。

23) 主语+系动词+表语

(1) This book is very valuable.

这本书很有价值。

(2) She is in good health.

她的健康情况良好。

(3) His job is teaching.

他的工作是教书。

(4) This house is to let.

此房出租。

24) There + be + 主语 + 状语

在这种句型中使用的是表示存在的动词。

(1) There is a table in the room.

房间里有一张桌子。

(2) There remains one more experiment to be carried out.

还有一个实验要完成。

(3) There is a pull of gravitation between the earth and the moon.

在地球和月球之间有一种引力。

(4) There seem too many factors influencing motion.

看来影响运动的因素似乎太多了。

25) 主语 + 动词 + 介词 + 宾语

(1) He is listening to the radio.

他正在听收音机。

(2) He succeeded in passing the exam.

他成功地通过了考试。

(3) It depends on the weather.

此事要根据天气而定。

(4) He will deal with the matter.

他将处理这件事。

26) 主语 + 动词 + 动词不定式

(1) They should stop to have a rest.

他们应该停下来休息一下。

(2) How does he come to know that?

他怎么知道了那件事情?

(3) We woke to find the house on fire.

我们醒来发现房子着火了。

(4) Do you happen to know where he has gone?

你是不是刚好知道他去哪儿啦?

(5) We are to do it tomorrow.

我们明天做这件事。

(6) Nobody is to know.

不许任何人知道。

27) SV（主语 + 谓语）结构

在这种句型中使用的是不及物动词。

(1) In a hydrogen atom, an electron whirls around the nucleus at a tremendous speed.

氢原子中,一个电子以极大的速度绕原子核旋转。

(2) Electro magnetic waves can move through great distance.

电磁波可以传播很远距离。

28) SVO(主语+谓语动词+宾语)结构

在这种句型中使用的是及物动词,又可分为如下三类。

- 动词后有一个宾语。

(1) Some computers can perform over a billion computations a second.

有些计算机每秒钟可以完成十亿次以上的运算。

(2) Color television breaks down pictures into three colors—red, green and blue.

彩色电视把图像分解成三种颜色——红色、绿色、蓝色。

- 动词后有一个宾语和一个宾语补语。

(1) During war, radar enables bombers to find their targets at night.

战时,雷达可以帮助轰炸机在黑夜找到目标。

(2) These new methods will make the electronic devices of the future quite small.

这些新方法将使将来的电子器件变得相当小。

- 动词后有两个宾语,即一个间接宾语和一个直接宾语。

(1) The turbo jet and the turboprop give airplanes an even thrust.

涡轮喷气发动机和涡轮螺桨发动机给飞机提供平稳的推力。

(2) This gives the work a good finish.

这使工件有良好的光洁度。

29) SVC(主语+系词+表语)结构

这种句型中使用的是系词。

(1) The laser is really amazingly simple in construction.

激光器在结构上是惊人的简单。

(2) At about 1 300 ℃ the metal becomes plastic.

在大约 1 300 ℃ 时金属变成塑性体。

2. 并列句和复合句的基本类型

如果句子中出现不止一个主谓结构,就要用连词组成并列句或复合句。以由两个分句组成句子为例,按照主谓结构安排有以下几种句型。

1)(主语+谓语)+(连词+主语+谓语)

这种句型适用于并列句及带有各种从句的复合句。

(1) Most sonar sets send out sounds that are millions of times more powerful than a shout.

多数声呐装置发出的声音比喊叫声要强数百万倍。(带有定语从句的复合句)

(2) A box resting on the floor has more than one force acting on it, but they do not produce a change in its position.

一个放在木板上的箱子有不止一个力作用于它,但是这些力并不使箱子的位置发生变化。(并列句)

2)(连词+主语+谓语)+(主语+谓语)

这种句型适用于带有除结果状语从句以外的各种状语从句、以 as 引起的特种定语从句的复合句。

(1) As load is added, the active component of the current increases.

加上负载后,有效电流增大。(带有时间状语从句的复合句)

(2) As we know, there are two kinds of steel, carbon steel and alloy steel.

如我们所知,钢有两种:碳钢和合金钢。(带有特种定语从句的复合句)

(3) As electricity has many advantages, it is widely used in production.

由于电有许多优点,因而它广泛用于生产中。(带有原因状语从句的复合句)

(4) If fuel is burnt, heat is given out.

如果燃烧燃料,就产生热。(带有条件状语从句的复合句)

3) 主语+(连词+主语+谓语)+谓语

这种句型适用于状语从句、定语从句插在主句当中的复合句。

(1) An earth satellite, whether it is natural or artificial, is held in orbit by the balance of gravity and the satellite's inertia.

地球卫星,不管是天然的还是人造的,都靠地心引力与卫星的惯性之间的平衡固定在轨道上。(带有让步状语从句的复合句)

如果中间为定语从句而省去关系代词,则成为"主语+(主语+谓语)+谓语"。

(2) The petrol you use to drive your car engine is fined product of crude oil.

你开动汽车发动机所用的汽油是由原油中提炼出来的。

4) (连词+主语+谓语)+谓语

这种句型适用于带有主语从句的复合句。

(1) That matter consists of atoms is known to all of us.

我们都知道物质由原子组成。

(2) Whether life may exist on the Moon or Mars remains a mystery.

生命能否在月球或火星上存在还是个谜。

3. 机电专业英语句型特点

1) 多重复合句

科技文体常常使用这种句型,以便能严谨地表达复杂的思想。如果把一句话分成几个独立的句子,就有可能影响到句子之间的密切联系。所以说,多重复句是能体现英语科技文体的一种句型。文章的论述性越强,多重复句用得越多,句子也越长。多重复句的分句之间有两种基本关系,一种是并列关系,另一种是主从关系;但是以主从关系为主。这两种关系常常同时出现在一个句子中。请看下面的例子。

This instrument works on the principle that each individual substance emits a characteristic spectrum of light when its molecules are caused to vibrate by the application of heat, electricity, etc., and after studying the spectrum which he had obtained on this occasion, Hillebrand reported the gas to be nitrogen.

这个句子的基本骨架是用"and"连接的两个并列的主句"this instrument works on the principle"和"after studying the spectrum Hillebrand reported the gas to be nitrogen"第一个主句有一个用"that"连接的同位语从句,说明主句中的"principle",而这个同位语从句又有一个用"when"连接的时间状语从句。第二个主句中包含了一个用"which"连接的

定语从句,说明"spectrum"从句在说明主句的时候,有三种可能的位置:在主句前、在主句后和插在主句中间。例如:

When we look into the matter carefully, we will find that the world we live in presents an endless variety of fascinating problems which excite our wonder and curiosity.

这句话由五个分句构成。主句 we will find 有两个从句:时间状语从句 when... 在前面,宾语从句 that 在后面。宾语从句又有两个定语从句:第一个定语从句 we live in 插在它中间,第二个定语从句 which... 跟在它后面。

插在主句中间的从句叫做嵌入句。由于它把主句分成两半,往往造成阅读理解的困难。例如:

This is not, of course, the case inhuman affairs, and the most that can be yet done is to seek for mathematical models which describe, however, imperfectly as yet they are, the presumed behavior of the system or situation under investigation.

定语从句 "that can be yet done" 把它的主句的主语和谓语分隔开,让步状语从句 "however imperfectly as yet they are" 把主句的谓语和宾语分隔开。

科技文体中有的句子可能很长,遇到这种句子时,不要眉毛胡子一把抓,而是要进行语法分析。语法分析主要从两点入手,第一是找出谓语(谓语的形式比较明显,容易发现),然后找出它的主语。英语句子不像汉语那样经常省略主语,而是由主语和谓语构成句子的核心。第二是找出连接词。英语和汉语的另一个不同是汉语句子分句时常常没有连接词,而英语句子的分句之间一般都有连接词连接。找出了连接词就找到了分句间的界限和它们之间的关系。这里说的连接词是广义的,包括连接代词、连接关系代词、关系副词等。

2)被动语态

在机电专业英语中大量存在被动语态,由于机电专业英语中往往不需要明确动作的执行者是谁,一般采用被动语态来表达;但翻译时可采用主动语态。

(1) No work can be done without energy.

没有能量就不能做功。

(2) All sorts of necessaries of life can be made of plastics.

各种生活必需品都能用塑料制造。

(3) All business decisions must now be made in the light of the market.

所有业务现在必须根据市场来作出决策。

(4) Automobiles may be manufactured with computer-driven robots or put together almost totally by hand.

汽车可以由计算机操纵的机器人来制造,或者几乎全部用手工装配。

以上四例都用被动语态;但译成汉语时都没有用被动语态,以便合乎汉语传统规范。例(4)的并列后句,其谓语本应是 may be put together。put 是三种变化形式一样的不规则动词,这里是过去分词,由于修辞学上避免用词重复出现的要求,略去了 may be 两词,所以并非现在时,而是被动语态。

机电专业英语之所以多用被动语态,为的是要强调所论述的客观事物(四例中的 work, necessaries, business decisions, automobiles);因此,放在句首,作为句子的主语,以突出其重要。

3）非谓语形式

机电专业英语中的句子一般比较简单，通常用一个谓语动词，如果有几个动作，就必须选出主要动词谓语，而将其余动词作为非谓语动词形式，才能符合英语语法要求。非谓语动词有三种：动名词、分词（包括现在分词和过去分词）和不定式。

（1）To be a true professional requires lifelong learning.

要成为一个名副其实的内行，需要学到老。这句中，有"成为"、"需要"和"学"三个表示动作的词，可以看出，选好"需要"（require）作为主要动词谓语，其余两个动作："成为"用不定式形式"to be"，而"学"用动名词形式"learning"，这样才能符合英语语法要求。

（2）Heating water does not change its chemical composition.

把水加热并不会改变水的化学成分。

这句中有"加热"和"改变"两个动作，本句的处理方式是将"改变"（change）用作主要谓语，而将"加热"（heating）处理为动名词，连同其宾语 water 作为本句主语。

（3）Matter is anything having weight and occupying space.

任何具有重量并占有空间的东西都是物质。

这句包含"是"（在英语中属于存在动词）、"具有"和"占有"三个动作，将"是"（is）当谓语（系动词），而"具有"（having）和"占有"（occupying）处理为现在分词，连同它们的宾语"weight"和"space"分别构成现在分词短语，作为修饰名词"anything"的定语。

（4）The two great divisions of this science known are inorganic chemistry and organic chemistry.

这门学科的两大分支是无机化学和有机化学，这是众所周知的。

这句有"众所周知"和"是"两个动词，这里将"是"（are）作为谓语系动词，而将"为人所知"（known）处理为过去分词。

上述四例，分别列举了四种非谓语动词的使用情况。每个简单句只允许有一个谓语动词。这就是英语为什么不同于其他语言，有非谓语动词，而且用得十分频繁的原因。

4）词性转换

英语单词有不少是多性词，即既是名词，又可用作动词、形容词、介词或副词，字形特殊，功能各异，含义也各不相同，如不仔细观察，必致谬误。例如：

（1）above

介词：above all（things）　首先，最重要的是。

形容词：for the above reason　由于上述理由。

副词：as（has been）indicated above　如上所指出。

（2）light

名词：（光）in（the）light of　由于，根据；highlight（s）　强光，精华；（灯）safety light　安全指示灯。

形容词：（轻）light industry　轻工业；（明亮）light room　明亮的房间；（淡）light blue　淡蓝色；（薄）light coating　薄涂层。

动词：（点燃）light up the lamp 点灯。

副词：（轻快）travel light 轻装旅行；（容易）light come, light go 来得容易去得快。

诸如此类的词性转换在机电专业英语中屡见不鲜，几乎每个技术名词都可转换为同义的形容词，如 capital goods（生产资料），space rocket（宇宙火箭）。词性转换增加了英语的灵活性和表现力，读者必须从上下文判明用词在句中是何种词性、含义如何，才能对全句得到正确无误的理解。

1.1.5 逻辑关系

在机电专业英语文章中，作者为了准确表达一个科学真理或一个科学事实或一个实验过程，文章是由句子、句群或段落组成，文章的各组成部分存在一定的逻辑关系，往往采用一些虚词来表达文章的逻辑关系，有连词、副词、介词短语、不定式短语等，这些词多出现在句首或句中，较少出现在句尾。

1. 列举：Firstly, secondly...; finally, for one thing... (and) for another (thing); in the first place, to begin with, initially, next, lastly, on the other hand, etc.

<u>To start with</u>, mathematicians become valued members of the industrial community, <u>and</u> are no longer destined merely to teach <u>or</u> lecture.

<u>First</u>, how do these new circumstances affect the position in the community of the politician? <u>Second</u>, how far is the scientist equipped to handle political and governmental affairs? ... <u>finally</u> (Lastly), what are the special responsibilities, if any, of the scientists towards the community?

2. 增补：And, and also, in addition (to), furthermore, moreover, what is more, as well as

This apparatus and its use have now become exceedingly complex and require the participation of large numbers of scientists and technologists. <u>Moreover</u>, many types of industry, including the largest, <u>e.g.</u> the aerospace industry, are strongly linked to defense requirements and again depend <u>increasingly</u> on scientific and technical personnel.

A person viewing the backlit film could see the three-dimensional image of the object. <u>In addition</u>, the image changed as the viewer moved to another position, just as if the real object were being seen.

3. 转折或对比：But, yet, nevertheless, instead, in fact, on the contrary; on the one hand..., however, on the other hand; as a matter of fact, etc.

The older methods of curing, smoking and drying reduced the number of micro-organisms, or else stopped them from acting. <u>But</u> these older methods almost always changed the food itself, so that it often looked and tasted different.

The limited number of quasars（星体）so far identified indicates that they become more abundant the more distant they are in space and time. <u>In other words</u>, the universe was different in the past, and is evolving.

4. 原因或结果：hence, therefore, thus, consequently, because of this, for this reason, in consequence, on account of this, as a result, etc.

As a result, governments are becoming increasingly dependent on biologists and social scientists for planning the programs and put them into effect.

　　The specific use of leisure varies from individual to individual. Even the same leisure activity may be used differently by different individuals. Thus, the following is possible used of television watching, a popular leisure activity.

　　5. 解释：that is to say, namely, for example, for instance, such as, in other words, i. e., etc.

　　These divisions hardly suggest the complexity of modern physics, but do hint at the opportunities for applying physics. For instance, the design of musical instruments now requires a detailed knowledge of sound.

　　6. 总结或结论：(all) in all, in conclusion, in short, in a word, in brief, on the whole, to conclude, to sum up, the result of, in conclusion, hence, evidently, apparently, clearly, seemingly, undoubtedly, etc.

　　To conclude, it seems clear that if we are to succeed in solving the many inter-related problems of underdevelopment, only the fullest and most intelligent use of the resources will enable us to do so.

　　Above all, we should avoid deciding what we think about people different from ourselves without first having learned a great deal about them and the kind of lives they have to live.

　　如果句子较长时，每个分句也有自己的逻辑关系，这时也可以表示句子内部的逻辑关系。例如：

　　Topology（拓扑学）seems a queer subject; it delves into（深入研究）strange implausible （不合理的）shapes and its propositions are either childishly obvious（that is, until you try to prove them）or so difficult and abstract that not even a topologist can explain their intuitive meaning.

　　Most commonly the decisive factor is money; in fact, most engineering problems are answered ultimately in dollars and cents.

　　It seems to us that on the one hand, he must make intensive efforts to give the ordinary citizen and the politician—the means of evaluating the role of science in the modern world, since in the long run it is only the existence of a large body of well-informed and energetic citizens which can control abuses of governmental power; on the other hand, he must take more trouble to prepare himself for his own growing role as decision-maker and administrator.

1.2　机电专业英语表达方式

1.2.1　动词的常用表达

　　1. 摘要部分常用的动词表达

　　常用动词有：present, state, specify, describe, introduce, illustrate, interpret, report, explain, support, deal with, account for, characterize, argue, propose, intent, decide, conclude, review, discuss, treat, address, show, concern, develop, extend, consider, suggest, relate to, look at, etc.

常用句型有：The paper is essentially about..., The author presents the theory/method/technology/facts that..., A dominant factor is determined/decided by..., The model is set up/established/built through..., To improve the process/method/technology/theory, we will use a new kind of standard/flow procedure..., The author suggests that..., To make full use of resource/energy/information/data..., we must adopt/make/take measure..., It is shown/probed/proved/investigated that..., It is concluded that....

(1) The author presents some new observations, both theoretical and experimental, concerning the effects of the mutual interaction between micro-sized particles in a standing wave.

作者阐述了对不动波中微粒子相互作用的效应进行一些新的理论和实验观测的结果。

(2) This paper discusses the relation between the sampling period and the stability of sampled-data.

本文讨论了抽样周期与抽样数据稳定性之间的相互关系。

(3) The paper looks at what is happening across the UK as well as at new design techniques and materials now in use.

本文考查了全英国发生的情况及现在使用的设计技术和材料。

(4) The paper addresses an important problem in data-base management systems.

本文讨论了基本数据管理系统的一个重要问题。

(5) The author describes a configuration of a high-field machine capable of working at leading or lagging power factor.

作者描述了一种强磁场机的构造，这种机器以超前或滞后的功率因数工作。

(6) The paper reviews these applications, summarizes the theory from materials science viewpoint, and discusses the instrumentation considerations or extension of the techniques to other studies, and presents more recent applications.

本文综述了这些用途，从材料科学的观点概述了这一理论，并考查了仪器手段或将这一技术用于其他研究，还阐述了更多的近期用途。

(7) The author describes the techniques of open-loop vibration control.

作者介绍了开环振动控制技术。

(8) The author proposes an approach to the creation of an integrated method of investigation and designing objects, based on a local computer system.

作者创立一种综合法，以当地计算机系统为基础来进行对象研讨与设计。

(9) The paper concluds that, for British place in the world to be restored, changes must be initiated in the areas of marketing, design, development and manufacture.

本文结论是，为了恢复英国在世界上的地位，必须在市场营销、规划开发和制造方面开始做出改变。

(10) The paper provides a new framework for the analysis of loss of power.

本文提出了一种功率损耗分析方法的框架。

(11) A triangulation technique consisting of participant observation, interviews, and questionnaires was used to collect data from one hundred and ten engineers and twenty project managers over a two-year period.

本文采用了一种三点式技术，即亲自观察、访谈和问卷调查，对110位工程师和20位项目经理作了两年的调查和资料收集。

(12) The paper describes the use and development trends of telecommunication.

本文对无线电通信的使用和发展趋势作了简要的叙述。

2. 用于表达介绍、描述、分析、推理等过程的动词和句型

动词有：Discuss, study, research, develop, design, conduct, make, perform, implement, accomplish, complete, equip with, mount, produce, install, describe, analyze, detect, find out, compute, constitute, insist, comprise of, communicate with, consist of, set up, establish, build, increase, decrease, deduce, induce, infer, refer to, explain, investigate, survey, prove, testify, divide into, accept, report, modify, repair, maintain, hold, pay for, indicate, show, stand for, be characterized by, faced with, based on, benefit from, emphasize, seem, conclude, create, change into, turn into, convert into, draw, aim at, focus on, highlight, attempt to, propose, advise, put forward, innovate, range from, vary from, separate from, point out, represent, employ, discharge, charge, be regarded as, direct, apply for, compare to/with, express, believe, include, control, lead to, state, illustrate, require, differ from, support, cite, quote, verify, valid, provide, supply, delivery, etc.

主要句型有：

There are also a number of expressions used to introduce the present work:

In this paper, ... is investigated (studied, discussed, presented, etc.)

The present work deals mainly with...

We report here..., in the presence of...

This paper reports on...

On the basis of existing literature data, we carried out studies in an effort to...

The present study will therefore focus on...

The primary goal of this research is...

The purpose of this paper (study, thesis, etc.) is...

In this paper, we aim at...

3. 表示讨论、结果和结论的句型

The research we have done suggests an increase in...

As a result of our experiments we concluded that...

This fruitful work gives an explanation of...

Our experimental data are briefly summarized as follows...

Figure 3 shows the results obtained from studies of...

Table 5 presents the data provided by the experiments on...

This table summarized the data collected during the experiment of...
Some of the author's findings are listed in tables.
The direct outcome was then reported in...
Sufficient result for... has been observed with the new method...
This work did provide...
Most recent experiments to the same effect have led the author to believe that...
As a result of our experiments, we concluded that...
On the basis of..., the following conclusion can be made...
From... we now conclude...
To sum up, we have revealed...
We have demonstrated in this paper...
The results of the experiment indicate...
In conclusion, the result shows...
We have described..., we found...
Our argument proceeds in...
The research work has brought about a discovery of...
Finally, a summary is given of...
These findings of the research have led the author to the conclusion that...
The research has resulted in a solution of...

1.2.2 时态、语态特点

动词的时态和语态特点是由于科技文章一般重在客观地叙述事实，力求严谨和清楚，避免主观成分和感情色彩，这就决定了机电科技文体具有以下语法特点。

（1）时态：时态形式使用比较单一。

（2）语态：经常使用被动语态，而且没有行为的执行者。

（3）谓语：经常使用静态结构，用来表示状态或情况，例如，不说 The airplane flies fast. 而是说 the speed of the airplane is very high.

（4）定语：经常使用名词做定语，以取得简洁的效果，如用 radar range-finder target selector switch 表达雷达测距目标选择开关。

（5）动词非限定形式：经常使用它们来扩展句子。

① 动词不定式短语。

② 动名词短语。

③ 分词短语和独立分词结构。

（6）名词化：以名词为中心词构成短语以取代句子，如 when the experiment has been completed 可改写成名词短语 on completion of the experiment。

（7）多重复合句：长复合句较多，句子中又镶嵌子句。例如：

The simple fact shows that the more of the force of friction is got rid of, the farther will the ball travel, and we are led to infer that, if all the impeding forces of gravitation and resistance could be removed, there is no reason why the ball, once in motion, should ever stop.

这一简单事实表明，摩擦力越小，球滚得越远。由此可以推断，如能除去一切起阻碍作用的引力和阻力，就没有理由认为，球一旦处于运动中还会再停下来。

（8）逻辑词语：使用很频繁，明确表示内容的内在联系，有助于清楚地叙述、归纳、推理、论证和概括，如 hence, consequently, as a result, however, nevertheless, on the contrary, in short, as mentioned above 等。

（9）叙述方式：常避免用第一人称单数，而用第一人称复数 we 或用 the author 等第三人称形式（paper, article）。例如：

The author is particularly grateful to Prof. Anne Anderson for helpful discussion.

We have decided to repeat the experiment.

前面曾经提到，英语科技文章中动词常用的时态种类较少和比较经常使用被动语态，现在分别介绍如下。

1.2.2.1 时态

英语动词的 16 个时态中在机电专业英语中最常用的有 5 个，即一般现在时、现在进行时、一般过去时、一般将来时和现在完成时。在科技文章中一般现在时、一般将来时和现在完成时要比另外两种更常用些。此外，它们的用法也不如普通英语那样丰富多样。

1. 一般现在时

一般现在时是机电科技文章中最常见的时态，主要有三种用法。

（1）叙述过程。

A scientist observes carefully, applies logical thought to his observations and tries to find relationships in data, etc.

（2）叙述客观事实或科学定理。

Sound travels through the air in waves.

A complete rotation of the earth in relation to the pole star takes four minutes short of twenty-four hours.

Work is equal to the product of force and the distance through which the force moves.

（3）通常或习惯发生的行为。

Alternating current is usually supplied to people's houses at 50 cycles per second.

2. 一般将来时

表示将来发生的行为或情况。口语中常用的 be + going to infinitive 形式很少用，而用 will, is to, is about to, 如 many things now unknown will become known.

3. 现在完成时

现在完成时表示到现在为止发生的行为，或者已经发生但对现在有影响的行为。

During the past few years, several countries have pooled their resources in order to carry out certain types of scientific investigation more efficiently.

Cast iron is more brittle than iron which has been heated but not to be melted, but it is easier to shape, as it can be poured into moulds.

1.2.2.2 被动语态

被动语态在科技文章中用得十分频繁，主要有两个原因。第一个原因是科技描写行为或状态本身，所以由谁或由什么作为行为或状态的主体就显得不重要，或状态的主体没有必要指出，或者根本指不出来。在科技文章中被动句带有 by 短语的数量不多，by 短语有时是被动行为的主体，例如：

All the insulating substances <u>were damaged by</u> sea water.

The heat loss can <u>be considerably reduced by</u> the use of firebricks, round the walls of boiler.

有时则是行为的方式或工具，下面两个句子中的 by 短语就表示工具或行为方式。

The spectrum of the substance could <u>be determined by</u> testing its effectiveness against various types of bacteria.

Most of the drugs in current use <u>were discovered by</u> accident or trial and error.

被动语态使用频繁的第二个原因是便于向后扩展句子，而不至于使句子显得头重脚轻，例如：

In the digital computer the numbers to be manipulated <u>are represented by</u> sequences of digits (which are first recorded in suitable code, then converted into positive and negative electrical pulses, and stored in electrical or magnetic registers).

在上面这个句子里，sequences of digits 是被动行为的主体，which 连接的定语从句作为它的定语。如果把这个被动句变成主动句，把 sequences of digits 改成句子的主语，整个句子会显得非常笨拙和不平衡，违反了英语造句的一般原则。

1.2.3 句型表达

1. 表示原因

（1）<u>Because/Since</u> silver is a very good conductor of electricity, it is widely used industry.

（2）<u>In view of the fact that/On account of the fact that/Owing to the fact that/Seeing that</u> silver is a very good conductor of electricity, it is widely used in industry.

（3）<u>The reason why</u> it is widely used in industry is that silver is a very good conductor.

（4）<u>This explains why</u> it is widely used in industry.

（5）<u>This accounts for</u> the fact that it is widely used in industry.

（6）<u>This accounts for</u> it is widely used in industry.

2. 表示结果

（1）The temperature of the gas rises. <u>Consequently/Therefore/As a result/Hence</u> it expands in the cylinder.

（2）After-burners have to be used. <u>Consequently/Therefore/As a result/Hence</u> fuel consumption is heavier.

（3）The aircraft speed is limited. <u>Consequently/Therefore/As a result/Hence</u> it will soon become obsolete.

（4）The temperature of the gas rises, <u>so that/with the result that</u> it expands in the cylinder.

（5）After-burners have to be used, <u>so that/with the result that</u> more fuel is consumed.

（6）<u>As a result of/In consequence of/Consequent upon</u> its rise in temperature the gas expanded.

(7) As a result of/In consequence of/Consequent upon having to use after-burners more fuel is consumed.

(8) As a result of/In consequence of/Consequent upon its limited speed the aircraft is now obsolete.

(9) A rise in the temperature of the gas results in/leads to its expansion.

3. 表示比例关系

(1) The professor and student ratio is 1:10.

(2) The air and fuel ratio is 15:1.

(3) The ratio of the clearance volume to the swept volume in a cylinder differs in different type of engine.

(4) A compression ratio of about 4:1 can be obtained with a turbo-compressor.

(5) The efficiency of a cyclic process is the ratio of the work done to the heat received.

(6) The proportion of students to professors is 10 to 1.

(7) The proportion of air to fuel in the combustion chamber is 15 to 1.

(8) The air and fuel are mixed in a proportion of 15 to 1.

(9) Manganese and magnesium are present in equal proportions in duralumin.

(10) The linear speed of rotation of a pulley is proportional to its diameter.

(11) The electromotive force induced is proportional to the rate of change of flux.

(12) The volume of a mass of gas at constant pressure is directly proportional to its absolute temperature.

(13) The power of an engine is directly proportional to the area of cross-section of the cylinder.

(14) The insulation resistance of a cable is inversely proportional to its length.

(15) As the demand for power increases, the supply is proportionately increased.

(16) The machine is simple but much too heavy. It is disproportionately heavy.

(17) The new machine is slightly better but twice as expensive. It is disproportionately expensive.

(18) This bridge will be very costly for/in relation to its limited usefulness.

(19) The evaporative capacity is large for/in relation to the size of the boiler.

(20) The machine is very heavy for/in relation to its small size.

4. 表示组成和具有

Contents: Contain, Consist, Comprise, Constitute, Include.

(1) The packet contains 20 cigarettes.

(2) The gas contains about 5% carbon monoxide.

(3) The alloy contains 5% nickel and 5% iron.

(4) The tank contains 100 gallons of oil.

(5) The carbon monoxide content was about 5%.

(6) The moisture content of the cylinder increased.

(7) Part of the heat content of the gases is lost.

(8) He emptied out the contents of the box.

(9) A tank is a large container for holding liquids.

(10) The class consists of twenty-four students.

(11) The atmosphere comprises a number of gases.

(12) The machine is composed of several different parts.

(13) Cast-iron is made up of about six different substances.

(14) The factory produces components for aircraft.

(15) The resultant force acting on an aircraft wing may be resolved into a vertical component and a horizontal component.

(16) The composition of cast-iron is different for different purposes.

(17) Twenty-four students constitute the class.

(18) A number of gases form the atmosphere.

(19) Ferrite and carbon make up mild steel.

(20) Ferrite and carbon are the constituents of mild steel.

(21) The students in the class include three from Germany and four from France.

(22) The gases in the atmosphere include oxygen and nitrogen.

(23) The mixture in the furnace includes a certain amount of limestone.

5. 表示能够、许可等

(1) The microscope enables scientists to examine very small objects.

(2) A thermometer enables the doctor to measure body temperature.

(3) Helicopters enable passengers to land in the city centre.

(4) Good production methods enable the factory to manufacture more cars.

(5) Expansion joints permit/allow the pipes to expand or contract.

(6) Safety valves permit/allow the steam to escape from the boiler.

(7) We permit/allow the metal to cool slowly.

(8) The heat caused the metal to melt.

(9) Weakness in the metal caused it to fracture under tension.

(10) The heat made the metal melt.

(11) Weakness in the metal made it fracture under tension.

6. 表示对比关系

There is the structure commonly used to show the contrast or opposition between two facts:

(1) At high speed the turbo-jet is more efficient, while/whilst/whereas at low speed the propeller is more efficient.

(2) While/whilst/whereas at high speeds the turbo-jet is more efficient, at low speeds the propeller is more efficient.

(3) The contrast can be emphasized by adding on the one hand, on the other hand.

① A hot engine will run on a weak mixture, while on the other hand a cold engine requires a richer mixture.

② Whereas on the one hand a hot engine can run on a weak mixture, a cold engine requires a richer mixture.

(4) On the other hand is often used alone, after a full-stop.

A hot engine will run on a weak mixture. On the other hand a cold engine requires a richer mixture.

(5) Notice the expression in contrast to + Noun.

In contrast to the rich mixture needed to start a cold engine, a weak mixture is sufficient to keep a warm engine running.

7. 表示目的、设想、假设

Here we are concerned with the idea of assuming or assumption.

We do not know whether something is true or not, but we are going to assume or suppose true for a certain limited purpose.

(1) A hypothesis is a kind of assumption which we make as a starting-point for a line of reasoning. Ancient geographers assumed that the world was flat. It is assumed that petroleum originates in marine deposits.

(2) For the purposes of some calculation or experiment, we assume certain facts: they may not be true, but it simplifies the calculation to assume that they are true.

(3) The medium is assumed to be atmospheric air only.

(4) The cylinder is assumed to be a perfect non-conductor of heat.

(5) The heat loss is assumed to be negligible, and is disregarded.

(6) The assumption is made that the cylinder is a perfect non-conductor.

(7) The assumption is made that there is no heat loss from the cylinder.

(8) Assuming (that) there is no loss of speed over the blades, calculate the outlet velocity of the steam.

(9) Assuming (that) the deflection of the galvanometer is 45 degrees, find the weight of copper deposited.

(10) Assuming (that) /Suppose (that) if "v" is the velocity of the steam, then R is its relative velocity.

(11) Assuming (that) /Suppose (that) if the rise in the temperature of the water is 15 degrees, how much water must be delivered to the condenser?

8. 表示计算、判断、决定等

1) Calculations (work out mathematically)

(1) Calculate/Work out/ (Determine) the brake horse power developed by the engine at 2 000 rev/min.

(2) Calculate/Work out/ (Determine) the amount of air required for complete combustion of the fuel.

(3) Calculate/Work out/Determine the mass of copper deposited in 40 minutes.

2) Determine (find out)

(1) The constituents of the fuel can be determined by chemical analysis.

(2) The purpose of the test is to determine the calorific value of the fuel.

（3）It is necessary to determine the effect of the particles on the flow.

（4）Other types of thermometer must be used for accurate determination of very high temperature.

3）Estimate, Gauge, Judge（roughly）

（1）The temperature of the metal may be estimated/judged/gauged from the color of the oxide film.

（2）The age of a rock may be estimated/judged/gauged from the fossils embedded in it.

（3）A pressure gauge gives an indication of the pressure in the boiler.

（4）A plug gauge is a tool used to measure dimensions accurately.

（5）A micrometer is a gauge which gives a very exact measurement of size.

（6）The surveyor estimates the quantity and cost of the materials.

（7）In the estimate produced by the surveyor, the cost of each item is noted down.

（8）The estimated time of arrival of the aircraft is 11:00 today.

（9）It is estimated that the world's oil resources will last for 100 years.

4）Deduce（one thing from another）

（1）From the information given, we can deduce the specific heat of the oil.

（2）From the fossils embedded in it, we deduce the age of a rock.

9. 表示转移、传输、移动等

1）Transmission

（1）The power from the engine is transmitted/communicated to the machine through a belt.

（2）The piston movement is transmitted/communicated to the wheels through a crankshaft.

（3）The movement of the spindle is transmitted/communicated to the lead-screw through gem.

2）Transfer

（1）The molten metal is transferred from the ladle to the mould.

（2）The heat from the reactor is transferred to the heat exchange by a liquid coolant.

（3）Heat is not easily transferred from a dry vapour to a metal surface.

3）Convection

（1）The warm air is conveyed/carried upwards and displaces the cold air.

（2）The heat from the engine is conveyed/carried away by the air-stream.

（3）The heat from the engine is transmitted by convection into the air.

（4）When the liquid is heated from the bottom, convection current is set up.

4）Conduction

（1）The heat from the furnace is conducted/transmitted through the cylinder walls.

（2）The heat of the soldering iron is conducted/transmitted to the metal of the joint.

（3）Power from the generator is conducted/transmitted through cables to every house.

（4）The heat from the steam is transmitted through the tubes by conduction.

（5）Some substances are better conductors of electric current than others.

（6）Copper is a better conductor of heat than iron.

5) Radiation
(1) The heat of the sun is radiated/transmitted to the earth by radiation.
(2) Heat from the fire is radiated/transmitted to the walls of the furnace.
6) Carry or Take
(1) Boiler tubes convey the water from the upper drums to the lower drums.
(2) Lorries convey the machinery to the decks ready for loading.
(3) The exhaust steam is conducted/led through a blast pipe.
(4) The steam is conducted/led through nozzles onto the blades.

第2章　机电专业英语词法基础

2.1　专业英语词法特点

专业技术词是用来记录和表述各种现象、过程、特性、关系、状态等不同名称，亦称术语（term）。它在通用的词汇中虽占少数，但举足轻重，往往是段落或文章所要论述的中心词语，如 Microprocessor（微处理器），welding（焊接），NC（Numerical Control，数控）。技术词的主要特征如下。

（1）涌现性：新学科的诞生、新化合物的合成、新物种的发现等，使科技术语随着技术的发展而不断出现。

（2）单义性：对于某一特定专业或其分支，其词义狭窄，形态单一，定义时尽可能避免同形异义或同义异形现象。

（3）中性：术语只有概念意义，没有任何附加色彩，如 cat 转化为"吊锚"、dog 转化为"卡爪器"后，就失去原来猫和狗的形象及人们在用词方式上可能反映的好恶。

（4）国际性：英语和其他印欧语中的部分技术词和半技术词汇来源于拉丁语和希腊语，且词汇的专业性越强，在印欧语中同形同义词越多，国际性也越强。另外，新创造的科技词语只要在一国使用和流行，英语国家和别的拼音文字国家就可按照语音对应规律和拼写体系转写过来，成为自己的文字，例如，transistor（晶体管）一词在英语、德语和法语中是完全一样的。

2.2　构　词　法

目前，各行各业都有一些本专业学科的专业词汇，有的是随着本专业发展应运而生的，有的是借用公共英语中的词汇，有的是借用外来语言词汇，有的则是人为构造成的词汇。

2.2.1　派生词

这类词汇非常多，它是根据已有的词加上某种前后缀，或以词根生成，或以构词成分构成新的词。机电英语词汇中有很大一部分来源于拉丁语、希腊语等外来语，有的是直接借用，有的是在它们之上不断创造出新的词汇。这些词汇的构词成分主要是由词根加上前缀或后缀，或加上前后缀构成。

1. 前缀

采用前缀构成的单词在机电专业英语中占了很大比例，通过下面的实例可以了解常用的前缀构成的单词。

(1) multi—many, poly 多

该前缀在机电英语中表达"多的"意思时几乎可以随便加在词根前。例如：multimedia（多媒体），multi-sensor（多传感器的），multi-processor（多处理器），multi-protocol（多协议），multi-program（多道程序），multi-state（多态性）。

(2) hyper- 超级，super- 超级

这两个词也可加在表达"超级"意义的词根前，在程度上 hyper 比 super 大。例如：hypercube（超立方），superhighway（超级公路），supermarket（超级市场），superconductor（超导体），hypertext（超文本），HyperCard（超级卡片），super-pipeline（超流水线），hypermedia（超媒体），superscalar（超标），hyper switch（超级交换机），super class（超类）。

(3) inter- 相互、在……间

例如：interface（接口、界面），interlace（隔行扫描），interlock（连锁），internet［互联网络（因特网）］，interaction（相互作用，互感），interconnection（互联）。

(4) micro- 微型，(macro- 宏大)

例如：microcode（微代码），microchannel（微通道），microprocessor（微处理器），micro motor（微电机），microfilm（微型胶片），Microsoft（微软）。

(5) tele- 远程的，电的

例如：telemarketing（电话购物），teleconference（远程会议），telephone（电话），telecom（电信），telegraph（电报机），Tele-immersion（远程沉浸）。

(6) by- 边、侧、偏、副、非正式

例如：by-product（副产品），by-effect（副作用），by-pass（旁通），by-road（小路）。

(7) centi- 百分之一

例如：centimeter（厘米），centigrade（百分度），centigram（厘克），centisecond（厘秒），centigrade thermometer（百分度温度计）。

(8) co- 共同、相互

例如：cooperation（合作），co-run（共同管理），coexist（共存），collaboration（合作，协作），cohabit（同居）。

(9) counter- 反

例如：counteraction（反作用），counterclockwise（逆时针方向），countermeasure（对策，措施），counter-current（反向电流），counterclaim（反索赔），counterbore（沉孔），countercharge（反指控）。

(10) dis- 否定、相反

例如：disorder（混乱），discharge（放电），disappear（消失），disassembly（拆卸），disconnection（切断，中断）。

(11) en- 使……

例如：enlarge（扩大），enclose（封闭），encode（编码），enforce（实行，实施，强制），endanger（使危险）。

(12) ex- 出自、向外

例如：export（出口），extract（抽出，提取），exterior（外部，外面），exchange

（交换）。

（13）in- 不、非、无

例如：incorrect（不正确的，错的），inseparable（不可分的），independency（独立），invisible（看不见的）。**注意**：在 b、m、p 前加 im，在 l 前加 il。impossible（不可能的），logical（逻辑的）—illogical（不合逻辑的）。

（14）kilo- 千

例如：kilogram（千克），kilometer（千米，公里），kilowatt（千瓦），kilo-Newton（千牛）。

（15）milli- 毫、千分之一

例如：millivolt（毫伏），liter（升）—milliliter（毫升），milligram（毫克）。

（16）mis- 误、错、坏

例如：misfortune（不幸），mislead（误导），misunderstand（误解），misuse（滥用，误用）。

（17）a- 无、非、不

例如：aperiodic（非周期的），acentric（无中心的），abnormal（不正常的）。

（18）anti- 反对、相反、防止、防治

例如：anti-virus（防病毒），antimagnetic（防磁的），antiwar（反战的），antibody（抗体）。

（19）auto- 自动、自身

例如：auto-alarm（自动报警器），autorotation（自动旋转），autobiography（自传），automat（自动售货机），autonomy（自治）。

（20）bi- 两、二、重

例如：bi-colored（双色的），bimonthly（两月一次的，双月刊），bilingual（双语的），bicycle（自行车），bi-wheel driven（两轮驱动的）。

（21）semi, hemi 相当于 half

例如：semiconductor（半导体），hemicycle（半圆形），semifinal（半决赛），semitone（半音）。

（22）mono- 单、一

例如：monoplane（单翼飞机），monorail（单轨铁道），monotone（单音，单调），monograph（专著，专论），monopoly（独有权，垄断）。

（23）non- 非、不、无

例如：nonstop（直达，中途不停），nonmetal（非金属），nonconductor（绝缘体），nonstandard（非标准的，不规范的）。

（24）over- 过分、在……上面、超过、压倒、额外

例如：overproduction（生产过剩），overload（过载），overcharge（要价太高），overhead（在头顶上的，在上头的），overrun（溢出，超越）。

（25）poly- 多、复、聚

例如：poly-crystal（多晶体），poly-technical（多工艺的），polyatomic（多原子的），polygon（多边形），polysyllable（多音节词）。

（26）post- after，后

例如：postwar（战后的），post-liberation（解放后的），postdate（在日期后），postgraduate（研究生）。

（27）pre- 预先、在前

例如：preheat（预热），preschool（学前），predetermine（先定，预定），precondition（前提，先决条件），prepay（预付，提前付）。

（28）re- 再、重新

例如：rerun（重新运行），rewrite（改写），reset（重新设置），restate（重述），reprint（重新打印）。

2. 后缀

后缀是在单词（主干）后部加上构词结构，形成新的单词。一般改变词性，词的基本意义一般不变，例如：work 是动词，表示"工作"的意思；加 er 构成名词，worker 表示"工人"的意思；加 able 构成形容词 workable，表示"可加工的"的意思。这一组词都与主干词"工作"有关。

1）常见的构成名词的后缀

（1）-age 场所；费用；行为或行为的结果；状态；情况

例如：mileage（英里数），passage（通道），postage（邮费），breakage（破碎，破损），wastage（耗损），shortage（不足，短缺），advantage（利益），teenage（十几岁的时期），usage（使用）。

（2）-ance 性质，状况，行动，过程

例如：abundance（丰富，充裕），ignorance（忽视），intelligence（智力），interference（干扰，干涉）。

（3）-ant, -ent ……者

例如：assistant（助手），participant（参加者），agent（代理人），client（委托人，当事人），attendant（服务员，随从人员）。

（4）-er ……者，……物，……的机械，……人

例如：teacher（教师，导师），beginner（初学者），lawyer（律师），reader（读者），customer（顾客），barrier（栅栏，障碍物），cooker（厨具），washer（洗衣机），Londoner（伦敦人）。

（5）-ese ……的人，……派的，……特色

例如：Chinese（中国人），Japanese（日本人）。

（6）-ess 女性

例如：actress（女演员），hostess（女主人），waitress（女服务员），princess（公主）。

（7）-graph 记录仪器

例如：barograph（气压记录仪），telegraph（电报），spectrograph（分光摄像仪）。

（8）-ing 动作，动作的结果，与某一动作有关

例如：engineering（工程，工程学），feeling（感觉），greeting（问候），fishing（钓鱼），findings（发现的东西），reading（读数）。

（9）-ism ……主义，宗教，行为，……学，……术，……论，……法，……学派，

具有某种特性、情况、状态。

例如：capitalism（资本主义），heroism（英雄行为），magnetism（磁力学），hypnotism（催眠术），atomism（原子论），cubism［（艺术上的）立体派］。

（10）-ist　某种主义者或某种信仰者，从事某种职业或研究的人

例如：socialist（社会主义者），typist（打字员），scientist（科学家）。

（11）-ivity　性质，情况，状态

例如：activity（活动性，活动），productivity（生产力，生产率），sensitivity（敏感性，灵敏度），passivity（被动性）。

（12）-ment　行为，状态，过程

例如：development（发展），agreement（同意，协议），equipment（设备），investment（投资），requirement（需要）。

（13）-meter　计量仪器

例如：barometer（气压表），telemeter（测距仪），spectrometer（分光仪）。

（14）-ness　性质，情况，状态

例如：illness（病，疾病），firmness（结实，坚定），idleness（懒惰），business（事物，商业）。

（15）-scope　探测仪器

例如：telescope（望远镜），spectroscope（分光镜）。

（16）-or　……的人

例如：editor（编辑），inventor（发明者），visitor（来访者），doctor（医生），director（指导者）。

（17）-ship　情况，技能，身份，职位

例如：friendship（友谊，友好），membership（成员资格），professorship（教授身份），ownership（所有权，所有制）。

（18）-th　动作，过程，状态，性质

例如：growth（成长，生长，增长），strength（力量），depth（深度），birth（起源，诞生）。

（19）-tion　行为的过程、结果、状况

例如：option（选择，选择权），function（作用），addition（增加），elimination（消灭，排除），execution（完成，执行），suggestion（建议），situation（位置，处境）。

（20）-ty　性质、状态、情况，构成抽象名词

例如：safety（安全），beauty（美丽），cruelty（残忍），liberty（自由）。

（21）-ure　行为，行为的结果、状态、情况

例如：culture（文化，教养），pressure（压力），failure（失败），flexure（弯曲）。

（22）-ware　件（部件）

例如：hardware（硬件），groupware（组件），freeware（赠件）。

（23）-y　性质、状态、行为，构成抽象名词及学术名

例如：difficulty（困难），discovery（发明，发现），possibility（可能性），philosophy（哲学）。

2）常见的构成形容词的后缀

（1）-able　能……的，可……的，易于……的

例如：usable（可用的），suitable（适当的，合适的），favorable（受人喜欢的，赞成的），considerable（值得考虑的，相当大的，相当多的，值得重视的）。

（2）-al　属于……的，与……有关的

例如：digital（数字的），decimal（小数的，十进位的），commercial（商业的），elemental（基本的，元素的），global（全球的，全面的），external（外部的）。

（3）-ant　……的，具有……，性质的

例如：abundant（丰富的，充分的），assistant（辅助的），vacant（空的），ascendant（上升的）。

（4）-ar　有……性质的，如……的，属于……的，有……的

例如：familiar（熟悉的），similar（同样的），solar（太阳的），nuclear（核子的，原子核的）。

（5）-ary　与……有关的，属于……的

例如：ordinary（普通的），necessary（必需的），customary（通常的，习惯的），elementary（初级的）。

（6）-ed　有……的；如……的

例如：coloured（有色的，彩色的），gifted（有天才的），skilled（熟练的，有技能的），complicated（复杂的，难懂的）。

（7）-en　由……制成的，含有……质的，似……的

例如：woolen（羊毛制的），wooden（木制的），golden（金制的，似金的），leaden（铅制的）。

（8）-ent　具有……性质的，关于……的，有……行为倾向的

例如：apparent（明显的），frequent（频繁的，经常的），patent（专利，特许的）。

（9）-ful　充满……的，具有……性质的，可……的

例如：useful（有用的），hopeful（富有希望的），powerful（有力的），wonderful（奇妙的，惊人的）。

（10）-ible　易于……的，可……的

例如：compatible（兼容的），visible（看得见的），flexible（易弯曲的），sensible（觉察的，感知的）。

（11）-ic　与……有关的，属于……的，有……特性的

例如：academic（学术的），elastic（弹性的，灵活的），atomic（原子的，原子能的），periodic（周期的）。

（12）-ive　有……性质的；属于……的；与……有关的；有……倾向

例如：attractive（有吸引力的），active（积极的，主动的），expensive（昂贵的），productive（生产的，生产性的）。

（13）-less　没有，无，不

例如：useless（无用的），harmless（无害的），careless（粗心的），wireless（无线的）。

(14) -ly 如……的，有……性质的

例如：friendly（友好的），lovely（可爱的，令人愉快的），early（早的），timely（及时的，适时的）。

(15) -ous 多……的，有……的

例如：dangerous（危险的），famous（著名的），poisonous（有毒的），enormous（巨大的）。

(16) -some 充满……的，易于……的，产生……的

例如：tiresome（令人厌倦的），handsome（漂亮的，美观的），troublesome（令人烦恼的）。

(17) -y 多……的，有……的，有点……的

例如：rainy（有雨的），ready（乐意的，准备好的），holy（神圣的），empty（空的，空虚的），funny（有趣的，滑稽可笑的），healthy（健康的），tricky（棘手的，难处理的），noisy（嘈杂的）。

3) 常见的构成动词的后缀

(1) -ate 成为……，处理，使，作用

例如：eliminate（排除，消除，消灭），circulate（循环，流通），terminate（终止），estimate（估计，估算）。

(2) -en 使成为，变成，引起

例如：widen（加宽），darken（使变暗，变黑），strengthen（加强，巩固），weaken（削弱，变弱）。

(3) -fy 弄成，使……化

例如：simplify（简化），specify（指定），testify（证明，表明），beautify（美化）。

(4) -ize 变成，……化，实行

例如：characterize（表示……的特性），emphasize（强调），realize（实现），industrialize（使工业化），recognize（认出，承认），optimize（完善）。

4) 常见的构成副词的后缀

(1) -ly 每……一次

例如：yearly（每年的），daily（每日地），greatly（大大地），quickly（迅速地），carefully（小心地，认真地），truly（真正地，确实地）。

(2) -wards 向……

例如：outwards（向外），eastwards（向东），forwards（向前），upwards（向上）。

(3) -wise 方向，方式，状态

例如：clockwise（顺时针方向），likewise（同样地），otherwise（否则），lengthwise（纵向地）。

2.2.2 合成词

合成词是机电专业英语中另一大类词汇，其组成面广，通常可构成复合名词、复合形容词、复合动词等。复合词通常以小横杠"-"连接单词构成，或者采用短语构成。有的复合词进一步扩展，去掉了小横杠，并经过缩略成为另一类词类。例如：-based 基于，

以……为基础，rate-based（基于速率的），credit-based（基于信誉的），Windows-based（以 Windows 为基础的），file-based（基于文件的）；-centered 以……为中心的，client-centered（以客户为中心的），user-centered（以用户为中心的），host-centered（以主机为中心的）；-oriented 面向……的，以……为导向的，object-oriented（面向对象的），thread-oriented（面向线程的），economy-oriented（以经济为导向的），market-oriented（以市场为导向的）。也可以省去连字符，如 handbook，hardware，software，blackboard，同时也可以由三个词构成，如 up-to-date（现代的），one-to-one（一对一），point-to-point（点对点），peer-to-peer（对等网络），two-year-old（两岁的），line-by-line（逐行地），plug-and-play（即插即用）。

1. 合成名词

（1）名词 + 名词

work + shop—workshop（车间），wave + length—wavelength（波长）。

（2）名词 + 动名词

machine + building—machine-building（机器制造），book + learning—book-learning（书本知识），hand + writing—handwriting（手迹）。

（3）动名词 + 名词

waiting + room—waiting-room（候车室），building + material—building-material（建筑材料），swimming + pool—swimming-pool（游泳池）。

（4）形容词 + 名词

short + hand—shorthand（速记），hard + ware—hardware（硬件），

soft + ware—software（软件），black + board—blackboard（黑板）。

（5）动词 + 名词

pick + pocket—pickpocket（小偷），break + water—breakwater（防水堤）。

（6）副词 + 动词

in + put—input（输入），out + put—output（输出，产量），

out + come—outcome（结果）。

（7）动词 + 副词

feed + back—feedback（反馈），get + together—get-together（联欢会），

stand + still—standstill（停顿）。

2. 合成形容词

（1）名词 + 现在分词

peace + loving—peace-loving（热爱和平的），epoch + making—epoch-making（划时代的）。

（2）名词 + 过去分词

man + made—man-made（人造的），hand + made—hand-made（手工制作的）。

（3）形容词 + 现在分词

good + looking—good-looking（好看的），fine + looking—fine-looking 美观的，deep + going—deep-going（深入的）。

（4）形容词 + 过去分词

ready + made—ready-made（现成的）。

(5) 形容词 + 名词

new + type—new-type（新型的），large + scale—large-scale（大规模的）。

(6) 形容词 + 名词 + ed

medium + sized—medium-sized（中型的），noble + minded—noble-minded（高尚的）。

(7) 形容词 + 形容词

red + hot—red-hot（炽热的），light + blue—light-blue（淡蓝的），dark + green—dark-green（深绿的）。

(8) 数词 + 名词

first + class—first-class（第一流的），three + way—three-way（三通的，三项的）。

(9) 数词 + 名词 + ed

four + cornered—four-cornered（有四个角的），one + sided—one-sided（单面的，片面的）。

(10) 副词 + 现在分词

hard + working—hard-working（勤劳的），ever + increasing—ever-increasing（不断增长的）。

(11) 副词 + 过去分词

well + known—well-known（著名的），newly + built—newly-built（新建的），above + mentioned—above-mentioned（上述的）。

(12) 介词或副词 + 名词

under + ground—underground（地下的），off + hand—offhand（即刻的）。

3. 合成动词

(1) 名词 + 动词

work + harden—to work-harden（加工硬化），heat + treat—to heat-treat（热处理），trial + produce—to trial-produce（试制）。

(2) 形容词 + 动词

safe + guard—to safeguard（保卫），white + wash—to whitewash（白刷）。

(3) 副词或介词 + 动词

over + heat—to overheat（过热），over + write—to overwrite（覆盖），up + set—to upset（推翻），under + line—to underline（在……下面划线）。

2.2.3 转化法

在英语中，一些单词可以从一种词类转换为另一种词类，这叫做"转化"。转化后的词义往往与原来的词义有密切的联系。转化的方法主要有以下几种。

1. 名词转化为动词

machine（机器）—to machine（机加工），time（时间）—to time（计时、定时），format（格式）—to format（格式化）。

2. 动词转化为名词

to talk（交谈）—talk（谈话，讲话），to test（测验，检查）—test（测验、检验），

to use（使用）—use［用途（注意发音不同）］，to increase（增加）—increase［增加、增量（注意重音不同）］。

3. 形容词转化为名词

mineral（矿物的）—mineral（矿物质），good（好的）—good（益处），final（最后的）—final（决赛）。

2.2.4 缩略词

词汇缩略是指将较长的单词取其首部或主干构成与原词同义的短单词，或者将组成词汇短语的各个单词的首字母拼接为一个大写字母的字符串，通常词汇缩略在文章索引、前序、摘要、文摘、电报、说明书、商标等科技文章中频繁采用。在计算机专业中，在程序语句、程序注释、软件文档、互联网信息、文件描述中也采用了大量的缩略词汇作为标识符、名称等。缩略词汇的出现方便了印刷、书写、速记及口语交流等，但也同时增加了阅读和理解的困难。词汇缩略有以下四种形式。

1. 节略词（clipped words）

为方便起见，某些词汇在发展过程中逐渐用它们的前几个字母来表示，这就是节略词，如 maths—mathematics，ad—advertisement，dir—directory lab—laboratory 等。

2. 首字词（Initials）

首字词与缩略词基本相同，区别在于首字词必须逐字母念出，如 CAD—Computer Aided Design，CAM—Computer Aided Manufacture，CAE—Computer Aided Engineering，VM—Virtual Manufacture，QIS—Quality Information System，DB—Database，ES—Expert System，CPU—Central Process Unit，DBMS—Data Base Management System（数据库管理系统），CGA—Color Graphics Adapter（彩色图形适配器），ROM—Read Only Memory，RAM—Random Access Memory 等。

3. 缩写词（Abbreviation）

缩写词并不一定由某个词组的首字母组成，有些缩写词由一个单词变化而来，而且大多数缩写词的每个字母后都附有一个句点，如 e.g.—for example，Ltd.—limited，sq.—square 等。

2.2.5 拼缀法

拼缀词以原有的两个或两个以上的词为基础，经过首尾剪裁（或保留其中一个原词）重新组合而成。拼缀词实际上也可看成是复合词的简化。但拼缀词与缩略词不同，它们符合普通词的使用规律，如可读出音节，有数的变化，句首需大写等。例如：

programmatic = program + automatic（自动编程序的），telecamera = television + camera（电视摄像机），comsat = communication + satellite（通信卫星），forex = foreign + exchange（外汇）。

2.3 词义的引申

英汉两种语言在表达方式上差别很大。翻译时，有些词或词组无法直接搬用辞典中的释义，若勉强按辞典中的释义，逐词死译，会使译文生硬晦涩，很难看懂，甚至会造成误解。所以，要在弄清原文词义的基础上，根据上下文的逻辑关系和汉语的搭配习惯，对词义加以引申［如 Who's who，直译时谁也看不懂，实际上它是美国的一本著名杂志（名人录）的英文名称］。若遇到有关专业方面的内容，必须选用专业方面的常用语。引申后的词义虽然同辞典中的释义稍有不同，但却能更确切地表达原文意义。举例如下。

（1）There is no physical contact between tool and work piece.

欠佳译法：在工具和工件之间没有有形的接触。

引申译法：工具和工件不直接接触。

（2）Public opinion is demanding more and more urgently that something must be done about noise.

欠佳译法：公众舆论越来越强烈地要求为消除噪声做某些事情。

引申译法：公众舆论越来越强烈地要求管一管噪声问题。

（3）There is a wide area of performance duplication between numerical control and automatics.

欠佳译法：在数控和自动化机床之间，有一个性能重复的广阔地带。

引申译法：数控和自动化机床有很多相同的性能。

（4）High-speed grinding does not know this disadvantage.

欠佳译法：高速磨床不知道这个缺点。

引申译法：高速磨床不存在这个缺点。

（5）You found that, in two experiments, hardness and greenness in apple went together with sourness.

欠佳译法：在有过两次经验之后，你发现苹果中的硬与青是和酸同行的。

引申译法：在有过两次经验之后，你发现凡是又硬又青的苹果总是酸的。

2.4　词性变化

有些句子由于英汉两种语言的表达方式不同，不能逐词对译。原文中有些词在译文中需要转换词性，才能使译文通顺自然。词性转译大体有以下几种情况。

1. 英语动词、形容词、副词译成汉语名词

（1）Gases differ from solids in that the former has greater compressibility than the latter.

气体和固体的区别在于气体的可压缩性比固体大。

（2）The instrument is characterized by its compactness, and portability.

这个仪器的特点是结构紧凑、携带方便。

（3）The cutting tools must be strong, tough, hard and wear resistant.

刀具必须有足够的强度、韧性、硬度，而且耐磨。

（4）Dynamics is divided into statics and kinetics, the former treating of force in equilibrium, the latter of the relation of force to motion.

力学分为静力学和动力学：前者研究平衡力，后者研究力和运动的关系。

（5）The image must be dimensionally correct.

图形的尺寸必须正确。

2. 英语名词、介词、形容词、副词译成汉语动词

（1）The application of electronic computers makes for a tremendous rise in labor productivity.

使用电子计算机可以大大提高劳动生产率。

（2）In any machine input work equals output work plus work done against friction.

任何机器的输入功，都等于输出功加上克服摩擦所做的功。

（3）Scientists are confident that all matter is indestructible.

科学家们深信一切物质是不灭的。

（4）Open the valve to let air in.

打开阀门，让空气进入。

3. 英语的名词、副词和动词译成汉语形容词

（1）The maiden voyage of the newly-built steamship was a success.

那艘新造轮船的处女航是成功的。

（2）It is a fact that no structural material is perfectly elastic.

事实上没有一种结构材料是十全十美的弹性体。

（3）They said that such knowledge is needed before they develop a successful early warning system for earthquakes.

他们说，这种知识对他们要发明一种有效的地震早期警报是必要的。

4. 英语形容词、名词译成汉语副词

（1）A continuous increase in the temperature of the gas confined in a container will lead to a continuous increase in the internal pressure within the gas.

不断提高密封容器内气体的温度，会使气体的内压力不断增大。

（2）It is our great pleasure to note that China will sooner join the WTO.

我们很高兴地注意到，中国不久就会加入世界贸易组织。

2.5　词义的差异

英语单词绝大多数为多义词，因此翻译时首先要选择一个最确切的词义。只有这样，才能使译文正确。选择词义通常从以下几个方面考虑。

1. 根据词义的差异选择准确词汇

同一个单词，因词类不同，其词义也不同。例如：like 在下面五个句子中，分属五种不同词类，弄错了词类，理解上就错了，译文也错了。

（1）Like charges repel, while unlike charges attract.

同性电荷相斥，异性电荷相吸（like 是形容词，作"同样的"讲）。

（2）Things like air, water or metals are matter.

像空气、水或金属之类的东西都是物质（like 是介词，作"像"讲）。

（3）Like knows like.

英雄识英雄（like 是名词，作"同类的人"讲）。

(4) I hope I can use the computer like you do.

我希望我使用计算机像你一样（like 是连接词，作"如同"讲）。

(5) Do you like this color TV set?

你喜欢这台彩电吗（like 是动词，作"喜欢"讲）？

2. 同一个词在不同的句子里，虽然其词类相同，词义却可能有差别。在下面三个句子中，light 均为形容词，但词义不相同。

(1) The instrument is very light.

这台仪器很轻（light 作"轻的"讲）。

(2) The cover of the meter is light blue.

这个仪表盖是浅蓝色的（light 作"浅的"讲）。

(3) The lamp is very light.

这盏灯是很明亮的（light 作"明亮的"讲）。

3. 根据名词的数不同选择词义

英语中有些名词的单数和复数所表示的词义完全不同。例如：

名词	单数词义	复数词义
facility	简易，灵巧	设施，工具
charge	负荷，电荷	费用
main	主线，干线	电源
spirit	精神	酒精
work	功，工作	著作，工厂，工程

2.6 词的搭配

英语和汉语是两种不同的语言，它们的词汇各有其搭配规律，在翻译时如果不分具体场合，机械地复制原文里的词汇搭配，孤立地译出每个词的字面意义，往往会破坏译文语言的规范，得不出正确的译文。因此，有时必须根据原文的上下文逻辑关系和译文语言习惯，适当地调整原文的字面意义，换用另一些词来表达。

1. 动词与名词的搭配

以动词"move"为例，其基本意思是"运动"，但在不同的句子里与不同的名词搭配，译法也就不同了。

(1) The earth moves round the sun.

地球绕太阳旋转。

(2) Heat moves from a hotter to a colder body.

热量从温度较高的物体传到温度较低的物体上。

(3) Move M to other work.

调 M 去做别的工作。

(4) The work moves slowly.

工作进展缓慢。

2. 副词与动词的搭配

以副词"successfully"为例。

(1) Spot-welding has already been used successfully in welding fuel tanks.

点焊已经成功地用来焊接油箱。

(2) The task was finished successfully.

圆满完成了任务。

(3) Our production plan has been successfully carried out.

我们的生产计划已顺利执行了。

3. 形容词与名词的搭配

以形容词"thick"为例。

(1) The book is 8 inches thick.

这本书有8英寸厚。

(2) He drew a thick line on the paper.

他在纸上划了一条粗线。

(3) Thick liquids pour much slowly than thin liquids.

稠的液体往外倒时比稀的液体慢得多。

(4) The conditions are too thick.

条件太过分了。

4. 动词与介词、动词与副词的搭配

电机机电专业英语中大量出现动词与介词及动词与副词的搭配使用，这些搭配常常是固定的，需要牢记。常见的搭配有：set up（建立），differ from（不同，区别），be characterized by（以……为特征），find out（发现，找到），work out（计算出，设计出，解决），figure out（计算出，解决），apply for（请求，申请），be applied to（应用到），be divided/separated into（分成，分为），use up（用完，耗尽），run out（用完，耗尽），give up（放弃），give in（屈服，让步，交上），give off［放出（光、热），长出］，remove from（从……取下，脱下），study/research on 研究……，be based on（基于，以……为基础），draw out（抽出，取出，说出，画出），link to（连接），connect with（连接，联系），provide...with（用……提供），stop...from（阻止，禁止），be equipped with（装备，安装），go down（下降，减少），be increased/decreased/reduced by［增加（减少）了］，change/turn/convert...into（变为，将……变成），aim at（以……为目标），sum up（总结），be used to（习惯于），used to（过去常常），fill in/out（填写），fall into（落在……，下降到），bring out（生产，制造），bring up（教育，培养，提出），bring on（引起，导致），put forward（提出），put up with（容忍，忍受），contribute to（贡献，有助于），care for（关心 照顾），call for（要求），lead to（导致），result in（导致），lie in（在于），vary from...to...（从……到……变化），make up（组成，分解，编造，化妆），make use for（利用），mix/blend with（混合），familiarize with（熟悉），break up（分解，打破，分裂，驱散），speed up（加速），interfere in（干涉），set aside（放在一边，备用），adapt to（适用），trace/go back to（追溯到）。

第2篇 阅读篇

第二篇 肉食

第3章 机电专业英语阅读概论

3.1 机电专业英语的阅读要求

所谓阅读，实际上就是语言知识、语言技能和智力的综合运用。在阅读过程中，这三个面的作用总是浑然一体、相辅相成的。词汇和语法结构是阅读所必备的语言知识；但仅仅如此是难以进行有效阅读的，学生还需具备运用这些语言知识的能力，即根据上下文来确定准确词义和猜测生词词义的能力，辨认主题和细节的能力，正确理解连贯的句与句之间、段与段之间的逻辑关系的能力。这里所指的智力是学生的认知能力，包括记忆、判断和推理的能力。因为在阅读专业英语文章时常常要求领悟文章的言外之意和作者的态度、倾向等。

阅读理解能力的提高是由多方面因素决定的，学生应从以下三个方面进行训练。

1. 打好语言基本功

扎实的语言基础是提高阅读能力的先决条件。首先，词汇是语言的建筑材料。提高专业英语资料的阅读能力必须扩大词汇量，尤其是掌握一定量的机电专业词汇。如词汇量掌握得不够，阅读时就会感到生词多，不但影响阅读的速度，而且影响理解的程度，从而不能进行有效的阅读。其次，语法是语言中的结构关系，用一定的规则把词或短语组织到句子中，表示一定的思想。熟练掌握英语语法和惯用法也是阅读理解的基础。在阅读理解中必须运用语法知识来辨认出正确的语法关系。如果语法基础知识掌握得不牢固，在阅读中遇到结构复杂的难句、长句，就会不知所措。

2. 在阅读实践中提高阅读能力

阅读能力的提高离不开阅读实践。在打好语言基本功的基础上，还要进行大量的阅读实践。词汇量和阅读能力的提高是一种辩证关系：要想读得懂，读得快，就必须扩大词汇量；反之，要想扩大词汇量，就必须大量阅读。同样，语法和阅读之间的关系也是如此：有了牢固的语法知识就能够促进阅读的顺利进行，提高阅读的速度和准确率；反之，通过大量的阅读实践又能够巩固已掌握的语法知识。只有在大量的阅读中，才能培养语感，掌握正确的阅读方法，提高阅读理解能力。同时在大量的阅读中，还能巩固机电专业知识及了解专业的发展趋势，这对于跟踪机电技术的发展很有好处。

3.2 掌握正确的阅读方法

阅读时，注意每次视线的停顿应以一个意群为单位，而不应以一个单词为单位。要是一个词一个词地读，当读完一个句子或一个段落时，前面读的是什么早就忘记了。这样读不仅速度慢，还影响理解。因此，采用正确的阅读方法可以提高阅读速度，同时提高阅读理解能力。常用的有效阅读方法有三种，即略读（Skimming）、查读（Scanning）、精读（Reading for full understanding/intensive reading）。

略读是指以尽可能快的速度进行阅读，了解文章的主旨和大意，对文章的结构和内容获得总的概念和印象。一般地说，400 字左右的短文要求在 6~8 min 完成。进行略读时精力必须特别集中，还要注意文中各细节分布的情况。略读过程中，学生不必去读细节，遇到个别生词及难懂的语法结构也应略而不读。不要逐词逐句读，力求一目数行而能知大体含义。略读时主要注意以下几点：

（1）注意短文的开头句和结尾句，力求抓住文章的主旨和大意；
（2）注意文章的体裁和写作特点，了解文章结构；
（3）注意了解文章的主题句及结论句；
（4）注意支持主题句或中心思想的信息句，其他细节可以不读。

查读的目的主要是要有目的地去找出文章中某些特定的信息，也就是说，在对文章有所了解的基础上，在文章中查找与某一问题、某一观点或某一单词有关的信息。查读时，要以很快的速度扫视文章，确定所查询的信息范围，注意所查信息的特点，如有关日期、专业词汇、某个事件、某个数字、某种观点等，寻找与此相关的关键词或关键段落。注意与所查信息无关的内容可以略过。

精读是指仔细地阅读，力求对文章有深层次的理解，以获得具体的信息，包括理解衬托主题句的细节，根据作者的意图和中心思想进行推论，根据上下文猜测词义等。对难句和长句要借助语法知识对其进行分析，达到准确的理解。总之，要想提高阅读理解能力，必须掌握以下六项基本的阅读技能：

（1）掌握所读材料的主旨和大意；
（2）了解阐述主旨的事实和细节；
（3）根据上下文判断某些词汇和短语的意义；
（4）既理解个别句子的意义，也理解上下文之间的逻辑关系；
（5）根据所读材料进行一定的判断、推理和引申；
（6）领会作者的观点、意图和态度。

第4章 机电专业英语阅读技巧

机电专业英语阅读不仅对于机电专业的学生而且对于从事机电专业的技术人员都是十分重要的。不同的读者在阅读科技文章时有不同的方法和技巧,但作为科技文献阅读本身总是存在一定的规律,有普遍通用的方法和技巧可以遵循。

4.1 获取主题思想

老练的作者通常都是围绕一个主题思想来组织写作材料的。许多读者在获取主题思想方面有困难。或许我们都遇到过这样的情形,谈话中双方在进行争论,但是似乎任何一方都没有抓到对方的要点。与此非常相似的是,或许我们看过一段文章后还不明白作者究竟在说什么。我们可以把获取主题思想的阅读技巧分为以下四步:

(1) 辨认主题名词;
(2) 找出主题句;
(3) 获取主题思想;
(4) 避免不相关的内容。

1. 辨认主题名词

就大多数文章而言,获取主题思想的第一步就是要确定一个最能描述作者思想中的某个人、某个地方或某件事的名词,这样的一个名词(有时是一个短语)就是主题名词。

(1) Rocks found on the surface of the earth are divided into three classes: igneous, sedimentary, and metamorphic. Molten material becomes igneous rock when it cools. Sedimentary rocks are formed from materials deposited by glaciers, plants, animals, streams, or winds. Metamorphic rocks are rocks that once were igneous or sedimentary but have changed as a result of pressure, heat, or the deposit of material from solution.

Topic noun: rocks: igneous, sedimentary, and metamorphic.

(2) Hieroglyphic writing was extremely difficult to read and write, even during the period when it was in common use. Trained professional, known as scribes, were employed to do all the writing and reading of hieroglyphics.

Topic noun: Hieroglyphics writing.

(3) At the beginning of the Expressionist movement, we see the work of Van Gogh. Not at all concerned with producing a copy of what he painted, he used color and form to express his feelings about his subject. He also used broad brushes and palette knives and sometimes squeezed paint directly from the tube in his haste to get his feelings.

Topic noun: Van Gogh, Expressionist.

2. 找出主题句

一个段落的主题句就是最能表达作者的主题思想的句子,多数情况是主题句位于句首，也可以位于句尾，少数情况位于句中。

(1) In the early days of big-city post offices, a great deal of time was spent in getting mail from the main station to the substations and from stations to trains. Then compressed air came into use as a means of speeding up the movement of mail from place to place, long tubes were built under the ground to connect different mail-handling sites, and hollow containers were made to fit the tubes. Mail was put into the containers, the containers were put into the tubes, and compressed air was used to propel the containers to their destinations. Some cities still have many miles of mail tubes. Smaller tubes are used in many libraries, stores, and factories.

Topic sentence: In the early days of big-city post offices in the early days of big-city post offices.

(2) The risk of premature death from all causes is much greater among cigarette smokers than among nonsmokers. This alone should be a good reason to quit smoking. The risk of premature death from coronary artery disease is 1.7 times greater among smokers. The risk of death from bronchitis and emphysema is 6 times greater among smokers. The risk of premature death from lung cancer is 10 times greater among smokers. It is clear that smoking affects not only your day-to-day health but your life span as well.

Topic sentence: The risk of premature death from all causes is much greater among cigarette smokers than among nonsmokers.

(3) Today's marketplace is crowded with sellers competing for your money and your attention by offering different services, prices, specials, bonuses, and quality of goods. There are so many kinds of stores and deals that it is hard to keep them straight. To get the best bargain you need to carefully weigh the advantages and disadvantages of each deal before making your final selection.

Topic sentence: To get the best bargain you need to carefully weigh the advantages and disadvantages of each deal before making your final selection.

(4) The class of drugs known as depressants act to slow down the functioning of the central nervous system. They relax the body and are often used to induce sleep or alleviate pain. When too large a dose is taken, depressant drugs induce a state of drunken intoxication and produce slurred speech, blurred vision, slowed reaction time, and loss of coordination. The depressant drugs are highly addictive and include alcohol, opiates, barbiturates, and minor tranquilizers.

Topic sentence: The class of drugs known as depressants act to slow down the functioning of the central nervous system.

(5) Poultry, ground meat, and seafood become unsafe to eat when they start to spoil. The bacteria present in these foods multiply rapidly. When these foods have thawed completely, they should not be refrozen. If the food still has ice crystals in it you may refreeze it immediately. Usually this is safe, although it may reduce the quality of the food. If the food is completely thawed and its condition appears poor or questionable, get rid of it. It might be dangerous.

Topic sentence: Poultry, ground meat, and seafood become unsafe to eat when they start to spoil.

(6) If your car is stopped in a blizzard, by all means stay in it. Trying to walk outside in a blizzard can be extremely dangerous. In blowing and drifting snow, disorientation comes, very rapidly. Being lost in open country during a blizzard can be fatal. If you stay in your car you are most likely to be found and the car will provide a great deal of protection from the elements.

Topic sentence: If your car is stopped in a blizzard, by all means stay in it.

3. 获取主题思想

在获取主题思想时，读者容易出现将主题的一小部分看作是主题思想，或概括内容过多并已超过了作者所表达的主题思想的范围的错误。

阅读下面各段文章，决定哪句是主题句，哪句过窄，哪句过宽。

(1) Nitrogen is sometimes called a "lazy" as there are not any very interesting simple experiments that can be done with it. It is, however, important to us. We are not built to survive in pure oxygen. The nitrogen in the atmosphere weakens or dilutes the oxygen so that the air is right for us. The nitrogen serves the same purpose in the air that water serves in lemonade, lemonade made of pure lemon juice and sugar would be too strong. To make lemonade right for us, we add water.

(a) Nitrogen is important because it dilutes oxygen so that the air is right for us. (main idea)

(b) Lemonade without water would not be very good. (too specific)

(c) Nitrogen is very important to us. (too general)

(2) Handling children's anger can be very distressing to adults. Often the distress is of being unable to deal with our own anger. Parents, teachers, counselors and others who deal with children need to remember that they may not be very good at dealing with their own anger. As children many of us were taught that anger was bad and were made to feel guilty for expressing anger.

(a) Children can be very hard for adults to deal with. (too general)

(b) Our own anger can make it hard to deal with children's anger. (main idea)

(c) Children sometimes make us angry. (too specific)

(d) Teachers must learn to handle their own anger in order to learn how to deal with children anger. (too general)

(3) Lead, cadmium, and mercury are elements that have been found to be harmful to humans. They seem to be completely unnecessary to health. Cadmium, for example, interferes with the functions of iron, copper, and calcium, which are necessary for health. People exposed to large amounts of cadmium may suffer anemia, kidney damage, and bone deficiencies.

(a) Cadmium is harmful to humans. (too specific)

(b) Lead, cadmium, and mercury are harmful to humans and are unnecessary for health (main idea).

(c) lead is harmful to humans and has no beneficial properties. (too specific)

(d) Some minerals are harmful to human health. (too general)

(4) With Lake Mead as its reservoir, Hoover Dam has proved very effective in the control

flooding. The dam controls not only the lesser flash floods that come anytime when there is heavy rain also the great flood-tide runoff that occurs each spring and summer.

(a) Hoover Dam has many benefits. (too general)

(b) Hoover Dam helps control spring flooding. (too specific)

(c) Hoover Dam helps control flash floods. (too specific)

(d) Hoover Dam has proved very effective in the controling flooding. (main idea)

(5) One cheap and effective way of advertising your home is to place a sign in your front yard. The sign should be placed so that it can be seen easily from the street. The lettering should be large enough so it can be read easily. It is especially important that the telephone numbers are bright easy to read. Block out your spacing before you start so your sign looks well balanced. A well-made lawn sign should put you in contact with many prospective customers.

(a) When selling your home it is important to advertise. (too general)

(b) A well-made lawn sign can help you sell your house. (main idea)

(c) Selling your home can be a lot of work. (too general)

(d) The letters on your lawn sign should be easy to read from the street. (too specific)

4. 避免不相关的内容

读者在获取主题思想时所犯的另一个普遍错误就是头脑中出现一些与文章主题思想不相关的概念，并把它们看作是文章的主题思想。在阅读文章之前读者有可能对作者表述的主题方面已有一些了解。如果读者过多地考虑已了解的那些内容，而不充分地关注作者所阐述的思想的话，就容易形成与文章的主题思想不相关的主题思想，尽管它本身的内容是真实的。总而言之，不能先入为主，不能用自己的想法代替文章的主题思想。

判断下面段落的主题思想是否与作者观点相符。

(1) Movies are actually separate still pictures shown so fast that the human eye cannot detect the break between them. When successive images are presented rapidly enough, we fuse them into single moving image.

(a) Movies are extremely popular. (irrelevant)

(b) Modern movies make much use of slow motion. (irrelevant)

(c) Motion pictures are separate pictures shown so fast that we see no break between them. (relevant)

(d) Motion pictures require an expensive camera, capable of making very rapid multiple exposures. (irrelevant)

(2) Blue dye is only one of the many chemicals that are changed by light. Any chemical which is changed by light is said to be "sensitive to light". If there were no light-sensitive chemicals, we would not be able to make photographs.

(a) Light-sensitive chemicals are always blue. (irrelevant)

(b) If a chemical, such as blue dye is changed by light, it is said to be sensitive to light. (relevant)

(c) Blue dye is the only chemical which is changed by light. (irrelevant)

(d) Without blue dye, there would be no photography. (irrelevant)

(3) Spelling skills are very important in modern life. People often form an impression based on what we have written. If what we have written is full of misspellings, their impression of us suffers. Some of us may have difficulty learning the principles of good spelling, but if we want to make a favorable impression on our teachers, associates, employers, and other people we communicate with in writing, these principles must be learned.

(a) Spelling skills are not very important for some people. (irrelevant)

(b) Spelling skills are very important. (relevant)

(c) Some words are harder to spell than others. (irrelevant)

(d) Spelling principles are very easy to learn. (irrelevant)

(4) Shampoos that are medicated, whether sold by prescription or not, are classified as drugs rather than cosmetics. They contain drug ingredients designed to cure or help certain conditions such as dandruff. The manufactures of these products are required to comply with the FDA's drag regulations or, if it is a new drug, to show that it is both safe and effective in meeting the claims on the label.

(a) Some shampoos are designed only to clean hair. (irrelevant)

(b) Some shampoos are classed as drugs. (relevant)

(c) Some shampoos are fairly expensive. (irrelevant)

(d) Shampoos that are classed as drugs tend to be more expensive. (irrelevant)

4.2 获取细节

在所有的文章中，作者都使用细节或事实来表达和支持他们的观点。阅读要想有效果，就要能够辨认并记住文章中重要的细节。一个细节就是一个段落中的一条信息或一个事实。它们或者给段落的主题提供证据，或者为其提供例子。有些细节或事实是完整的句子，而有一些只是简单的短语。只判断出哪些是细节这往往并不够。在很多情况下，还必须能区分哪些是重要细节，哪些是次要细节。想记住所有的细节是不可能的，但是在阅读过程中要尽量发现重要细节并记住它们，判断下列各段中哪些部分是<u>最重要的细节</u>。

Madame Curie and her husband discovered that a piece of pitchblende produced a darkening of photographic plates out of all proportion to its uranium content. This meant to them that the pitchblende contained some other element.

(a) The Curies decided to try and isolate this new element.

(b) The task took all their time for two years.

(c) When they were through, the Curies had discovered not one but two new elements.

(d) The first to be discovered was called polonium, after Madame Curie's native Poland; the other element was the famous metal radium.

4.3 领 悟 词 义

在阅读英文科技文章时，你可能会碰到许多不认识的词汇。从英汉词典中查出它们的意思既费时又令人厌倦。有时长时间的查找甚至令你心灰意冷而不能继续读下去。在阅读英文资料时不可能不查词典，但是可以通过上下文来领悟生词，从而减少查词典的时间。作者常常用"or"这个词来引导出一个词或一个短语的定义，特别是当他认为这个词或短语对于读者来说是比较生疏的时候，就更会这样做。科技文章常常会阐述一些新思想、新概念，所以在文章中常常就会出现一些生词。"or"这个词就像是一个信号，把新词语的定义告诉你，从而可以使你不用查词典就可以明白这个新词语的意思。有时也可能用一同位语来解释这个词，或用括号来说明，或用":"和"-"来提示。在阅读机电英语时可以利用词缀来猜出词义，知道了主干词义可通过前缀和后缀的意思来猜测不认识的词汇。

4.4 弄清文中的指代关系

机电专业英语中经常使用 it 来指代名词、代词，可作形式主语或宾语，可指代某一客观事物、自然现象等，在文中可指代上下逻辑关系。

1. it 用作代词，指代无生命的东西、物体及抽象概念，也可指代在前面出现过名词。

(1) The book is about science. It is not about mathematics. (It = book)

(2) Science is my main interest. It is also my best subject. (It = science)

(3) Science is my main interest. I know a lot about it. (It = science)

(4) Her research project was on some aspect of genetics. I'm not sure what it was. (It = some aspect)

(5) The amoeba is a one-celled organism. It reproduces by dividing in two parts. (It = amoeba)

2. it 用在习语中的组成部分及与天气、时间有关的非人称主语。

(1) It is hot in the tropics.

(2) It rains from May to October.

(3) It was snowing last week when we got there.

(4) It is three o'clock.

(5) It will be dark in an hour.

(6) It will be three months before we know the results of the test.

(7) It is 4 200 kilometers from Caracas to Hudson Bay.

(8) It costs a lot to do research.

3. it 用作形式主语，起先行作用，没有具体意义。

It is known that plaque builds up on artery walls. (It = that which is known, namely: plaque builds up on artery walls) This means: Plaque builds up on artery walls. This is known.

It has been shown that laser surgery is painless. (It = that which has been shown, namely: laser surgery is painless) This means: Laser surgery is painless. This has been shown.

It has been discovered that amaranth is nutritious. (It = that which has been discovered, namely: amaranth is nutritious) This means: Amaranth is nutritious. This has been discovered.

It is essential to understand genetics if you want to work on hybridization. (It = that which is essential, namely: to understand genetics) This means: To understand genetics is essential if you want to work on hybridization.

4.5　把握文中的对比逻辑关系

作者常常用读者比较熟悉的概念或事物作为陪衬来帮助读者理解或记住他们所表述的概念或事物。例如：

Unlike laser surgery, which can be performed in a doctor's office, traditional surgery must be performed in a hospital because of the danger of complications.

表示陪衬和对比的词和词组可以帮助读者理解含有生词的句子。只要认识这样的表示陪衬和对比的词语，就可以猜测出不认识的词语的意思。例如：

Most strong earthquakes in lonely outposts are not dangerous. On the other hand, even a fairly minor one in a city can cause great damage.

即使从没见"lonely outpost"，你也可以根据"on the other hand"来猜出它的含义。从对比中可以看出 lonely outpost 肯定与 city 非常不同，所以意思一定是没有什么人居住的地方。在阅读过程中如果特别留意这些表示陪衬和对比的词语，对文章的理解就会更深入，而且可以节省查词典的时间。常见的表示对比的词有 while，however，unlike，but，although，in contrast 和 on the other hand。

(1) Sharks have a cartilaginous skeleton, while bony fish have a skeleton made of bone.

(Contrast: skeleton. Explanation: There is something unusual about the shark's skeleton. It is unlike that of other fish.)

(2) Earthquakes occur most frequently in the western part of the United States. However, they also occur in all parts of North America.

(Contrast: earthquake locations. Explanation: You probably already know that earthquakes occur in the western part of America. You probably do not know that they also occur in Nova Scotia.)

(3) Amaranth and other wild plants can be hard to farm because, unlike corn, wheat, and oats they do not have a known harvest time.

(Contrast: harvest times for various grains. Explanation: The reason amaranth is hard to farm is that it doesn't have a predictable harvest time.)

(4) Most eye surgery is still performed in the traditional manner. But more and more conditions are beginning to be treated with lasers, making true surgery unnecessary.

(Contrast: surgical methods. Explanation: The reality of the situation is that lasers have not made eye surgery a thing of the past.)

(5) Although studies have shown an association between high blood lipid levels and arterial plaque many scientists feel the relationship is not yet entirely understood.

(Contrast: assumptions and proven fact. Explanation: There is still controversy about this subject.)

(6) The English system of measurement is based on multiples of twelve. In contrast, the metric system is always based on multiples of ten.

(Contrast: systems of measurement. Explanation: See just how different two systems of measurement can be.)

(7) Having an advanced degree in science does not help a teacher teach. On the other hand, it is impossible to get a science teaching position without having an advanced degree in science.

(Contrast: methods of preparing for teaching. Explanation: Absurdity of situation pointed out.)

4.6　把握文中描述的位置关系

尽管表示位置关系的词都十分简单，但在专业英语中表述位置关系非常重要也很普遍，对这些词的理解是否准确是搞清位置关系的重要前提，在机电专业英语中经常使用这些词来描述设备、装置等的工作原理，部件的空间位置；因此必须掌握以下表示位置关系的词汇。

(1) Noun

front/back	middle/edge	rear	corner
left/right	north/south	top/bottom	east/west
interior/exterior	inside/outside	center/side	

(2) Adjectives

horizontal/vertical/diagonal	inner/outer	perpendicular/parallel	forward/after
upper/lower			

(3) Prepositions, Adverbs, and other Expressions

aboard	beneath	near	through
above	beside	off	throughout
across	between	on	to
against	beyond	onto	toward
along	by	on either side of	under
alongside	down	on top of	underneath
around	in	out	up
at	in front of	outside	upon
behind	inside	over	with
below	into	surrounded by	within

4.7　两种快速阅读方法

1. 略读 (Skimming)

在时间有限而又不想仔细了解一篇文章的总内容时，就常常需要进行略读。与浏览不同，略读不需要寻找特定的数目和名称，只是制定主题；所以进行略读的一种方法就是判定可能的主题句。

在英语文章的段落中通常包含着本篇文章主题中的某一方面的信息。而每一段的第一句话往往就是了解这一段落内容的线索,这样的句子就是主题句。

略读下列短文,判定主题。

Credit can cost you pennies or dollars. It depends on your character, your capital and your capability to repay, the money market, and other economic factors.

Two choices you frequently have are closed-end and revolving transactions. Under the closed-end plans you ordinarily sign a promissory note, if you are borrowing cash, or a retail installment contract, if you are using sales credit. You agree in advance on the specific a mount to borrow, the number and size of weekly or monthly payments, and a due date.

On the other hand, the revolving charge plan is open-ended. A top limit is agreed upon purchases which are added as they are made and finance charges are figured on the unpaid balance each month.

(1) The topic is

(a) money market funds.

(b) cost of credit. (main idea)

(c) shopping suggestions.

(d) economic conditions.

Cost increases may make it necessary for the Superintendent of Documents to increase the selling price of publications. Therefore, the prices listed in the Catalog may differ from those in the publications.

Operating rules require that receipts must be deposited in the U.S. Treasury within 48 hours. Therefore, your cancelled check may be returned before your order arrives. If this happens, be assured that your order is being processed as rapidly as possible.

(2) The topic is

(a) the U.S. Treasury.

(b) government services.

(c) document ordering information. (main idea)

(d) how to write a check.

2. 浏览(Scanning)

浏览和略读一样也是非常重要的阅读技巧。所不同的是,略读使你对一篇文章或一本书籍的内容获得一个总的了解,而浏览可以帮助你得到你想得到的特定信息。在你已经知道一篇文章或一本书籍的大概内容后,而你又想从中得到你对某些特定问题的答案时,就可以应用浏览方式。

浏览使你或者进行选择性阅读,或者只是得到特定信息。在通过对文章的题目、副标题和主题句进行略读后,你或者浏览你所感兴趣的段落,或者浏览整篇文章;但注意力只是集中在你所感兴趣的特定信息上。

第3篇 翻译篇

第三篇 關聯篇

第 5 章　专业英语翻译的标准与过程

5.1　翻译的标准

翻译是将一种语言表示的内容用另一种语言准确无误地重新表达出来，翻译不是原文的翻版或者复制，从某种意义上说是原文的再创作。其目的是使不懂原文的读者能够了解原文所表达的科技内容。科技文章翻译要求必须文理清楚。忠实于原文并不等于死抠语法、逐词死译，而要使译文符合本民族语言的习惯，不必迁就原文语言形式。一篇修辞正确、逻辑合理、语言简洁、文理通顺的译文，让读者感觉不到翻译腔的存在，这正是人们为之苦苦追求的目标。

如果把一种语言的所有词汇作为一个词汇总集来看待，则各种词汇的分布情况和运用频率就不一样。在词汇的总体分布中，有些词属于语言的共核部分，如功能词和日常用词，这些词构成了语言的基础词汇；此外，各个学术领域的技术术语和行业词构成了词汇总集，而各个学科领域又存在大量的行业专用表达方法和语汇，正是这些词汇在双语翻译中构成了真正的难度。在科技翻译中，一方面，准确是第一要素，如果为追求译文的流畅而牺牲准确，就会造成科技信息的丢失。另一方面，译文语言必须符合规范，用词造句应符合本民族语言习惯，要使用民族科学的、大众的语言，力求通顺易懂，不应有文理不通、逐字死译和生硬晦涩等现象。专业英语翻译的标准如下。

科技文献主要为叙事说理，其特点一般是平铺直叙，结构严密，逻辑性强，公式、数据和专业术语繁多；所以专业英语的翻译应特别强调"明确"、"通顺"和"简练"。所谓明确，就是要在技术内容上准确无误地表达原文的含义，做到概念清楚，逻辑正确，公式、数据准确无误，符合专业要求，不应有模糊不清、模棱两可之处。专业科技文献中的一个概念、一个数据翻译不准将会带来严重的后果，甚至巨大的经济损失。通顺不但指选词造句应该正确，而且译文的语气表达也应正确无误，尤其是要恰当地表达出原文的语气、情态、语态、时态及所强调的重点。简练就是要求译文尽可能简短、精练，没有冗词废字，在明确、通顺的基础上力求简洁明快、精练流畅，这就是专业英语翻译的客观标准。

5.2　翻译的过程

翻译的过程大致可分为理解、表达、校对三个阶段。

1. 理解阶段

透彻理解原著是确切表达的前提。理解原文必须从整体出发，不能孤立地看待一词一句，每种语言几乎都存在着一词多义的现象。因此，同样一个词或词组，在不同的上下文搭配中，在不同的句法结构中就可能有不同的意义。一个词、一个词组脱离上下文是不能被正确理解的。因此，译者首先应该结合上下文，通过对词义的选择，语法的分析，彻底弄清楚原文的内容和逻辑关系。通常情况下，理解是第一位的，表达是第二位的。正确理解原作是翻译的基础,没有正确的理解就不可能有正确的翻译。当然,虽然理解了原文,但不能用确切的汉语表达出来,词不达意,文理不通,晦涩难懂,也无法达到忠实表达原作思想内容的目的,为了透彻理解原文,应注意以下几个方面。

(1) 结合上下文,推敲词义。理解必须通过原文的上下文来进行。只有结合上下文才能了解单词在某一特定语言环境中的确切意义,否则翻译时往往容易出错。例如:

Various speeds may be obtained by the use of large and small pulleys.

(误) 利用大小滑轮可以获得不同的转速。

(正) 利用大小皮带轮可以获得不同的转速。

"pulleys"一般做"滑轮"、"辘轳"理解,但影响机器转速的应为"皮带轮"而不是"滑轮"。

(2) 辨明语法,弄清关系。机电专业英语的特点之一是句子长,语法结构复杂;因此,根据原文的句子结构,弄清每句话的语法关系对正确理解原文具有重要意义。例如:

Intense light and heat in the open contrasted with the coolness of shaded avenues and the interiors of building.

(误) 强烈的光线和露天场所的炎热,同林荫道上的凉爽和建筑内部形成了对比。

(正) 露天场所的强烈光线和酷热,同林荫道上和建筑物内部的凉爽形成了对比。

(3) 理解原文所涉及的事物。对有些机电专业英语句子的翻译,不能单靠语法关系来理解,还必须从逻辑意义或专业内容上来判断,应特别注意某些特有事物、典故和专门术语所表示的概念。例如:

Do you know that the bee navigates by polarized light and the fly controls its flight by its back wings?

(误) 你知道蜜蜂借助极光飞行,而苍蝇用后翅控制飞行吗?

(正) 你知道蜜蜂借助偏振光飞行,而苍蝇用后翅控制飞行吗?

2. 表达阶段

表达就是要寻找和选择恰当的词汇,把已经理解了的原作内容重新叙述出来。表达的好坏一般取决于理解原著的深度和对归宿语言的掌握程度。故理解正确并不意味着表达一定正确。表达阶段的任务就是把已经理解了的原文内容,用汉语恰如其分地重述出来。如果说,在理解阶段必须"钻进去",把原文内容吃透,那么在表达阶段就必须"跳出来",不受原文形式的束缚,要放开思路,按照汉语的规律和习惯从容自如地遣词造句。在表达阶段最重要的是表达手段的选择,也就是如何"跳出来"的问题,这也是机电专业英语翻译的技巧问题。机电专业英语翻译的创造性也就表现在这方面。表达涉及的问题很多,这里只介绍两种基本的方法,即直译和意译。

(1) 直译。所谓直译,是指译文采取原作的表现手法,既忠于原文内容,又考虑原文形式。也就是说,在译文条件许可时,按照字面意思进行翻译,但直译绝不是逐字死译。例如:

Industrial regions of the world suffer much more acidic fall – out than they did before Industrial Revolution.

世界上的工业化地区现在遭受的酸性回落物的危害,比工业革命前要大得多。

(2) 意译。所谓意译,是指在译文中用创新的表现法来表现原文的逻辑内容和形象内容。当使用直译法不能使文章达到准确通顺时,就要用意译。例如:

Mankind has always reverenced what Tennyson called "the useful trouble of the rain".

直译：人类一直很推崇坦尼森所说的："雨有用的麻烦"。

意译：人类一直很推崇坦尼森所说的这句话："雨既有用，又带来麻烦"。

在翻译实践中，应根据最能忠实、通顺地表达原文含义的原则，灵活机动地选用或替换使用这两种翻译方法。翻译时应考虑到原作的整体性，最好以"段"而不是"句"为单位，一小段一小段地翻译，这不仅有利于辨别词义而且有利于句与句的衔接、段与段的联系，译文不致成为一个个孤立句子的堆积。

3. 校对与修改阶段

校对阶段，是理解和表达的进一步深化，是使译文符合标准的一个必不可少阶段，是对原文内容的进一步核实和对译文语言的进一步推敲。校对对于科技文献的译文来说尤为重要，因为科技文章要求高度精确，公式、数据较多，稍一疏忽就会给工作造成严重的损失。理解和表达都不是一次完成的，而是逐步深入，最后才能达到完全理解和准确表达所反映的客观现实。因此，校改译文是使译文翻译准确必不可少的一步。校改译文时，不仅要对译文做进一步的推敲，使之合乎汉语规范，而且要特别注意译文的准确性，这对科技作品尤其重要。因此，译文只有经过再三校改，直到符合原文意思时才能最后定稿。

Erasable Optical Disks

Erasable optical disks use lasers to read and write information to and from the disk but use a magnetic material on the surface of the disk and a magnetic write head to achieve erasing ability. To write on such a disk, a laser beam heats a tiny spot on it; then a magnetic field is applied to reverse the magnetic polarity of the spot.

Erasable optical disk systems are still in the early stages of commercial development. They offer the same storage capabilities of the non-erasable optical disks, along with the same reusability capabilities of conventional magnetic disks, such as Winchester systems.

这篇短文讲述的是可擦除光盘，因此在对一些词的理解上就要注意准确性及合理性。如 Erasable optical disks, magnetic material, a laser beam, a magnetic field, the magnetic polarity, storage capability, reusability capability 和 conventional magnetic disks 可分别翻译成"可擦除光盘"、"磁性材料"、"激光束"、"磁场"、"磁性"、"存储能力"、"重复使用能力"和"常规磁盘"。

在对这篇短文的关键词理解的基础上，人们可以给出每句话的表达。可能还存在对原文表达不准确的地方，因此需要对原文内容进行进一步地核实和推敲。最后，就可以得出忠于原文、准确并合理的关于可擦除光盘的译文。译文如下。

可擦除光盘

可擦除光盘使用激光从光盘读出或向光盘写入信息，不过盘的表面也使用磁性材料和磁性写磁头以获得可擦性。为了向光盘写入，激光束在盘上加热成小点，接着提供一个磁场以改变点的磁性。

可擦除光盘系统还处于商业开发的早期阶段。它们既提供了与非擦除光盘相同的存储能力，又具有同温彻斯特系统那样的常规磁盘的重复使用能力。

第 6 章　翻译的方法与技巧

6.1　词的增减翻译法

在英译汉中，由于英汉两种语言的语法结构的差异、词类差异及修辞手段的不同，在翻译过程中往往会出现词的增补或减少的现象。增减翻译法包括加词译法、减词译法。

6.1.1　增词译法

增词译法是经常采用的翻译技巧之一。为了确切表达原文，在译文中增加原文中未出现的某些词。词的增补主要有以下几种情况：重复英语省略的某些词、给动名词加汉语名词、增加概括性的词、增加解说性的词、增加加强上下文连贯性的词语、语法加词、虚拟语气加词、分词独立结构和分词短语的加词等。

（1）High voltage is necessary for long transmission while low voltage for safe use.

远距离输电需要高压，安全用电则需要低压。（增加英语句子省略的词）

（2）The lower the frequency is, the greater the refraction of a wave will be.

频率越低，波的折射作用就越强。（给动作名词加汉语名词）

（3）This report summed up the new achievements made in electron tubes, semiconductors; components.

这篇报告总结了电子管、半导体和元件三方面的新成就。（增加数量说明）

（4）Many persons learned to program with little understanding of computers or applications to which computer could or should be applied.

许多人虽然已经学会了编程序，但对计算机及计算机能够或必备的种种用途所知甚少。（增加加强上下文连贯性的词）

（5）The development in science to be brought about due to a fuller knowledge of atom is expected to be even more extensive and fundamental.

可以预期，由于对原子更加充分的认识而引起的科学发展必将更加广泛，更加重要。（将来时态加词）

（6）Steam still provides power, of which electricity is the obedient carrier, it being capable of transmitting power in any desired amount and to any place where it is necessary to use it.

蒸汽仍旧是提供动力，而电则是动力的驯服手段，因为电能够把任何数量的动力输送到任何需要用的地方。（分词独立结构加词）

6.1.2　减词译法

减词译法也是英译汉经常采用的翻译技巧之一。在英语中，有些词如冠词、介词、连词和代词等，在汉语中要么没有，要么用得不多，主要是因为汉语可以借助词序来表达逻辑关系。因此，英汉翻译中词的减少主要出现在英语冠词、介词、代词、连词及关系代词的省略翻译中。

（1）The alternating current supplies the greatest part of the electric power for industry today.

如今交流电占了工业用电的绝大部分。（冠词的省略）

（2）Because they are neutral electrically, they are called "neutrons".

由于它们呈电中性，所以被称为"中子"。（代词的省略）

（3）Because copper possesses good conductivity, it is widely used in electrical engineering.

因为铜具有良好的导电性，所以被广泛地应用于电力工程。（it 的省略）

（4）They have found a method for solving this problem.

他们已经找到了解决这个问题的方法。（介词的省略）

（5）Check the circuit before you begin in the experiment.

检查好线路后再开始做实验。（连词的省略）

6.2　词性的转译

英语和汉语属于不同的语系，英语属于印欧语系，汉语属于汉藏语系。不同语系的语言，无论在词汇方面或在语法方面都有很大的不同。就词类来说，同一意思在不同语言中可以用不同词类来表达。

（1）It is possible to convert energy from one form into another.

能量可以从一种形式转化为另一种形式。

（2）Nylon is nearly twice as strong as natural silk.

尼龙的强度约为真丝的两倍。

这里的"possible"和"strong"都是形容词，但翻译时将其转化为动词"可以"和名词"强度"。翻译时适当改变一下原文某些词的词类，以适应汉语的表达习惯，或达到一定的修饰目的。这种改变原词词类的翻译方法就叫词类转换。

1. 译成汉语动词

根据汉语动词在使用中的灵活性和广泛性的特点，除动词非谓语形式外，还可以把名词、形容词和介词译成汉语动词。

1）名词译成动词

（1）Were there no friction, transmission of motion would be impossible.

没有摩擦就不可能传递运动。

（2）The flow of electrons is from the negative zinc plate to the positive copper plate.

电子是从负的锌极流向正的铜极。

2）形容词译成动词

（1）When metal is cut, the shining surface is visible, but it turns gray almost immediately.

切削金属时，可以看到光亮的表面，但立刻就变成灰色。

（2）Copper and gold were available long before man has discovered the way of getting metal from compound.

早在人们找到从化合物中提取金属的方法以前，铜和金就已经开始使用了。

3）介词译成动词

(1) In general, positive or negative rake tools can be used <u>on</u> stainless steel.

通常正前角和负前角的刀具都可以用来加工不锈钢。

(2) Atomic power <u>for</u> ocean-going vessels is already a reality.

原子能动力用于远洋船只已经成为现实。

2. 译成汉语名词

1）动词译成名词

(1) A voltmeter connected across A B would <u>read</u> 10 Volts.

接在 AB 两点间的伏特计的读数应当是 10 V。

(2) Momentum is <u>defined</u> as the product of velocity and a quantity called the mass of the body.

动量的定义是物体的速度和质量的乘积。

2）形容词译成名词

机电专业英语往往习惯于用表示特征的形容词及其比较级来说明物质的特性，因此在汉译英时，可以在这类形容词后加"度"、"性"等词，使之成为名词。

(1) The more carbon the steel contains, <u>the harder and stronger</u> it is.

钢的含碳量越高，强度和硬度就越大。

(2) As most metals are <u>malleable and ductile</u>, they can be beaten into plates and drawn into wire.

由于大多数金属具有韧性和延展性，所以它们可以压成薄板和拉成细丝。

3. 译成汉语形容词

1）副词译成形容词

(1) The electronic computer is <u>chiefly</u> characterized by its accurate and rapid computations.

电子计算机的主要特点是计算准确而且迅速。

(2) Low cycle fatigue properties are affected <u>adversely</u> by abusive grinding.

过量磨削对低循环疲劳性起着有害的作用。

(3) It is a fact that no structural material is <u>perfectly</u> elastic.

事实上，没有一种结构材料是十全十美的弹性体。

2）名词译成形容词

(1) The low stretches of the rivers show considerable <u>variety</u>.

河下游的情况是多种多样的。

(2) The electrical conductivity has great importance in selecting electrical materials.

导电性在选择电气材料时是很重要的。

6.3 句子成分转译

英语汉语两种语言，由于表达方式不尽相同，翻译时往往需要改变原文的语法结构。其所用的主要方法除了词类转换之外，还有句子成分的转换。在一定情况下，适当改变原文中的某些句子成分，以达到译文逻辑正确、通顺流畅、重点突出等目的。

1. 介词宾语译成主语

英译汉时，为了符合汉语的表达方式，有时需要用原文中的介词宾语更换原来的主语使译文重点突出，行文流畅。现分别举例说明如下。

(1) Rivers differ greatly in character.
各种河流的特点彼此很不相同。

(2) Iron comes between manganese and cobalt in atomic weight.
铁的原子量在锰与钴之间。

(3) The electric arc may grow to an inch in length.
电弧长度可以增长到1英寸。

(4) A motor is similar to a generator in construction.
电动机的结构与发电机类似。

2. 动词 have 的宾语译成主语

(1) The proton has considerably more mass than the electron.
质子的质量比电子大得多。

(2) Levers have little friction to overcome.
杠杆要克服的摩擦力很小。

(3) At high temperature the semiconductor has the same conductivity as the conductor.
高温下半导体的导电性与导体相同。

(4) Evidently semiconductors have a lesser conducting capacity than metals.
半导体的导电能力显然比金属差。

(5) Water has a density of 62.5 pounds per cubic foot.
水的密度是每立方英尺62.5磅。

3. 其他动词的宾语译成主语

除动词 have 的宾语以外，其他及物动词的宾语有时也可以译成主语，译法基本相同，不过动词（省略不译除外）有时需要与主语一起译成定语。

(1) We need frequencies even higher than those we call very high frequency.
我们所需要的频率甚至比我们称之为甚高频的频率还要高。

(2) Hot-set systems produce higher strengths and age better than cold-set systems.
热固系统比冷固系统的强度高，而且老化情况也较好。

(3) This device (FET) exhibits a high impedance.
这种器件（场效应晶体管）的输入阻抗很高。

(4) Light beams can carry more information than radio signals.
光束运载的信息比无线电信号运载的信息多。

(5) Most cylinder cushions provide a relatively small velocity change.
大多数缸体缓冲器所引起的速率变化均较小。

4. 主语译成定语

翻译时，往往由于更换主语，而将原来的主语译成定语。

1) 形容词译成名词

当形容词译成名词并译作主语时，原来的主语通常都需要译成定语。

(1) Medium carbon steel is much stronger than low carbon steel.

中碳钢的强度比低碳钢大得多。

(2) The wings are responsible for keeping the airplane in the air.

机翼的用途是使飞机在空中保持不下坠。

(3) The oxygen atom is nearly 16 times as heavy as the hydrogen.

氧原子的重量几乎是氢的 16 倍。

(4) This steam engine is only about 15 percent efficient.

这种蒸汽机的效率只有百分之十五左右。

(5) In fission processes the fission fragments are very radioactive.

在裂变过程中，裂变碎块的放射性很强。

2）动词译成名词

当动词译成名词并译作主语时，原来的主语一般需要译成定语。

(1) The earth acts like a big magnet.

地球的作用像一块大磁铁。

(2) Mercury weighs about 13 times as much as water.

水银的重量约为水的 13 倍。

(3) A cathode ray tube is shaped like a large bell.

阴极射线管的形状像个大铃铛。

(4) The vertical spindle-drilling machine is characterized by a single vertical spindle rotating fixed position.

立式钻床的特点是具有一根单独在固定位置上旋转的垂直主轴。

5. 定语译成谓语

1）动词宾语的定语译成谓语

(1) Copper and tin have a low ability of combining with oxygen.

铜和锡的氧化能力低。

(2) Water has a greater heat capacity than sand.

水的热容比沙大。

(3) Manganese has the same effect on the strength of steel as silicon.

锰对钢的强度的影响和硅相同。

(4) Neutron has a mass slightly larger than that of proton.

中子的质量略大于质子的质量。

(5) A semiconductor has a poor conductivity at room temperature, but it may become a good conductor at high temperature.

在室温下，半导体导电率差，但在高温下，它可能成为良导体。

2）介词宾语的定语译成谓语

在介词宾语译作主语的同时，有时还需要把该宾语的定语译成谓语，原来的谓语都译成定语。

(1) Gear pumps operate on the very simple principle.

齿轮泵的工作原理很简单。

此句中，将介词宾语"principle"译作主语，其定语"very simple"译成谓语，原来的"operate"译成定语。

（2）Nylon is produced by much the same process as rayon.

尼龙的生产过程与人造丝大体相同。

（3）The molecules of ice and steam are exactly the same except that they are moving at different speeds.

冰的分子和蒸汽的分子完全相同，只不过运动速度不相同。

（4）Though each cam appears to be quite different from the other, all the cams work in a similar way.

虽然每种凸轮都大不相同，但所有凸轮的动作方式都相同。

（5）Radar works in very much the same way as the flashlight.

雷达的工作原理和手电筒极为相似。

6. 译成汉语主谓结构中的谓语

有时出于修辞的目的，将某一名词前面的形容词，即名词的定语与该名词颠倒翻译，一起译成汉语的主谓结构，在句子中充当一个成分。原来作定语的形容词成为主谓结构中名词的谓语。

（1）Among the advantages of numerical control are more flexibility, higher accuracy, quicker changes, and less machine down time.

数控的优点中有适应性大、精度高、非加工时间短。（试比较：在数控的优点中有大的适应性、高的精度、短的非加工时间。）

（2）These pumps are featured by their simple operation, easy maintenance, low oil consumption and durable service.

这些水泵的特点是操作简便、维修容易、耗油量少、经久耐用。

（3）Other requirements of the lathe tool are long life, low power consumption, and low cost.

车刀的其他要求是使用寿命长，动力消耗少并且造价低。

（4）Heating in the bearings may be due to the lack of oil, dirty oil, or to an overtight belt.

轴承发热可能是由于缺油、油不干净或皮带过紧所造成的。

（5）Briefly, a long thin wire has a high resistance, a short thick wire has a low resistance.

简单地说，长而细的导线电阻大，短而粗的导线电阻小。

6.4 被动语态的翻译

英语有别于汉语的特点之一，就是被动语态的广泛使用。这一特点在机电专业英语中反映更为突出。因为被动语态把所要论证、说明的科技问题放在句子的主语位置上，这就能引起人们的注意。此外，被动语态比主动语态更少带有主观色彩，这正是科技作品所需要的。因此，在机电专业英语中，凡是不需要或不能指出行为主体的场合，或在需要突出行为客体的场合都使用被动语态。但汉语的被动语态使用的范围要窄得多，因为汉语具有英语所没有的无主句，许多被动语态可以用汉语的无主句代替。翻译英语的被动语态时，既可以译成汉语的被动句，也可以译成汉语的主动句，而且译法灵活多样。常见的有以下几种译法。

1. 在谓语前加"被"、"受"或"由"字

（1）Energy from different sources has been used to do useful work.

各种能源均被用来做有用功。

（2）When a spring is tightly stretched, it is ready to do work.

当弹簧被拉紧时，它随时都可以做功。

（3）Once the impurities have been removed, the actual reduction to the metal is an easy step.

杂质一旦被除掉，金属的真正还原就容易了。

（4）Besides voltage, resistance and capacitance, all alternating current is also influenced by inductance.

除了电压、电阻和电容以外，交流电还受电感的影响。

（5）The first stage of a rocket is thrown away only minutes after the rocket takes off.

火箭的第一级在火箭起飞后几分钟就被扔掉了。

2. 在谓语前省略"被"字

在不出现行为主体的被动句中，当其被动意义很明显时，汉语习惯不用"被"字，例如，汉语说"工件加工完了"，而不说"工件被加工完了"。这种不用"被"字的被动句在形式上与主动句相似，但意义上是被动的。在现代汉语中，不用"被"字的被动句比用"被"字的要多得多。

（1）Plastics have been applied to mechanical engineering.

塑料已应用于机械工程。

（2）All radio sets used large, heavy vacuum tubes before transistors were invented.

在晶体管发明之前，所有收音机都使用大而重的真空管。

（3）Much progress has been made in electrical engineering in less than a century.

不到一个世纪，电气工程就取得了很大的进展。

（4）Since numerical control was adopted at machine tools, the productivity has been raised greatly.

自从机床采用数控以来，生产率大大提高了。

（5）The head stock is mounted at the left end of the lathe bed.

床头箱安装在车床床身的左端。

3. 在行为主体前加"被"、"由"、"受"、"为……所"等字

当句中出现行为主体时，可以在其前面加"被"字来表示被动意义。

（1）Steam, oil, and water power have been used by mankind for doing work.

蒸汽、石油和水力已被人们用来做功。

（2）The magnetic field is produced by an electric current.

磁场由电流产生。

（3）Magnetic substances are those that are attracted by magnets.

磁性物质就是受磁铁吸引的物质。

(4) Only a small part of the sun's energy reaching the earth is used by us.

传到地球的太阳能只有一小部分为我们所利用。

(5) Air is attracted by the earth as every other substance.

空气像任何其他物质一样被地球吸引着。

4. 译成"是……的"结构

汉语中还有一种不用"被"字的被动句，这就是具有"是……的"结构的句子。凡是着重说明一件事情是"怎样做"或"什么时候、什么地点做"的等，就不用"被"字，而用"是……的"结构。

(1) Iron is extracted from the ore of the blast furnace.

铁是用高炉从铁矿中提炼出来的。

(2) The material first used was copper because it was easily obtained in its pure state.

最先使用的材料是铜，因为纯铜是最容易得到的。

(3) Although electricity was discovered about two thousand years ago, it came into practice long after.

虽然早在两千年前就发现了电，但是过了很久以后它才得到实际应用。

(4) This kind of device is much needed in the mechanical watch-making industry.

这种装置在机械表业制造工业中是很需要的。

5. 译成汉语主动句

1) 更换主语

翻译时把原文的主语译成宾语，而把行为的主体或相当于行为主体的介词宾语译成主语。

(1) More than one hundred elements have been found by chemical workers at present.

目前化学工作者已经发现了一百多种元素。

(2) A right kind of fuel is needed for an atomic reactor.

原子反应堆需要一种适宜的燃料。

(3) Two factors, force and distance, are included in the units of work.

功的单位包含两个因素，即力和距离。

(4) Semiconductors have been known to mankind for many years.

人们知道半导体已有多年了。

(5) In chemistry, symbols are used to represent elements.

化学用符号代表元素。

2) 增加主语

翻译时，把原文的主语译成宾语，并增译泛指性的主语，如"大家"、"人们"、"我们"、"有人"等。

(1) All bodies on the earth are known to possess weight.

大家知道地球上的一切物质都具有重量。

(2) To explore the moon's surface, rockets were launched again and again.

为了探测月球的表面，人们一次又一次地发射火箭。

(3) When water falls a great distance, energy is known to change from potential to kinetic.

当水从高处通过很长的距离流下时，我们知道能量从位能转变为动能。

（4）At one time it was thought that all atoms of the same element were exactly alike.

人们曾认为同一种元素的所有原子都是完全相同的。

（5）It was also said earlier that NC is the operation of machine tools by numbers.

大家早就听说，数控就是机床采用数字操纵。

（6）With the development of modern electrical engineering, power can be transmitted to wherever it is needed.

随着现代化电气工程的发展，人们能把电能输送到所需要的任何地方。

6. 译成无主句

当无法知道或无需说出行为主体时，往往可以把英语的被动语态译成汉语的无主句。翻译时，把原文的主语译成动词的宾语，有时还可以把原文的主语并入谓语一起翻译。

1）主语译成宾语

（1）Work is done, when an object is lifted.

当举起一个物体时，就做了功。

（2）To get all the stages off the ground, a first big push is needed.

为了使火箭各级全部离开地面，需要有一个巨大的第一次推力。

（3）If 250 million hydrogen atoms were placed side by side, they would extend about one inch.

如果将两亿五千万个氢原子并排排列起来，也不过一英寸左右长。

（4）So attention is now being given to possible uses of atomic energy.

因此，现在正把注意力放在原子能的可利用上。

（5）Mercury freezes if it is cooled to too low a temperature.

如果水银被冷却到太低的温度，它就冻结。

（6）Much of the energy is absorbed as the sun's rays pass through our atmosphere.

太阳光线通过大气层时，许多能量被吸收了。

2）主语与谓语合译

英语中有些成语动词含有名词（如make use of, pay attention to等），变成被动语态时将该名词译作主语，这是一种特殊的被动语态。翻译时可以把主语和谓语合译，译成汉语无主句的谓语。

（1）Use can be made of laser beams to burn a hole in a diamond.

可以利用激光在金刚石上打孔。

（2）Attention must be paid to safety in handling radio active materials.

处理放射性材料时必须注意安全。

（3）Brief reference should be made here to one of the alkyl oxides.

这里应该简单提一提一种烷基化氧。

（4）Allowance must, no doubt, be made for the astonishing rapidity of communication in these days.

毫无疑问地要考虑到现代通信的惊人速度。

（5）Account should be taken of the low melting point of this substance.

应该考虑到这种物质的熔点低。

6.5 It 结构的翻译

it 也是英语的多用词之一，它可以构成多种用法不同的结构。这里着重介绍引导词 it 和无人称代词 it 所构成的某些疑难结构。it 在这些结构中只有语法意义而无词汇意义，所以均省略不译，要是翻译成代词"它"或"这"就错了。

1. It follows that

动词 follow 作及物动词时表示"跟随"、"遵循"等意思，这是大家比较熟悉的。因此，这里的 that 从句容易被看作是宾语从句，而 it 当作指示代词"这"。其实，这一结构是属于"It + 不及物动词 + that"句型的一种具体形式。that 从句是主语从句，it 是引导词作形式主语，follow 是不及物动词，表示"归结"的意思。这一结构常用来引出某一结论，可以译为"由此可见"、"由此得出"、"可以推断"等。

（1）It follows that action and reaction always act on different bodies but never act on the same body.

由此可见，作用力和反作用力总是作用在不同的物体上，而永不作用在同一物体上。

（2）It follows that the greater conductance a substance has, the less is the resistance.

由此得出，一种物质的导电率越大，电阻越小。

2. it is + 形容词 + for... + 不定式

这是常见的"it is + 形容词 + 不定式"结构的变形，不定式作主语时习惯放在句末，而句首用形式主语 it，这里的 for 引出不定式的逻辑主语，与不定式一起构成不定式复合结构，作主语放在句末，it 是引导词作形式主语，其谓语是"系动词 be + 形容词表语"。这一结构相当于 that 引出的主语从句。翻译时一般有两种处理方法：一是把不定式复合结构译成汉语的主谓结构仍作主语，即"……是……的"；二是把不定式的逻辑主语译作主语，而把形容词转成动词，与不定式一起译成谓语。

（1）It is important for a scientist to look at matter from the view point of movement.

科学家从运动的观点来看待问题是重要的。

（2）It is necessary for us to know how to convert energy.

我们必须弄清楚能量是怎样转换的。

3. it takes... for... + 不定式

这一结构与前一结构类似，都是不定式复合结构作主语放在句末，句首用引导词 it 作形式主语。两者的区别在于谓语，这里的谓语动词 take 作为"花费"理解，整个结构表示"某人或某物做某事需要若干时间"的意思。这一结构的真正主语也可以用不带逻辑主语的不定式。翻译时要先翻译主语，it 省略不译。

（1）It takes about 28 days for the moon to revolve around the earth.

月亮绕地球一周约需 28 天。

（2）It took millions of years for fossil fuel to be formed from plants.

从植物变成矿物燃料需要数百万年。

4. It is no use + 动名词

这也是 it 作形式主语的结构,但真正主语是动名词,它表示"……是无用的"的意思。动名词作主语,而用 it 作形式主语的情况不很普遍。翻译时先译动名词。

(1) It is no use employing radar to detect objects in water.

使用雷达探测水下目标是不行的。

(2) It is no use learning a theory without practice.

学习理论而不实践是无用的。

5. 动词 + it + 形容词 + that

这里的 it 是引导词作形式宾语。这一结构是由"动词 + 宾语 + 宾语补足语"结构变化而来的,宾语若是从句,通常放在作宾语补足语的形容词之后,以保持句子结构的平衡。适用这一结构的动词有 think,make,find,consider,believe 等。翻译时,形式宾语 it 省略不译,把 that 从句译成汉语的兼语式,即宾语兼主语(下例(1)),或者把 that 从句与形容词一起译成宾语(下例(2))。

(1) Do you think it possible that the electronic computer will replace man?

你认为电子计算机取代人是可能的吗?

(2) People consider it true that all types of radiant energy move through a vacuum at the speed of light.

人们认为各种辐射能确实是以光速通过真空管的。

6. 动词 + it + 形容词 + for + ... 不定式

这是"动词 + it + 形容词 + that"结构的变形,真正的宾语是不定式复合结构,相当于 that 从句。这一结构的宾语也可以用不带逻辑主语的不定式。

(1) Heat from the sun makes it possible for plants to grow.

来自太阳的热量使植物的生长成为可能。

(2) Radio makes it easy for us to be in touch with what is happening.

无线电使人们及时了解周围所发生的事情。

7. 动词 + it + 形容词 + 动名词

这一结构也是用引导词 it 作形式宾语,不同点在于这里的宾语是动名词。这种用法不常见,其翻译方法基本相同。

(1) We find it useless employing radar to detect objects in water.

我们发现使用雷达探测水下目标是不行的。

(2) People found it possible exerting a large force by the application of a small force.

人们发现有可能用一个小的力来产生一个大的力。

8. 动词 + 介词 + it + that

这里的 it 也是一个引导词,但是其作用是充当介词的形式宾语,真正的宾语是 that 从句。当 that 从句作某些成语动词(动词 + 介词)的宾语时,一般不直接跟在介词之后,而用一个形式宾语 it 插在介词和 that 之间。翻译时,it 省略不译,that 从句仍译作宾语。

(1) We will answer for it that this test is reliable.

我们保证这项试验是可靠的。

(2) This is why every aircrew member must see to it that this shape is maintained as accurately as possible.

这就是为什么每个飞行员都必须使（机翼的）这种形状尽可能保持正确的原因。

9. It is (was) + not until... + that

这里的引导词 it 不是形式主语，而是用来加强语气的。这一结构是常见的强调句型"It is (was) ... that"的一种形式，用来强调时间状语。习惯译作"直到……才……"。

(1) It was not until 1886 that aluminum came into wide use.

直到 1886 年，铝才得到广泛的应用。

(2) It is not until meteors strike the earth's atmosphere that they can be seen.

直到流星划过大气层时才能看见。

6.6 专业术语的翻译

专业术语是指自然科学和社会科学领域里的专业性名词。由于现代高新技术的迅速发展，在科技文献和专业资料中常常会出现一些新词，翻译时必须首先弄清原词的专业含义，再选择或创造相应的汉语术语。

6.6.1 意译

专业术语应尽量采用意译，这便于读者直接理解术语的确切含义。例如：operating system（操作系统），multimedia（多媒体），NC（Numerical Control，数控），semiconductor（半导体），radio active isotopes（放射性同位素），guided missile（导弹），holograph（全息摄影），damping resistance（阻尼，阻力）。

(1) 意译时，分析词的构成有助于确切定义。

codec = coder + decoder（编码译码器），cermet = ceramics + metal（金属陶瓷），insullac = insulation + lacquer（绝缘漆），astronics = astronomical + electronics（天文电子学），voder = voice operation demonstrator（语音合成专业术语）。

(2) 意译时，若译名太长，在不影响词义的情况下还可进一步简化。

modem = 调制解调器——解调器，transfer molding = 传递模塑法——递模法。

(3) 意译时，掌握前缀、后缀的意义和译法，对术语定义也会有很大帮助。

coaxial（同轴的，共轴），counteraction（反作用），superconductor（超导体），preheating（预热），telecommunication（电信），water-proof（防水的），noiseless（无噪声的），dust-free（无尘的）。

6.6.2 音译

有些科技术语有时采用意译不方便，常常采用音译法或部分音译法。

(1) 有些术语或新词是由几个词的第一个字母组合而来的，若用意译，则译名太长，这时可采用音译。例如：

radio detection and ranging = radar（无线电侦探及测距设备 = 雷达）；

sound navigation and ranging = sonar（声波导航与测距设备 = 声呐）；

light amplification by stimulated emission of radiation = laser（受激辐射式，光频放大——激光）。

（2）计量单位名称一般用音译，有些还可进一步简化。例如：hertz—赫兹（频率）＝赫，newton—牛顿（力，重量）＝牛，pascal—帕斯卡（压力，强度）＝帕，watt—瓦特（功率）＝瓦，volt—伏特（电位，电压，电动势）＝伏，ohm—欧姆（电阻）＝欧，Celsius scale—摄氏度（温度）＝度，lux—勒克司（光照度）＝勒，calorie—卡路里（热量）＝卡，bit—比特（二进制信息单位），morphine—吗啡，nylon—尼龙（酰胺纤维）。

（3）有些词采用音、意合译法，即在词头或词尾加上意译的词。例如：logic（逻辑电路），rifle（来复枪），topology（拓扑学），tank（坦克），card（卡片）。

（4）有些科技术语随着历史的发展已为人们熟悉或掌握，往往又由音译转为意译，或音译与意译同时兼用。例如：motor（马达，电动机），modern（摩登的，现代的），microphone（麦克风，扩音器），engine（引擎，发动机），vitamin（维他命，维生素），penicillin（盘尼西林，青霉素）。

6.6.3 形译

英语原文用字母等表示事物的外形时，汉语译文也按事物外形用各种办法表示。例如：T-square（丁字尺），I-steel（工字钢），cross-road（十字路口），crossheading（十字节，联轴节），herringbone gear（人字齿轮），A-frame（A形架），C-washer（C形垫圈），U-tube（U形管），V-slot（V形槽），Y-connection［Y形连接（星形连接）］，zigzag wave（锯齿形波），U-shaped magnet（马蹄形磁铁），V-belt（三角皮带），cabinet file（半圆锉），twist drill（麻花钻），O-ring（O形环），X-ray（X射线）。

6.7 从句的翻译

6.7.1 定语从句的翻译

定语从句是在复合句中起定语作用的主谓结构，它所修饰的是名词、代词或句子，被修饰的词是它的先行词。定语从句由关系代词（who，whom，whose，which，that，so，but）或关系副词（when，where，why，how）引导，放置在其所修饰的先行词后面。这种句法结构与汉语中修饰语多置于中心词之前的习惯不同。在翻译定语从句时，通常采取把定语翻译在先行词前，即用倒译法翻译，把从句译为主句的并列结构，即用顺译法翻译，或把定语从句译为状语从句，即用结构转化法进行翻译。对于特殊的定语从句也可采取分译法或合译法进行翻译。

1. 限定性定语从句的译法

限定性定语从句在结构上通常放置在先行词后，并且与先行词之间无逗号相隔。在意思上，此类定语从句是整个句子中密不可分的一部分，对先行词起到限制、修饰作用，一旦将其剥离，主句的表达便不清晰、不完整。对限定性定语从句主要采用倒译法、顺译法、合译法进行翻译。

（1）倒译法：将定语从句译成汉语后，放在其先行词前，使译文紧凑，符合汉语习惯。这种翻译方法主要适用于短小且与先行词的关系极其密切的定语从句，译后形成汉语中"……的"结构。

(a) Objects that do not transfer light cause shadows.

不透光的物体会造成阴影。

(b) The thin valley in the Mid-Atlantic Ridge is a place where the ocean floor splits.

中大西洋山脉里的浅谷是海底分裂的地方。

(c) A computer is a machine whose function is to accept data and process them into information.

计算机是一种能接受数据并把它们处理成信息的机器。

(d) "Genetic engineering" is the name used to describe the techniques that scientists have developed to change the genes of living things.

"基因工程"这一名称是用来说明科研人员所开发的改变生物基因的技术。

(e) The virus (HIV) invades healthy cells, including white blood cells that are part our defense system against disease.

这种病毒（HIV）侵入健康细胞，其中包括组成部分疾病抵御系统的白血球细胞。

有时连接代词 that 会被省略，翻译时可遵循相同的原则。

(f) Scientists think the first loss of ozone reduces the amount of solar energy the atmosphere can take in.

科学家认为，臭氧层的首次变薄减少了大气层能够摄入的太阳能量。

(g) By measuring the time it takes for the wave to travel to the object and bounce, we can find out exactly how far away the object is.

测得电磁波达到物体然后反射回来所花时间，我们就可以精确地求出该物体的距离。

(2) 顺译法：科技文献的特点是精确简练，因此当定语从句过长时，我们通常就会保持原句顺序，即将定语从句译成汉语后，放置在主句后，与主句形成并列的句式。

(a) Another kind of rectifier consists of a large pear-shaped glass bulb from which all the air has been removed.

另一种整流器由一个大的梨形玻璃灯泡构成，泡内的空气已全部被抽出。

(b) Until then, they will continue to study moon dust cement and other materials that can make it possible for people to live in the severe environment of the moon.

在此之前，他们将继续研究月球尘土水泥及其他建筑材料，使人们可以在月球的恶劣环境下生活。

(c) The base is the foundation of all machines and is the part on (upon) which all other parts are mounted.

底座是所有机器的基础，其他部件都装在它上面。

以上例句中关系代词所代表的含义并没有直接译出。其实，还可以将关系代词译为"它"、"这"、"这样"来代替先行词。

(d) AIDS is a life-threatening sickness that attacks the body's natural defense system against disease.

艾滋病是一种威胁生命的疾病，它侵袭人体内的自然免疫系统。

(e) The only effective control system is one that is capable of informing the operator of the progress of the refining path during the entire course of the blow, so that he can, before the end of blow, take the action necessary to reach the desired end point conditions.

唯一有效的控制系统是这样一种系统,它能把整个吹炼时期内精炼过程的进展情况通知操作工,从而使他能够在吹炼结束前采取必要的措施来达到所要求的停吹条件。

此外,也可利用"该"或"这"、"这种",并重复先行词。

(f) CD-4 is a man-made copy of protein that appears naturally on some of our major disease fighting cells.

CD-4是一种人类复制的蛋白质,这种蛋白质自然地出现于我们的一些主要的抗病细胞中。

(g) On the southern side of your home, you might select a deciduous tree that gives shade in the summer but loses leaves in winter and lets the sunshine through.

你可以选一棵落叶树种在你家南侧,这种树夏季枝繁叶茂给你阴凉,冬天叶落枝秃让阳光透射进屋。

(3) 合译法:将原主句和分句的界限打破,利用从句的关系代词与主句某成分的替代关系,根据意思重新组织成汉语单句,从句在其中可充当定语、谓语、主语或状语。

(a) For a long time, scientists could find little use for the material which remained after the oil has been refined. Later on they found that it could be turned into plastics.

科学家们很长时间都没有发现炼油渣有什么用途,后来才发现能将它制成塑料。

(b) Wegener pointed out a line of mountains that appears from east to west in south Africa.

魏格纳指出南非的一列山脉的走向是由西向东的。

(c) Then he (Wegener) pointed out another line of mountains that looks almost exactly the same in Argentina on the other side of Atlantic Ocean.

他(魏格纳)又指出大洋彼岸阿根廷的另一列山脉走向几乎完全一样。

(d) Will there be a time when a whole organ of the body—a lung, a kidney, the heart—can be frozen for later use?

将来是否有一天可以把人体中像肺、肾、心脏这样完整的器官进行冷冻储存以备后用呢?

(e) All of the principal units of the lathe are mounted on a bed having ways along which the carriage and tailstock travel.

车床的主要部件都装在具有导轨的床身上,刀架与尾架可沿着该导轨滑动。

2. 非限定性定语从句的译法

非限定性定语从句与它所修饰的先行词或句子的关系不甚紧密,只起到补充和说明的作用。它经常由关系代词"which",有时也由"when"、"where"等关系副词引导,并以逗号与其中心词隔开。翻译非限定性定语从句最常采用的方法是顺译法,根据具体情形不同,也可采用倒译法。

(1) 顺译法:如前所述,顺译法即是在翻译的过程中保持原句的顺序,将从句译成与主句具有并列关系的句式。

(a) Fig. 9 shows the effect of continuous charging on energy and electrode consumption, which not only eliminates the need for back charging, but also accomplishes refining during the continuous feed period.

图 9 表示了（电炉）连续装料对耗电量和电极消耗的影响，连续装料不仅不再需要补充装料，而且也能在连续装料阶段内完成精炼操作。

(b) Power is equal to work divided by the time, as has been said before.

功率等于功除以时间，这在前面已讲过。

(c) When it comes to communication, we already have Traffic Master, which operates from transducers on motorway bridges to gauge the speed of the traffic and warn of blockage ahead.

至于交通通信，"通霸"已经问世，这种装置通过高速路桥上的传感器对过往车辆的行驶速度进行监测，并警示前方堵车现象。

(2) 倒译法：当非限定性定语从句相对短小时，也不妨使用倒译法。

(a) The carbon, of which coal is largely composed, has combined with oxygen from the air and formed an invisible gas called carbon dioxide.

煤的主要组分——碳，同空气中的氧化合，生成一种看不见的气体，叫做二氧化碳。

(b) For pyrite and pyrrhotite, which have had limited commercial value to date, the desulphurization process offers an economical means of producing both elemental sulphur and high grade iron oxide.

对于迄今只具有有限工业价值的黄铁矿及磁黄铁矿而言，这种脱硫法为同时生产元素硫和高级氧化铁提供了一种经济实用的手段。

6.7.2 同位语从句的翻译

名词性从句在句子中也可以作同位语，称为同位语从句。其特点是，从句的先行词常为 idea, fact, theory, sense, question, conclusion, experience, evidence, proof, condition；同位语从句不是用来修饰先行词，而是用来明确先行词的内容。同位语从句在形式和表现上与定语从句相似，因此在翻译方法上也基本相同。对于同位语我们主要采用以下两种翻译方法。

(1) 同位语前置法：将同位语从句翻译成定语放置到先行词前，形成"……的"、"这一……"结构。

These uses are based on the fact that silicon is a semiconductor of electricity.

这些用途是基于硅是半导体这一事实。

(2) 顺译法：按照原句的语序译出，使用"："、"—"或"就是"、"即"等进行连接。

(a) We have settled to the idea that the earth's surface is something fixed, and will not be extended any more.

我们确立了这样的概念：地球的陆地表面基本上是固定的，不会再扩大了。

(b) These uses are based on the fact that silicon is a semiconductor of electricity.

这些用途是基于这一事实，即硅是半导体。

6.7.3 状语从句的翻译

英语的状语从句也是一个比较复杂的语言现象,它形式多样,变化繁多。状语从句由从属连词引导,通常用来修饰主句的谓语动词、形容词、副词而起状语作用。根据其不同含义,可分为时间、原因、条件、让步、目的等各种状语从句。由于英汉两种语言的差异,英汉复合句的形式颇有不同。英语复合句多取形合式,而现代汉语中的复句则多取意合式。因此,英译汉时尤其要注意状语从句的位置,连词的译法和省略及状语从句的转译等。

一般来说,在汉语中,状语从句多半在主句前面;英语的状语从句既可放在主句后面,也可放在主句前面,甚至有时放在整个句子当中。当然,这只是一般倾向,在实际翻译中必须灵活掌握。

汉语中,连词用得不多,语句的上下逻辑关系是靠词序或语序表示的。这就是汉语意合式的特点。因此,英译汉时,连词常可省略,这在时间、条件和原因状语从句中尤为常见。翻译时,不要碰到 when 就译成"当",碰到 if 就译成"如果",碰到 because 就译成"因为",应该酌情进行变化或简化。例如:

The computer will find the route when you send your signal to it.

把信号输入计算机,它就会找到行车路线。试比较:当你把信号输入计算机时,它就会找到行车路线。

1. 时间状语从句的译法

(1) 译成相应的时间状语并放在句首,不论原文中表示时间的从句是前置还是后置,按照汉语的习惯,时间状语从句要放在其主句的前面。例如:

Heat is always given out by one substance and taken in by another when heat-exchange takes place.

热交换发生时,总是某一物质放出热量,另一物质吸入热量。

(2) 译成并列句。有的连词(as,while,when 等)引导时间状语从句,在表达主句和从句的谓语动作同时进行时,翻译时可省略连词,译成汉语并列句。例如:

She sang as she prepared the experiment.

她一边唱着歌,一边准备实验。

(3) 译成条件状语从句。when 等引导的状语从句,有时从形式上看是时间状语,但从逻辑上判断则具有条件状语连接词的意义。因此,这类时间状语从句往往可转译为条件状语从句。例如:

(a) When the molecules of a solid move fast enough, the solid melts and becomes a liquid.

如果固体内的分子达到一定的运动速度,固体就融化为液体。

(b) Our whole physical universe, when reduced to the simplest terms, is made up of two things, energy and matter.

我们的整个物质世界,如果用最简单的话来说,是由两样东西组成的,即能量和物质。

(c) Aluminum, with a weight one-third that of steel, can be given a strength approaching that of steel when it is alloyed with small quantities of copper, manganese and magnesium, and subjected to heat treatment processes.

铝的重量是钢的三分之一，如果和少量铜、锰、镁熔合，并加以热处理，能获得接近于钢的强度。

2. 地点状语从句的译法

（1）译成相应的地点状语。一般可采用前置译法，将地点状语从句译在句首。例如：
Make a mark where you have any doubts or questions.

在有疑问的地方做个记号。

（2）译成条件状语从句或结果状语从句。一些以连接词 where 或 wherever 引导的状语从句，有时从形式上看是地点状语从句，但从逻辑上判断则具有条件状语或结果状语的意义；因而可将其译为条件状语从句或结果状语从句。

（a）The materials are excellent for use where the value of the work pieces is not high.

如果零件价值不高，最好使用这种材料。

（b）Where the volt is too large a unit, we use the millivolt or microvolt.

如果用伏特作为单位太大，我们可用毫伏或微伏。

（c）No relief valve is required where two pressure reducing valves are installed.

如果装上两个减压阀，就不需要安全阀。

（d）Where there is nothing in the path of the beam of light, nothing is seen.

如果光束通道上没有东西，就什么也看不到。

3. 原因状语从句的译法

（1）译成表"因"的分句。汉语中常用来表"原因"的关联词有"由于"、"因为"。一般说来，汉语表"因"的分句置于句首，英语则较灵活。但在现代汉语中，受西方语言的影响，表"因"的分句也有放在后面的，这种情况往往含有补充说明的意义。

（a）Some sulfuric dioxide is liberated when coal, heavy oil and gas burn, because they all contain sulfuric compounds.

因为煤、重油和煤气都含有硫化物，所以它们在燃烧时会放出一些二氧化硫。

（b）As the moon's gravity is only about 1/6 the gravity of the earth, a 200-pound man weighs only 33 pounds on the moon.

由于月球的引力只有地球引力的六分之一，所以一个体重200磅的人在月球上仅有33磅重。

（2）译成因果偏正复句的主句。实际上这是一种省略连词的译法，把从句译成主句。例如：
Since information is continuously sent into the system as it becomes available, teletext is always kept up-to-date.

新获得的资料不断地输入，所以电视传真文字系统总是保持最新水平。

4. 条件状语从句的译法

（1）译成表示"条件"或"假设"的分句。在汉语中，"只要"、"要是"、"如果"等是表示"条件"的常用关联词。在语气上，"只要"最强，"如果"最弱。常用来表示"假设"的关联词则有"如果"、"要是"、"假如"等。按照汉语的习惯，不管表示条件还是假设，分句都放在复句的前部；因此英语的条件从句在翻译时绝大多数置于句首。

(a) If something has the ability to adjust itself to the environment, we say it has intelligence.

如果某物具有适应环境的能力,我们就说它具有智力。

在英语的非真实条件句中,谓语用虚拟语气。这类从句一般位于句首,因此翻译时采用顺译法。当省略从属连词 if,而把 were, had, should, could 等移至主语之前,引起倒装语序时,翻译的方法也是将这类从句置于句首。

(b) If a laser beam diffused as it goes on, it could not be used to follow a satellite or other far-away targets.

如果激光光束前进时扩散开来,就不能用来跟踪卫星或其他远距离目标。

(c) Should there be no transformers to adjust the voltage, long-distance transmission of electricity would be impossible.

如果没有变压器调节电压,远距离输电是不可能的。

(2) 译成补充说明情况的分句。绝大多数条件状语从句翻译时都置于句首,但少数可译在主句后面,作为补充说明情况的分句。例如:

Iron or steel parts will rust, if they are unprotected.

铁件或钢件是会生锈的,如果不加保护的话。

5. 让步状语从句的译法

英语的让步状语从句,可翻译为汉语的让步分句或无条件的条件分句。

(1) 译成表示"让步"的分句。汉语中用以表示"让步"的常用关联词有"虽然"、"尽管"、"即使"等,让步分句一般前置(但现在也逐渐出现后置现象),英语中则比较灵活。例如:

Although planets give off no light of their own, they reflect the light from the sun and look like stars at night.

虽然行星自己不发光,但是它们反射太阳的光线,夜晚时看起来很像星星。

(2) 译成表示"无条件"的条件分句。汉语里有一种复句,前一分句排除某一方面的一切条件,后一分句说出在任何条件下都有同样的结果。这类复句的前一分句称为"无条件"的条件分句。通常以"不管"、"不论"、"无论"、"任凭"等作为关联词。英语中有些让步状语从句可以译为汉语的"无条件"的条件分句。

(a) All science students, no matter whether they should be physicists or chemists, should have a good foundation in basic sciences.

所有理科学生,不论他们是未来的物理学家还是化学家,均需打下基础科学的基础。

(b) However carefully boiler casing and steam pipes are sealed, some heat escapes and is lost.

锅炉壳体和蒸汽管无论怎样仔细地密封,总有一些热量泄出并损耗掉。

6. 目的状语从句的译法

(1) 译成表示"目的"的后置分句。英语的目的状语从句通常位于句末;因此翻译时一般采用顺译法,即译成后置分句。汉语里常用于表"目的"的关联词有"以便"、"以免"、"使得"等。例如:

A rocket must attain a speed of about five miles per second so that it may put a satellite into orbit.

火箭必须获得大约每秒五英里的速度才能把卫星送入轨道。

（2）译成表示"目的"的前置分句。汉语里表示"目的"的分句常用"为了"作为关联词，置于句首，往往有强调的含意。

（a）All the parts for this kind of machine must be made of especially strong materials in order that they will not break while in use.

为了在使用时不致断裂，这种机器的所有部件都应该采用特别坚固的材料制成。

（b）An atomic furnace must be surrounded by heavy thick walls so that the rays can not get out.

为了使射线不致逸出，必须用很厚的屏障将原子反应堆屏蔽。

7. 结果状语从句的译法

英语和汉语都把表示"结果"的状语从句置于主句之后；因此翻译这类从句时可采用顺译法，但又不能拘泥于引导结果状语从句的连词 that, so...that 等的词义，把它们一律译为"因而"、"结果"、"如此……以致"等，以免译文过于欧化。另外，翻译时应少用连词，或省掉连词。

（a）Newton's head was usually so full of ideas that he was quite lost in thought.

牛顿的头脑里充满着各种各样的想法，以致他常常想问题而出神。

（b）Some people can not accept the idea that animals might have intelligence so that they are even more surprised at the suggestion that machine might.

有些人不能接受动物可能有智力的想法，因此他们对机器可能有智力的设想就更为惊讶。

6.8 长句的翻译

由于其内容、使用域和语篇功能的特殊性，长句在许多表达方面有别于日常英语，其差别主要表现在句法和词汇上。大量使用长句结构是英语科技文章的特点之一。

英语长句之所以长，主要长在修辞成分上。英语句子的修辞成分主要是名词后面的定语短语或定语从句，以及动词后面或句首的介词短语或状语从句。这些修饰成分可以一个套一个连用，形成长句结构。显然，英语的一句话可以表达好几层意思，而汉语习惯用一个小句表达一层意思，一般好几层意思要通过几个小句来表达（俗称流水句）。由此可见，将英语译成汉语时，有必要采用拆句译法和改变顺序方法，再按汉语习惯重新组句。长句拆译的方法基本上有四种，即顺序法、逆序法、分译法和综合法。下面分别举例说明。

1. 顺序法

英语长句结构的顺序与汉语相同，即英语长句中所描述的一连串动作是按时间顺序安排的，可以采用顺序法翻译。

（a）Some of these causes are completely reasonable results of social needs. Others are reasonable consequences of particular advances in science being to some extent self-accelerating.

在这些原因中，有些完全是自然而然地来自社会需求，而另一些则是由于科学在一定程度上自我加速而产生某些特定发展的必然结果。

(b) Typically, when a customer places an order, that order begins a mostly paper-based journey from in-basket to in-basket around the company, often being keyed and re-keyed into different departments' computer systems along the way.

一般情况下，当一位顾客预定了一份订单后，那张订单就会在公司里被传阅，并经常以这种方式被发送和再转发到不同部门的计算机系统中。

2. 逆序法

所谓逆序法就是从长句的后面或中间译起，把长句的开头放在译文的结尾。这是由于英语和汉语的表达习惯不同：英语习惯于用前置性陈述，先结果后原因；而汉语习惯则相反，一般先原因后结果，层层递进，最后综合。处理这类句子，就要采用逆序法。

(a) Additional social stresses may also occur because of the population explosion or problems arising from mass migration movements——themselves made relatively easy nowadays by modern means of transport.

由于人口的猛增或大量人口的流动（现代交通工具使这种流动相对容易）造成的种种问题也会对社会造成新的压力。

(b) There is no agreement whether methodology refers to the concepts peculiar to historical work in general or to the research techniques appropriate to the various branches of historical in query.

所谓方法论是指一般的历史研究中的特有的概念，还是指历史探究中各个具体使用的研究手段，人们对此意见不一。

3. 分译法

有时英语长句包含多层意思，而汉语习惯于一个小句表达一层意思。为了使行文简洁，翻译时可把长句中的从句或介词短语分开叙述，顺序基本不变，保持前后的连贯，但是有时为了语气上的连贯，须加译适当的词语。

(a) The loads a structure is subjected to are divided into dead loads, which include the weights of all the parts of the structure, and live loads, which are due to the weights of people movable equipment, etc.

一个结构受到的载荷可以分为静载和动载两类。静载包括该结构各部分的重量，动载则是由于人和可移动设备等的重量而引起的载荷。

(b) When error correction is not required, UDP provides unreliable datagram service that enhances network through put at the host-to-host transport layer.

如果没有要求更改错误，则 UDP 提供不可靠的数据服务，从而增加了网络在传输的吞吐量。

4. 综合法

有些长句使用以上三种方法都不合适，那么可按照时空顺序，夹顺夹逆，主次分明，综合处理。

(a) Noise can be unpleasant to live even several miles from an aerodrome; if you think what it must be like to share the deck of a ship with several squadrons of jet aircraft, you will realize a modern navy is a good place to study noise.

噪声甚至会使住在远离飞机场几英里以外的人感到不适。如果你能想象到站在板上的几个中队喷气式飞机中间将是什么滋味的话,那你就会意识到现代海军是研究声的理想场所。

(b) The super-cooling effects of the cryogenics which convert liquid helium and other gases into "superfluids" and metals into "superconductors", making them non-resistant to electricity, could change the world in a number of ways.

低温学的过冷作用将液态氦及某些气体变成"超流体",将某些金属变成"超导体"使它们没有电阻,从而可以用许多方法改变世界。

6.9　否定结构的翻译

英语的否定形式是一个常见而又比较复杂的问题,使用非常灵活、微妙,被认为是英语的特点之一。机电专业英语里否定形式的应用也很广泛。在表达否定概念时,英语在用词、语法和逻辑等方面与汉语有很大的不同。有的句子形式上是肯定的而事实上是否定的,而有的句子形式上是否定的但事实上却是肯定的。英语否定词的否定范围和重点有时难于判断,否定词在句子中表示强调的方法与汉语不相同,某些否定词和词组的习惯用法较难掌握。因此,在翻译英语否定形式时,必须细心揣摩,真正彻底理解其意义及否定的重点,然后根据汉语的习惯进行翻译。

(a) The earth does not move round in the empty space.

(误) 不是地球在空无一物的空间中不运转。

(正) 地球不是在空无一物的空间中运转。

(b) All metals are not good conductors.

(误) 不是所有金属都不是良导体。

(正) 并非所有金属都是良导体。

从上面例句中可以看出,英语的否定形式与否定概念并非永远一致。如例(a)那样的句子,形式上是一般否定(谓语否定),但实际上却是特指否定(其他成分否定);又如例(b),句子看上去似乎是全部否定,但却是部分否定。下面我们就针对翻译英语否定结构时应注意的几个问题,逐一举例加以说明。

1. 否定成分的转译

一般来说,否定形式仍翻译成否定形式。但由于英语和汉语两种语言其表达手段和习惯的不同,有些否定应译成肯定形式。这种正反、反正表达法是翻译的一门重要技巧。有些英语否定句,虽然是用一般否定(否定谓语)的形式,但在意义上却是特指否定,即其他成分的否定;反之,有些句子形式上是特指否定,而意义上却是一般否定。翻译时,要根据汉语的习惯进行否定成分的转译。

(a) Sound does not travel so fast as light.

声音不像光传播得那样快。(原文否定谓语,译文否定状语)

(b) Neutrons carry no charge.

中子不带电荷。(原文否定宾语,译文否定谓语)

(c) The sun's rays do not warm the water so much as they do the land.

太阳光线使水增温,不如它使陆地增温那样高。(原文否定谓语,译文否定状语)

(d) Matter must move, or no work is done.

物质必须运动,否则就没有做功。(原文否定主语,译文否定谓语)

(e) The mountain is not valued because it is high.

山的价值并不是因为它高。(原文否定谓语,译文否定谓语)

(f) Nobody can be set in motion without having a force act upon it.

如果不让力作用在物体上,就不能使物体运动。(原文否定主语,译文否定谓语)

(g) Green plants can not grow strong and healthy without sunlight.

没有阳光,绿色植物就长不结实,长不好。(原文否定主语,译文否定谓语)

(h) But for the heat of the sun, nothing could live.

要是没有太阳的热,什么东西都不能生存。(原文否定主语,译文否定谓语)

(i) We do not consider melting or boiling to be chemical changes.

我们认为熔化或沸腾不是化学反应。(原文否定谓语,译文否定兼语式的第二谓语)

2. 部分否定的译法

英语的否定有全部否定与部分否定。全部否定指否定整个句子的全部意思,可用 none, neither, no, not, nothing, nobody 等否定词。部分否定则主要由 all, every, both, always 等含全体意义的词与否定词 not 构成,其表达的意义是部分否定,相当于汉语"不是所有都"、"不是两者都"、"不总是"之意。当否定词 not 放在这些词(not all, not every, not both)之前时,其部分否定的意义就很明显,一般不会翻译错。然而,否定词 not 有时却与谓语在一起,构成谓语否定,形式上很像全部否定;但实际上却是部分否定,翻译中应当特别注意。

(a) All minerals do not come from mines. (= Not all minerals come from mines.)

并非所有矿物都来自矿山。(不是"所有矿物都不来自矿山"。)

(b) Every color is not reflected back. (= Not every color is reflected back.)

并非每种色光都会反射回来。(不是"每种光都不反射回来"。)

(c) Both of the substances do not dissolve in water.

不是两种物质都溶于水。

(d) But friction is not always useless, in certain cases it becomes a helpful necessity.

摩擦并非总是无用的,在某些场合下,它是有益的、必需的。

(e) All the chemical energy of fuel is not converted into heat.

并非所有燃料的化学能都转变成热量。

3. 否定语气的改变

英语的否定句并非一概译成汉语的否定句,因为英语中有些否定句表达的是肯定的意思,还有些否定句在特定场合下可以表达肯定的意思。试看下面带否定词 nothing 的句子的译法。

(a) Energy is nothing but the capacity to do work.

能就是做功的能力。

(b) An explosion is nothing more than a tremendously rapid burning.

爆炸仅仅是非常急速的燃烧。

(c) Ball bearings are precision-made bearings which make use of the principle that "nothing rolls like a ball".

滚珠轴承是精密轴承,采用了"球形最善于滚动"的原理。

4. 否定意义的表达

英语中还有许多肯定句,所表达的却是否定的概念。在这类句子中虽然没有出现否定词,但句子中有些词组却含有否定的意义。翻译时一般都要将其否定意义译出,译成汉语的否定句。这类句子的理解和翻译,只要掌握了词汇意义,就不会有什么困难。在机电专业英语中,常见的含有否定意义的词组有 too...to(太……不), free from(没有), too...for(太……不), fall short of(没有达到), fail to(不能), instead of(而不是), far from(完全不), in the absence of(没有……时)。

(a) Of all metals silver is the best conductor, but it is too expensive to be used in industry.

所有金属中,银是最好的导体;但成本太高,不能在工业上使用。

(b) The distance from the sun to the earth is too great to imagine.

太阳到地球的距离大得不可想象。

(c) The angularity of the parts is too great for proper assembly.

零件的斜度太大,不适于装配。

(d) Hardened steel is too hard and too brittle for many tools.

淬火钢太硬、太脆,许多刀具不能用它来制造。

(e) If the follower loses contact with the cam, it will fail to work.

随动元件如果与凸轮脱开,就不能工作。

5. 双重否定的译法

英语和汉语一样,也有双重否定结构。英语的双重否定是由两个否定词(no, not, never 等)连用或一个否定词与某些表示否定意义的词连用而构成的。双重否定表示否定之否定,即强调肯定;因此翻译时有两种译法,既可以译成双重否定,也可以译成肯定。

双重否定从语气的强弱上分,有弱化的双重否定和强化的双重否定两种。弱化的双重否定中包含的两个否定词,一个常由否定前后缀构成,由于两个否定词中一个为另一个所否定,使否定的语气弱化,从而将否定的效果抵消了一部分。

(1) 译成双重否定。

(a) There is no steel not containing carbon.

没有不含碳的钢。

(b) Sodium is never found uncombined in nature.

自然界中从未发现不处于化合状态的钠。

(c) No flow of water occurs unless there is a difference in pressure.

没有压力差,水就不会流动。

(d) It is impossible for heat to be converted into a certain energy without something lost.

热转换成某种能而没有什么损耗是不可能的。

(2) 译成肯定。

(a) There is no law that has not exceptions.

凡是规律都有例外。

(b) A radar screen is not unlike a television screen.

雷达荧光屏跟电视荧光屏一样。
(c) There is nothing unexpected about it.
一切都在意料之中。
(d) One body never exerts a force upon another without the second reacting against the first.
一个物体对另一物体施加作用力就必然会受到另一物体的反作用力。

第4篇 应 用 篇

第7章　Mechatronics Technology

7.1　Intensive Reading

Lesson 1　Mechatronics

Mechatronics is nothing new; it is simply the application of the latest techniques in precision mechanical engineering, controls theory, computer science, and electronics to the design process to create more functional and adaptable products. This, of course, is something many forward-thinking designers and engineers have been doing for years.[1]

As shown in figure 7.1, mechatronics is the interdisciplinary fusion (not just a simple mixture!) of mechatronics, electronics and information technology. The objective is for engineer to complete development, which is why it is currently so popular with industry.

A Japanese engineer from Yasukawa Electric Company coined the term "mechatronics" in 1969 to reflect the merging of mechanical and electrical engineering disciplines.[2] Until the early 1980s, mechatronics meant a mechanism that is electrified. In the mid-1980s, mechatronics came to mean engineering that is the boundary between mechanics and electronics. Today, the term encompasses a large array of technologies, many of

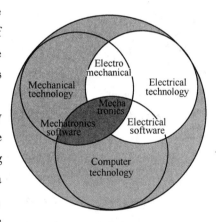

Figure 7.1　The interdisciplinary nature of Mechatronics

which have become well-known in their own right. Each technology still has the basic element of the merging of mechanics and electronics but now many also involve much more, particularly software and information technology. For example, many early robots resulting from mechanical and electrical systems became central to mechatronics.

Mechatronics gained legitimacy in academic circles in 1996 with the publication of the first referred journal: IEEE/ASME Transactions on mechatronics[3]. In the premier issue, the authors worked to define mechatronics. After acknowledging that many definitions have circulated, they selected the following for articles to be included in Transactions[4]: "The synergistic integration of mechanical engineering with electronics and intelligent computer control in the design and manufacture of industrial products and processes." The authors suggested 11 topics that should fall, at least in part, under the general category of mechatronics:

- modeling and design

- system integration
- actuators and sensors
- intelligent control
- robotics
- manufacturing
- motion control
- vibration and noise control
- micro devices and optoelectronics systems
- automotive systems
- other applications

New Words and Phrases

(1) mechatronics [ˌmekə'trɔniks] n. 机电一体化（技术）
(2) interdisciplinary [ˌintə'disiplinəri] adj. 跨学科的，多领域的
(3) modeling ['mɔdəliŋ] n. 建模，造型
(4) sensor ['sensə] n. 传感器，灵敏元件
(5) automotive [ˌɔːtəu'məutiv] adj. 自动的，汽车的
(6) optoelectronic [ˌɔptəui,lek'trɔnik] adj. 光电（子）的，光电子学的
(7) intelligent [in'telidʒent] adj. 聪明的，有智力的
(8) actuator ['æktjueitə] n. 调节器，激励器，执行元件
(9) robotics [rəu'bɔtiks] n. 机器人学
(10) encompass [in'kʌmpəs] v. 围绕，包含
(11) transaction [træn'zækʃən] n. 事项，记录，处理，交易；(pl) 学报，会刊
(12) synergistic [ˌsinə'dʒistik] adj. 协作的，合作的
(13) integration [ˌinti'greiʃən] n. 整体化，集成，综合
(14) category ['kætigəri] n. 种类，目录，部门
(15) fusion ['fjuːʒən] n. 融合，联合，聚变
(16) mechanical [mi'kænikəl] adj. 机械的，力学的，机械般的
(17) discipline ['disiplin] n. 纪律，训练（法），学科

Notes to the Text

(1) This, of course, is something ... have been doing for years.
当然，这也是很多具有超前思想的设计师和工程师多年来一直致力于做的事情。这里的 this 指代的是上句 to create more functional and adaptable products, something 后省略了 that，不定代词如 something, anything, nothing, everything, etc. 后面的定语从句只能用 that 引导。

(2) A Japanese engineer from Yasukawa Electric Company coined ... of mechanical and electrical engineering disciplines.
1969 年，Yasukawa 电气公司的一位日本工程师杜撰出了这个新词"mechatronics"（机电一体化），来反映机械与电气工程学科的融合。coin 作动词用，是杜撰之意，to

reflect the merging of... 是不定式作目的状语。

(3) Mechatronics gained legitimacy... journal: IEEE/ASME Transactions on Mechatronics.

1996 年，随着电气和电子工程师协会和美国机械工程师协会关于"机电一体化技术"的学报出版发行，机电一体化技术在学术界才得到正式承认。with the publication of... 随着……的出版。IEEE/ASME 是电气电子工程师协会和美国机械工程师协会的缩写词。

(4) After acknowledging that many definitions have circulated,... to be included in Transactions.

在承认了许多已流行的关于机电一体化方面的定义后，人们选择了如下一段并收入了学报。that many definitions have circulated 是 acknowledging 的宾语从句。

Exercises

Ⅰ．选择题

1. Mechatronics is nothing new; it is simply the application of the _____ techniques in precision mechanical engineering.

　　A. newly　　　　B. complex　　　　C. latest　　　　D. advanced

2. This, of course, is something many forward-thinking designers and engineers _____ for years.

　　A. has been doing　　B. have been doing　　C. have done　　D. will be doing

3. Mechatronics is the interdisciplinary fusion (not just a simple mixture!) of mechanics, _____ and information technology.

　　A. optics　　　　B. physics　　　　C. biology　　　　D. electronics

4. A Japanese engineer from Yasukawa Electric Company _____ the term "mechatronics" in 1969 to reflect the merging of mechanical and electrical engineering disciplines.

　　A. made　　　　B. used　　　　C. discovered　　　　D. coined

5. Today, the term encompasses a large array of technologies; many of _____ have become well-known in their own right.

　　A. what　　　　B. that　　　　B. which　　　　D. where

6. For example, many early robots resulting _____ mechanical and electrical systems, became central to mechatronics.

　　A. in　　　　B. of　　　　C. from　　　　D. by

7. Mechatronics gained legitimacy in academic circles in 1996 _____ the publication of the first referred journal: IEEE/ASME Transactions on Mechatronics.

　　A. in　　　　B. as　　　　C. at　　　　D. with

8. After acknowledging that many definitions have circulated, they selected the following for articles to _____ in Transactions.

　　A. include　　　　B. be included　　　　C. including　　　　D. have been included

9. In the mid-1980s, mechatronics came to mean engineering that is the boundary _____ mechanics and electronics.

  A. among   B. between   C. mid   D. middle

  10. The authors suggested 11 topics that should fall, at least in part, _____ the general category of mechatronics.

  A. under   B. below   C. in   D. at

Ⅱ. 将下列句子译成中文

  1. Mechatronics is the interdisciplinary fusion (not just a simple mixture!) of mechanics, electronics and information technology. The objective is for engineer to complete development, which is why it is currently so popular with industry.

  2. In the mid-1980s, mechatronics came to mean engineering that is the boundary between mechanics and electronics.

  3. For example, many early robots resulting from mechanical and electrical systems became central to mechatronics.

Ⅲ. 将下列短语或句子译成英语

  1. 机电一体化技术，电子学，机械学，智能控制，机器人学，信息技术，科学术语。

  2. 机电一体化技术是一门关于机械学、电子学和信息技术的跨学科技术。

  3. 机器人是机电一体化技术发展的产物，它涉及机械学、电子学、智能控制技术等。

  4. 机电一体化技术广泛用于汽车工业、机械工业及国防工业。

  5. 今天，机电一体化技术已成为研制机器人的关键技术。

Lesson 2   Mechanization and Automation

  Processes of mechanization have been developing and becoming more complex ever since the beginning of the Industrial Revolution at the end of the 18th century. The current developments of automatic processes are, however, different from the old ones. The "automation" of the 20th century is distinct from the mechanization of the 18th and 19th centuries in as much as mechanization was applied to individual operations, whereas "automation" is concerned with the operation and control of a complete producing unit.$^{(1)}$ And in many, though not all, instances the element of control is so great that whereas mechanization displaces muscle, "automation" displaces brain as well.$^{(2)}$

  The distinction between the mechanization of the past and what is happening now is, however, not a sharp one. At one extreme we have the electronic computer with its quite remarkable capacity for discrimination and control, while at the other end of the scale are "transfer machines", as they are now called, which may be as simple as a convey or belt to another. An automatic mechanism is one which has a capacity for self-regulate; that is, it can regulate or control the system or process without the need for constant human attention or adjustment.$^{(3)}$ Now people often talk about "feedback" as being an essential factor of the new industrial techniques, upon which is based an automatic self-regulating system and by virtue of which any deviation in the system from desired conditions can be detected, measured, reported and corrected. When "feedback" is applied to the process by which a large digital computer runs at the immense speed through a long series of sums, constantly rejecting the answers until it finds one to fit a complex set of facts that have been put to it, it is perhaps different in degree from what we have previously been accustomed to machines. But "feedback", as such, is a familiar mechanical conception. The old-fashioned steam engine was fitted with a centrifugal governor, two balls on levers spinning round and round an upright shaft. If the steam pressure rose and the engine started to go too fast, the increased speed of the spinning governor caused it to rise up the vertical rod and shut down a valve. This cut off some of the steam and thus the engine brought itself back to its proper speed.

The mechanization, which was introduced with the Industrial Revolution, because it was limited to individual processes, required the employment of human labor to control each machine as well as to load and unload materials and transfer them from one place to another. Only in a few instances were processes automatically linked together and was production organized as a continuous flow.

In general, however, although modern industry has been highly mechanized ever since the 1920s, the mechanized parts have not as a rule been linked together. Electric-light bulbs, bottles and the components of innumerable mass-produced articles are made in mechanized factories in which a degree of automatic control has gradually been building up. [4] The development of the electronic computer in the 1940s suggested that there were a number of other devices less complicated and expensive than the computer which could share the field of mechanical control. [5] These devices mechanical, pneumatic and hydraulic have been considerably developed in recent years and will continue to advance now that the common opinion is favoring the extension of "automation". Electronic devices, of course, although not the sole cause of what is happening, are nevertheless in a key position. They are gaining in importance and unquestionably hold out exceptional promise for development in the future.

New Words and Phrases

(1) mechanization [ˌmekənaiˈzeiʃən] n. 机械化
(2) in as much as 因为，由于，鉴于
(3) discrimination [disˌkrimiˈneiʃən] n. 辨别，鉴别，识别
(4) feedback [ˈfiːdbæk] n. 反馈，回馈
(5) deviation [ˌdiːviˈeiʃən] n. 偏差，偏移
(6) spinning [ˈspiniŋ] adj. 旋转的
(7) pneumatic [njuːˈmætik] adj. 空气的，气动的
(8) hydraulic [haiˈdrɔːlik] adj. 液压的
(9) remarkable [riˈmɑːkəbl] adj. 显著的，非凡的，值得注意的
(10) displace [disˈpleis] v. 移置，取代，转移
(11) old-fashioned [ˈəuldˈfæʃənd] adj. 老式的，旧的
(12) immense [iˈmens] adj. 巨大的，极大的

Notes to the Text

(1) The "automation" of the 20th century is distinct ... of a complete producing unit.

20 世纪的工业自动化之所以有别于 18、19 世纪的机械化，是因为机械化仅应用于操纵（执行）机构，而自动化则涉及整个生产单元中的执行和控制两个（核心）部分。be distinct from（与……有显著的区别），in as much as（因为……）引导一个原因状语从句，相当于 because，whereas 表示转折关系，相当于 while，表示相反的、但是、反之的意思，be concerned with（与……有关）。

（2）And in many, though not all, instances the element of control is so great that whereas mechanization displaces muscle, "automation" displaces brain as well.

尽管不是所有的情况，但在大多数情况下，控制元件依然发挥着强大的力量，机械化已经代替了手工劳动，自动化代替了脑力劳动。muscle（肌肉）在这里是暗喻，表示体力劳动；brain（脑）同样也是暗喻，表示脑力劳动，as well (as) 相当于 and。

（3）An automatic mechanism is one which has a capacity... without the need for constant human attention or adjustment.

自动调整机构能够自动调节系统，也就是说，它能在没有人干预和调整的情况下，自动对系统或生产过程进行控制和调节。which 引导后面的定语从句，修饰 one，self-regulate（自我调节控制），without the need...（在不需要……的情况下）。

（4）In general, however, although modern industry has been highly mechanized... in which a degree of automatic control has gradually been building up.

一般而言，从 20 世纪 20 年代以来，尽管现代工业已经实现了高度机械化，然而通常机械化的部分还没有联系在一起。机械化的工厂生产了光电灯泡、瓶子和大量生产的产品元件，这些机械化工厂的自动化程度日益得到了加强。in general（通常，大体，一般而言），ever since（自从……），主句要用完成式被动语态 has been highly mechanized, as a rule（通常），in which = where 引导地点状语从句，修饰 factories，building up（加强）。

（5）The development of the electronic computer in the 1940s suggested that... which could share the field of mechanical control.

20 世纪 40 年代电子计算机的发展，意味着在机械控制领域内将出现大量比计算机更简单，更廉价的产品。

Exercises

I. 根据课文填空

1. Processes of mechanization have been developing and becoming more complex _____ the beginning of the Industrial Revolution at the end of the 18th century.

2. The current developments of automatic processes are, however, different _____ the old ones.

3. The "automation" of the 20th century is distinct from the mechanization of the 18th and 19th centuries _____ mechanization was applied to individual operations, whereas "automation" is concerned with the operation and control of a complete producing unit.

4. And in many, though not all, instances the element of control is so great that whereas mechanization displaces muscle, "automation" displaces _____ as well.

5. An automatic mechanism is one which has a capacity for self-regulate; that is, it can regulate or control the system or process _____ the need for constant human attention or adjustment.

6. The system is based an automatic self-regulating system and by virtue _____ which any deviation in the system from desired conditions can be detected, measured, reported and corrected.

7. The old-fashioned steam engine was fitted _____ a centrifugal governor, two balls on levers.

8. The mechanization, which was introduced with the Industrial Revolution, because it was limited _____ individual processes.

9. The components of innumerable mass-produced articles are made in mechanized factories _____ which a degree of automatic control has gradually been building up.

10. The development of the electronic computer in the 1940s suggested that there were a number of other devices less complicated and expensive _____ the computer which could share the field of mechanical control.

Ⅱ. 将下列短语和句子译成中文

1. Industrial Revolution, mechanization and automatization, self-regulating system, feedback, mass-produced articles, hydraulic control, component, load and unload.

2. Now people often talk about "feedback" as being an essential factor of the new industrial techniques, upon which is based an automatic self-regulating system and by virtue of which any deviation in the system from desired conditions can be detected, measured, reported and corrected.

3. The mechanization, which was introduced with the Industrial Revolution, because it was limited to individual processes, required the employment of human labor to control each machine as well as to load and unload materials and transfer them from one place to another.

Ⅲ. 将下列句子译成英文

1. 一般来说，自从20世纪80年代计算机技术和信息技术就已经发展得很快。

2. 借助自动调节系统，这个生产线生产的产品质量已经越来越高，生产成本越来越低。

3. 机械化引入工业革命，由于局限于单个生产过程。因此，需要使用人工控制每部机器及装卸材料，并把材料从一个地方运到另一个地方。

4. 自动机械装置是一个能够自行调节，不需要人工调整的系统。

5. 这台机器人装备有先进的智能控制元件。

Lesson 3　Numerical Control and Automatic Machines

The major disadvantage of machine tool lies in the economics of the process. It is expensive to a machine tool for automatic production. Therefore, unless the part is to be made in very large numbers, the cost becomes prohibitive. Great need exists for a method that permits rapid automatic production, economical in job-lot amounts. The answer has been found in the numerical control of machine tools. In numerical control, the blueprint for a part is converted into a punched paper-type instruction, which is adapted via a computer to direct the operation of a specific machine tool. [1] Thus general purpose machine tools described in previous chapters— are instructed to machine a part according to information stored on a roll of tape. The tape can be rerun for copies of the same part or can be stored for future use. Furthermore, other tapes can be used to command the same machine tool to make other parts. There is a wide area of performance duplication between numerical control and automatics. Numerical control, however, offers more flexibility, lower tooling cost, quicker changes, and less machine down-time.

In machining contours, numerical control can mathematically translate the defined curve into a finished product, saving time and eliminating templates. [2] This can in turn improve accuracy. Another advantage appears to be great saving of machine time, the equivalent of increasing productive capacity with no increase in facilities.

Automation is no new development. Semiautomatic machines have been used in the textile industry and in engineering for many years. These machines merely require to be set up, loaded and started. Then, for a limited time, they will run on their own, with only an operator to watch them. From these have been developed machines known as transfer machines, found mostly in the motor-manufacturing industry. In production units using these, each stage in the manufacture of an article is carried out by one fully-automatic machine in a line of machines. The loading of the article to be machined is automatic, as is its transfer from one machine to the next.

Most of the transfer machines currently in operation employ electrical, pneumatic or hydraulic techniques.

Although automatic control by pneumatic and hydraulic means has been developed to a high degree of efficiency, the more recently developed electronic techniques offer many advantages over them. Electronic methods allow for greater speed, accuracy and flexibility in the operation of control systems. They also make possible the processing of information. Information, both from within the control system itself and from outside sources, can be electronically processed. Thus the control of extremely complex processes can be carried out automatically. [3]

New words and phrases

(1) tool　　[tu:l]　　v. 给……装配（配上）工具、机床和仪器；用工具加工，使用工具

(2) prohibitive　　[prəu'hibitiv]　　adj. 禁止（性）的，抑制的

(3) job lot　　杂乱（五花八门）的一堆，论堆的廉价品
　　job lot amount　　单批量

(4) rerun　　[ri:'rʌn]　　(reran, rerun; rerunning)　　v. （使）再开动（运转），（使）重新开动

(5) down-time　　[daun taim]　　n. 停机时间

(6) template　　['templit]　　n. 样（模，型）板，样规

(7) semiautomatic　　['semi,ɔ:tə'mætik]　　adj. 半自动的

Notes to the Text

(1) In numerical control, the blueprint for a part is converted into ... to direct the operation of a specific machine tool.

采用数控技术时,零件的图纸先转换成穿孔纸带型的指令,经计算机改编后用来控制专用机床进行作业。be converted into...译为"被转化成……",which 指 instruction,它引导后面的非限定性定语从句子,via 为介词,译为"经过、由、通过",这里相当于through,by,to direct 不定式作目的状语。

(2) In machining contours, numerical control can mathematically translate ... saving time and eliminating templates.

在加工外形轮廓时,数控能够用数学方法将确定的曲线转换成成品,既节省时间,又无需样板。machining 作动词用,词性变化,表示机加工,translate...to...译为"将……转换,翻译成……",a finished product 表示完工的产品,即成品。

(3) They also make possible the processing of information. Information... be carried out automatically.

它们还使信息处理成为可能。无论是控制系统本身的内部信息还是来自外部的信息,都可以利用电子技术进行处理。这样,就可以对极其复杂的工序进行自动控制。both...and 译为"两者,两方面,既……又",can be electronically processed 的主语是information,carry out 译为"执行、处理。"

Exercises

Ⅰ. 根据课文填空

The major __1__ of machine tool automation thus far described lies __2__ the economics of the process. It is expensive to a machine tool __3__ automatic production. Therefore, __4__ the part is to be made in very large numbers, the cost becomes prohibitive. Great need exists for a method __5__ permits rapid automatic production, economical in job-lot amounts.

Although automatic control __6__ pneumatic and hydraulic means has been developed to a high degree of efficiency, the more recently developed electronic techniques offer many advantages __7__ them. Electronic methods allow for greater speed, accuracy and flexibility in the operation of control systems. They also __8__ possible the processing of information. Information, both from within the control system itself __9__ from outside sources, can be electronically processed. Thus the control of extremely complex processes can be carried __10__ automatically.

Ⅱ. 将下列句子翻译成中文

1. The major disadvantage of machine tool lies in the economics of the process. It is expensive to a machine tool for automatic production.

2. Numerical control, however, offers more flexibility, lower tooling cost, quicker changes, and less machine down-time.

3. Most of the transfer machines currently in operation employ electrical, pneumatic or hydraulic techniques.

4. Although automatic control by pneumatic and hydraulic means has been developed to a high degree of efficiency.

Ⅲ. 将下列短语或句子翻译成英文
1. 机床，数控，全自动机器，制造商，气动和液压技术，柔性制造
2. 数控技术能提高加工精度，减少加工时间，提高生产能力。
3. 数控技术能自动执行特别复杂的加工过程的控制。
4. 使用数控技术把零件的图纸转化为计算机指令。

Lesson 4 Computer-Integrated Manufacturing System (CIMS)

A CIM system is commonly thought of as an integrated system that encompasses all the activities in the production system from the planning and design of a product through the manufacturing system, including control. CIM is an attempt to combine existing computer technologies in order to manage and control the entire business[1]. CIM is the approach that many companies are using to get to the automated factory of the future.

As with the traditional manufacturing approaches, the purpose of CIM is to transform product designs and materials into salable goods at a minimum cost in the shortest possible period of time.[2] CIM begins with the design of a product and with the manufacture of that product. With CIM, the customary split between the design and manufacturing functions is eliminated.

The element of CIM differs from the traditional job shop manufacturing system in the role the computer plays in the manufacturing process. Computer-integrated manufacturing systems are basically a network of computer systems tied together by a single integrated database. Using the information in the database, a CIS system can direct manufacturing activities, record results, and maintain accurate data. CIM is the computerization of design, manufacturing, distribution, and financial function into one coherent system.

A major element of a CIS system is a computer-assisted design (CAD) system. CAD involves any type of design activity that makes use of the computer to develop, analyze, or modify an engineering design. The design-related tasks performed by a CAD system are:
- Geometric modeling;
- Engineering analysis;
- Design review and evaluation;
- Automated drafting.

Another major element of CIM is computer-aided manufacturing (CAM). An important reason for using a CAD system is that it provides a database for manufacturing the product.[3] However, not all CAD data bases are compatible with manufacturing software. The tasks performed by a CAM system are:
- Numerical control (NC) or computer numerical control (CNC) programming.
- Computer-aided process planning (CAPP).
- Production planning and scheduling.
- Tool and fixture design.

New words and phrases

(1) integrate   ['intigreit]   v. 集成，使成整体，使一体化
(2) encompass   [in'kʌmpəs]   v. 包围，环绕，包含或包括某事物
(3) coherent   [kəu'hiərənt]   adj. 连贯的，一致的
(4) geometric   [dʒiəu'metrik]   adj. 几何学（的）
(5) compatible   [kəm'pætəbl]   adj. 兼容的，谐调的，一致的
(6) fixture   ['fikstʃə]   n. 夹具
(7) be thought of as…   被认为是……
(8) transform…into…   转变成……

Notes to the Text

(1) CIM is an attempt to combine existing computer technologies in order to manage and control the entire business.

CIM 旨在将现有的计算机技术结合起来，以对整个生产过程进行管理和控制。attempt to + v（企图，意图），后跟不定式；in order to + v（为了），后跟不定式。

(2) As with the traditional manufacturing approaches, the purpose of CIM is to … at a minimum cost in the shortest possible period of time.

与传统的生产模式相比，CIM 的目的是以最低的成本，在最短可能的时间内将产品设计及材料转变成适销对路的商品。approaches 相当于 methods or technique，transform…into… 相当于 turn/change/alter…into…，把……变成……，at a minimum cost 译为"以最小的成本"。

(3) An important reason for using a CAD system is that it provides a database for manufacturing the product.

采用 CAD 系统的一个重要因素是 CAD 系统为制造产品提供了一个数据库。reason for（理由，原因），that 引导的是表语从句。

Exercises

Ⅰ. 选择题

1. A CIM system is commonly thought of as an _____ system that encompasses all the activities in the production system from the planning and design of a product through the manufacturing system, including control.

　　A. integrated　　　B. combined　　　C. stable　　　D. special

2. CIM is the approach _____ many companies are using to get to the automated factory of the future.

　　A. to　　　B. of　　　C. that　　　D. when

3. The purpose of CIM is to transform product designs and materials into salable goods _____ a minimum cost in the shortest possible period of time.

　　A. on　　　B. in　　　C. to　　　D. at

4. The element of CIM differs _____ the traditional job shop manufacturing system in the role the computer plays in the manufacturing process.
   A. from   B. between   C. in   D. on
5. CIM is the _____ of design, manufacturing, distribution, and financial function into one coherent system.
   A. automatics   B. robotic   C. computerization D. methodology
6. Computer-integrated manufacturing systems are basically a network of computer systems tied together by a single integrated database.
   A. fastens   B. links   C. ties   D. tightens
7. A CIS system can direct _____ activities, record results, and maintain accurate data.
   A. design   B. manufacturing   C. measuring   D. marketing
8. A major element of a CIS system is a _____ system.
   A. CAM   B. CAPP   C. CAE   D. CAD
9. The design-related tasks performed by a CAD system are _____, engineering analysis, design review and evaluation and automated drafting.
   A. geometric modeling   B. physical modeling
   C. finite element analysis   D. productive planning
10. However, not all CAD data bases are _____ with manufacturing software.
   A. adapted   B. fitted   C. compatible   D. usable

Ⅱ. 将下列短语和句子译成中文

1. CIMS, CAE, CAD, CAM, FMS, CAPP, CNC, geometric modeling
2. CIM is the approach that many companies are using to get to the automated factory of the future.
3. Computer-integrated manufacturing systems are basically a network of computer systems tied together by a single integrated database.

Ⅲ. 将下列句子译成英文

1. 计算机集成制造系统的主要目的是以最小的成本和最短的时间将产品设计和材料转化成适销对路的商品。
2. 计算机集成制造系统能使用数据库的信息控制加工行为，记录加工结果，维护加工精度。
3. 然而，并非所有的 CAD 数据库可与制造软件兼容。

7.2 Extensive Reading

Lesson 1　Flexible Manufacturing System（FMS）

The most publicized type of modern manufacturing system is known as the flexible manufacturing system. The development of FMSs began in the United States in the 1960s. The idea was to combine the high reliability and productivity of the transfer line with the programmable flexibility of the NC machine in order to be able to produce a variety of parts. (1) In the later 1960s, such a system was installed for machining aircraft speed drive housings that is still in use today. However, very few of these systems were sold until the late 1970s and early 1980s, when a worldwide FMS movement began. (2)

The FMS is fundamentally an automated, conveyorized, computerized job shop. The system is complex to schedule. Because the machining time for different parts varies greatly, the FMS is difficult to link to an integrated system and often remains an island of expensive automation.

Some common features of FMSs are pallet changers, under floor a conveyor system that delivers parts to the machine.

A FMS system can usually monitor pieces part counts, tool changes, and machine utilization, with the computer providing supervisory control of the production. The workpieces are launched randomly into the system, which identifies each part in the family and routes it to the proper machines. The system generally displays reduced manufacturing lead time, low in-process inventory, and high machine tool utilization, with reduced indirect and direct labor. The materials-handling system must be able to route any part to any machine in any order and provide each machine with a small queue of "banked parts" waiting to be processed so as to maximize machine utilization. Convenient access to loading and unloading parts, compatibility with the control system, and accessibility to the machine tools are other necessary design features for the materials-handing system. The computer control for an FMS system has three levels. The master control monitors the entire system for tool failures or machine breakdowns, schedules the work, and routes the parts to the appropriate machine.

A FMS generally needs about three or four workers per shift to load and unload parts, change tools, and perform general maintenance. The workers in the FMS are usually high skilled and trained in NC and CNC. (3)

New words and phrases

(1) flexible   ['fleksibl]   adj. 柔韧性的，易曲的，灵活的，柔软的
(2) programmable   [ˌprəu'græməbl]   adj. 可设计的，可编程的
(3) conveyorize   [kən'veiəraiz]   v. 在……装设转运带
(4) pallet   ['pælit]   n. 随行夹具
(5) accessibility   [əkˌsesə'biləti]   n. 易接近，可到达
(6) inventory   ['invəntəri]   n. 库存，存货，详细目录，财产清册，总量

Notes to the Text

(1) The development of FMS began in the United States in the 1960s. The idea was to combine ... be able to produce a variety of parts.

20世纪60年代，FMS的发展始于美国，其设计思想是把生产线的高可靠性和高生产率同数控机床可编程的柔性相结合，以便能生产更多的零件。combine ... with, (将……结合，化合，合并)，transfer line 相当于 productive line, programmable 译为可编程序, NC machine (tool) 译为数控机床, in order to (为了), a variety of (许多的, 多种多样的)。

(2) However, very few of these systems were sold until the late 1970s and early 1980s, when a worldwide FMS movement began.

然而, FMS 直到 20 世纪 70 年代后期和 20 世纪 80 年代初期才开始在全球范围内发展, 这些 FMS 系统才卖得出去。very few of... (非常少), 表否定, until... (直到……才), when 引导定语从句。

(3) A FMS generally needs about three or four workers per shift to load and unload... in the FMS are usually high skilled and trained in NC and CNC.

一个 FMS 系统在加工每根轴时需要三四个工人来装卸零件、更换刀具和进行日常性维护, FMS 系统的工人通常都是经过数控和计算机数控培训的高技术人员。to load and unload, change tools, and perform general maintenance 不定式短语作目的状语, tool 这里指刀具和夹具, perform 相当于 make/do/conduct, NC 译为数控, CNC 译为计算机数控。

Lesson 2　Robot

You see robots at work around your home every day although you may not have thought of them as such. But, according to one definition, washing machines, electric heaters, etc., are all robots. Robots can also be designed to do the dangerous work in research laboratories or in outer space.

All the satellites launched into outer space have had robots on board.[1] These robots have sent back to their masters on earth, by way of radio, such important information on space as temperature, radiation, and so on. From their high position in space they have even taken photographs of the earth and other planets.

When the first spaceship lands on Mars and Venus, it will probably have on board robots rather than human beings. Robots can map the surfaces of these heavenly bodies, make necessary geological studies, explore unknown places, and even build landing areas for future spaceships.[2]

Of all the robots that we have with us today, those with electronic brains, called computers, are playing the most wonderful part in revolutionizing our way of life.[3] Computers were first developed to help in the solution of certain scientific problems, and now they have turned out to be so generally useful that they are being used in many different types of work. They have freed humans from heavy work and offer much more free time to their human masters.

Over the past two decades, industry has realized that in order to be competitive in world markets, it had to increase productivity and reduce manufacturing costs.[4] Since the source of skilled workers was dwindling and it was difficult to find people who would perform tasks which were considered to be monotonous, physically difficult, or environmentally unpleasant, industry has found it necessary to automate many manufacturing processes. The development of the computer has made it possible for industry to produce reliable machine tools and robots, which are making manufacturing processes more productive and reliable, thereby improving their user's competitive position in the world market.

The industrial robot of today is basically a single-arm device that can manipulate parts or tools through a sequence of operations or motions as programmed by the computer[5]. These operations or sequences may or may not necessarily be repetitive, because the robot, through the computer, has the ability to make logical decisions. The robot can be applied to many different operations in industry and is capable of being taken from one operation and easily "taught" to do another. This ability is based on the concept of flexible automation, where one machine is capable of economically performing many different operations with a minimum amount of special engineering or debugging.[6]

The industrial robot is finding many applications. The most common robot applications include:
- Loading and unloading machine tools.
- Welding.
- Moving heavy parts.
- Spraying painting
- Assembly
- Machining operations

New words and phrases

(1) robot　　　['rəubɔt]　　n. 机器人
(2) heater　　　['hi:tə]　　n. 加热器
(3) radiation　　[ˌreidi'eiʃən]　v. 放射，辐射
(4) position　　[pə'ziʃən]　　n. 位置，方法
(5) photograph　['fəutəgrɑ:f]　n. 照片
(6) rather…than…　而不是
(7) map　　　[mæp]　　v. 绘制……的地图
(8) geological　[dʒiə'lɔdʒikəl]　adj. 地质学的
(9) solution　　[sə'lju:ʃən]　　n. 解决办法，解答
(10) take photograph　拍照片
(11) free…from…　使……从……中解放出来

Notes the Text

(1) All the satellites launched into outer space have had robots on board.
发射到太空中的卫星都安装了机器人。launched 过去分词短语修饰 satellites，launched into... 译为"发射到……"。

(2) When the first spaceship lands on Mars and Venus, it will probably … and even build landing areas for future spaceships.
当第一条太空船在火星和金星上着陆时，它上面很可能带的是机器人而不是人类。机器人能够描绘出这些天体的表面，做必要的地理研究，开发未知的地方，并为将来的太空

船建造着陆地。when 引导时间状语从句，Mars and Venus（火星和金星），it 指 first spaceship，rather than（而不是），map 这里作动词，译为绘地图，explore unknown places（探索未知地方）。

（3）Of all the robots that we have with us today, those with electronic brains, called computers, are playing the most wonderful part in revolutionizing our way of life.

在我们今天使用的所有机器人中，装有电脑即计算机的机器人在彻底改革我们的生活方式方面正起着极其奇妙的作用。that 引导定语从句修饰 robots，of all...（所有……的），with electronic brains（有电脑的），called computers 是前面的同位语，playing the most wonderful part（起着神奇的作用），revolutionize（使……彻底改革）。

（4）Over the past two decades, industry has realized that in order to be competitive in world markets, it had to increase productivity and reduce manufacturing costs.

在过去20年，工业界认识到：为了提高在世界市场的竞争力，必须提高生产率，降低生产成本。decade = ten years，that 引导宾语从句，increase productivity（提高生产率）。

（5）The industrial robot of today is basically a single-arm device that can manipulate parts or tools through a sequence of operations or motions as programmed by the computer.

目前的工业机器人主要是单臂装置，该装置能根据计算机程序的设定，按操作或运动顺序来操作部件或工具。a single-arm device（单臂装置），that 引导定语从句，manipulate = control/operate，a sequence of（一系列，一连串）。

（6）This ability is based on the concept of flexible automation, where one machine is capable of economically performing many different operations with a minimum amount of special engineering or debugging.

这种能力是基于灵活（可调）自动化的概念，即一台机器能经济地，经过最少量的设计和调试而执行不同的生产操作。be based on...，（基于……），where 引导定语从句，is capable of...（能够……），a minimum amount of...（最小量的）。

第 8 章 Mechanical Technology

8.1 Intensive Reading

Lesson 1 Mechanisms

Mechanisms may be categorized in several different ways to emphasize their similarities and differences. One such grouping divides mechanisms into planar, spherical, and spatial categories. All three groups have many things in common; the criterion which distinguishes the groups, however, is to be found in the characteristics of the motions of the links. [1]

A planar mechanism is one in which all particles describe plane curves in space and all these curves lie in parallel places; i.e. the loci of all points are plane curves parallel to a single common plane. This characteristic makes it possible to represent the locus of any chosen point of a planar mechanism in its true size and shape on a single drawing or figure. [2] The motion transformation of any such mechanism is called coplanar. The plane four-bar linkage, the plate cam and follow, and the slider-crank mechanism are familiar examples of planar mechanism. The vast majority of mechanism in use today is planar.

Planar mechanisms utilizing only lower pairs are called planar linkages; they may include only revolute and prismatic pairs. Although a planar pair might theoretically be included, this would impose no constraint and thus be equivalent to an opening in the kinematics chain. Planar motion also requires that axes of all prismatic pairs and all revolute axes be normal to the plane motion.

A spherical mechanism is one in which each link has some point which remains stationary as the linkage moves and in which the stationary points of all links lie at a common location; i.e. the locus of each point is a curve contained in a spherical surface, and the spherical surfaces defined by several arbitrarily chosen points axes all concentric. The motions of all particles can therefore be completely described by their radial projections, or "shadows", on the surface of a sphere with properly chosen center.

Spherical linkages are constituted entirely of revolute pairs. A spherical pair would produce no additional constraints and would thus be equivalent to an opening in the chain, while all other tower pairs have no spherical motion. In spherical linkages, the axes of all revolute pairs must intersect at a point.

Spatial mechanisms, on the other hand, include no restrictions on the relative motions of the particles. The motion transformation is not necessary coplanar, nor must it be concentric [3]. A spatial mechanism may have particles with loci of double curvature. Any linkage which contains a screw pair, for example, is a spatial mechanism, since the relative motion within a screw pair is helical.

New Words and phrases

(1) mechanism ['mekənizəm] n. 机械装置，机构，机制
(2) categorize ['kætigəraiz] v. 加以类别，分类
(3) category ['kætigəri] n. 种类，逻辑范畴
(4) spherical ['sferikəl] adj. 球的，球形的
(5) spatial ['speiʃəl] adj. 空间的
(6) criterion [krai'tiəriən] n. 标准，规范
(7) distinguish [dis'tiŋgwiʃ] v. 区别，辨别
(8) particle ['pɑːtikl] n. 微粒，质点
(9) coplanar [kəu'pleinə] adj. 共面的
(10) loci ['ləusai] n. （拉丁语，locus 的复数形式）点的轨迹
(11) plane four bar linkage 平面四连杆机构
(12) cam [kæm] n. 凸轮
(13) follow ['fɔləu] n. 从动件
(14) slider crank mechanism 曲柄滑块机构
(15) planar mechanism 平面机构
(16) constraint [kən'streint] n. 约束，强制
(17) prismatic pair 棱形副
(18) concentric [kən'sentrik] adj. 同心的
(19) radial projection 径向投影
(20) planar pair 平面副
(21) intersect [,intə'sekt] v. 相交，交叉
(22) helical ['helikəl] adj. 螺旋的
(23) divide... into... 将……分成……
(24) in common 共同，共有

Notes to the Text

（1）The criterion which distinguishes the groups, however, is to be found in the characteristics of the motions of the links.

然而，区别分类的标准在于连杆运动的特性。which 引导定语从句，修饰 criterion，to be found 为不定式被动语态，links 译为连杆装置。

（2）This characteristic makes it possible to represent the locus of any chosen point of a planar mechanism in its true size and shape on a single drawing or figure.

这一特点能使在单一图形或图形上，以实际的尺寸和形状来绘出平面机构的任意选择点的轨迹。makes it possible（使……可能），represent（描绘，展现），planar mechanism（平面机构），in size and shape（在大小和形状方面）。

(3) The motion transformation is not necessary coplanar, nor must it be concentric.

运动的转换既不需要共面，也不需要同轴(中心)。nor must it be concentric 为倒装句，以否定词 nor 开头句子要用倒装，这类词有 not, no, never, hardly, seldom, scarcely, not until, not only, neither, in no way, no longer, nowhere, etc.

Exercises

Ⅰ. 根据课文完形填空

Mechanisms may be categorized in several different __1__ to emphasize their similarities and differences. One such grouping divides mechanisms __2__ planar, spherical, and spatial categories. All three groups have many things in __3__ ; the criterion which distinguishes the groups, however, is to be found in the characteristics of the motions of the links.

This characteristic __4__ it possible to represent the locus of any chosen point of a planar mechanism in its true size and __5__ on a single drawing or figure. The motion transformation of any such mechanism is called __6__ . The plane four-bar linkage, the plate cam and follow, and the slider-crank mechanism are familiar examples of planar mechanism. The vast __7__ of mechanism in use today is planar.

Spherical linkages are constituted entirely __8__ revolute pairs. A spherical pair would produce no additional constraints and would thus be equivalent to an opening in the chain, while all other tower pairs have no spherical motion. In __9__ linkages, the axes of all revolute pairs must intersect __10__ a point.

1. A. means   B. ways   C. methods   D. area
2. A. in   B. at   C. into   D. on
3. A. common   B. average   C. ordinary   D. commonly
4. A. does   B. lets   C. takes   D. makes
5. A. shape   B. form   C. type   D. model
6. A. coplanar   B. co-line   C. concentric   D. co-axes
7. A. minority   B. majority   C. all   D. total
8. A. at   B. in   C. of   D. with
9. A. planar   B. spherical   C. spatial   D. dimension
10. A. on   B. in   C. at   D. above

Ⅱ. 将下列句子译成中文

1. A spherical mechanism is one in which each link has some point which remains stationary as the linkage moves and in which the stationary points of all links lie at a common location.

2. A spherical pair would produce no additional constraints and would thus be equivalent to an opening in the chain.

3. Spatial mechanisms, on the other hand, include no restrictions on the relative motions of the particles.

Ⅲ. 将下列句子译成英文

1. 机构可分为平面的、球形的和空间的结构形式。

2. 理论上讲,在这个复杂的结构中可能包含了一个平面副,并且没有约束。

3. 运动的转换既不需要共面也不需要同心。

Lesson 2 Machine Elements

However, any simple machine is a combination of individual components generally referred to as machine elements or parts. Thus, if a machine is completely dismantled, a collection of simple parts remains such as nuts, bolts, springs, gears, cams, and shafts the building blocks of all machinery. A machine element is, therefore, a single unit designed to perform a specific function and capable of combining with other elements. Sometimes certain elements are associated in pairs, such as nuts and bolts or keys and shafts. In other instances, a group of elements is combined to form a subassembly, such as bearings, couplings, and clutches.

The most common example of a machine element is a gear, which, fundamentally, is a combination of the wheel and the lever to form a toothed wheel. The rotation of this gear on a hub or shaft drives other gears which may rotate faster or slower, depending upon the number of teeth on the basic wheels.

Other fundamental machine elements have evolved from wheel and levers. A wheel must have a shaft on which it may rotate. The wheel is fastened to the shaft with a key, and the shaft is joined to other shafts with couplings.[1] The shaft must rest in bearings, may be started by a clutch or stopped with a brake. It may be turned by a pulley with a belt or a chain connecting it to a pulley on a second shaft. The supporting structure may be assembled with bolts or rivets or by welding. Proper application of these machine elements depends upon knowledge of the force on the structure and the strength of the materials employed.

The individual reliability of machine elements becomes the basis for estimating the overall life expectancy of a complete machine.[2] Many machine elements are thoroughly standardized. Testing and practical experience have established the most suitable dimensions for common structural and mechanical parts. Through standardization, uniformity of practice and resulting economies are obtained. Not all machine parts in use are standardized, however, in the automotive industry only fasteners, bearings, bushings, chains, and belts are standardized, crankshafts and connecting rods are not standardized.[3]

New Words and Phrases

(1) dismantle [dis'mæntl] v. 拆除

(2) nut [nʌt] n. 螺母,螺帽

(3) bolt [bəult] n. 螺栓

(4) spring [spriŋ] n. 弹簧

(5) key [kiː] n. 键,花键,栓

(6) shaft [ʃɑːft] n. 轴

(7) subassembly [sʌbə'sembli] n. 组件,部件

(8) bearing ['bɛəriŋ] n. 轴承

第8章　Mechanical Technology

(9) coupling ['kʌpliŋ] n. 联结器
(10) clutch [klʌtʃ] n. 离合器
(11) lever ['li:və] n. 杠杆
(12) rotation [rəu'teiʃən] n. 旋转
(13) hub [hʌb] n. 轮毂
(14) pulley ['puli] n. 滑轮，皮带轮
(15) rivet ['rivit] n. 铆钉；v. 铆钉固定
(16) bushing ['buʃiŋ] n. 轴衬，套管
(17) crankshaft ['kræŋkˌʃɑ:ft] n. 机轴，转轴，曲轴
(18) life expectancy 寿命
(19) standardize ['stændədaiz] v. 使符合标准
(20) combine with... 将……组合（结合）在一起，
(21) associate... with... 与……有关，与……有联系
(22) depend on 依靠

Notes

(1) Other fundamental machine elements have evolved from wheel and levers. A wheel must have a shaft on which it may rotate. The wheel is fastened to the shaft with a key, and the shaft is joined to other shafts with couplings

其他的基本机械零件是由轮子和轴发展而成的。轮子必须要装在一根轴上才能转动，将轮子用花键固定在轴上；轴与另一个轴之间用联轴器联结。have evolved from（从……进化，发展而来），on which = where，引导地点状语从句，it 这里指 wheel，be fastened with 表示"用……固定……"，key（连接键），couplings（联轴器）。

(2) The individual reliability of machine elements becomes the basis for estimating the overall life expectancy of a complete machine.

单个机械零件的可靠性是估计整机全寿命的根据。individual reliability（单个零件的可靠性）；life expectancy（寿命），相当于 life span。

(3) Not all machine parts in use are standardized, however, in the automotive industry only fasteners, bearings, bushings, chains, and belts are standardized, crankshafts and connecting rods are not standardized.

然而，并非所有的机械零件已经标准化。在汽车工业领域，只有紧固件、轴承、轴套、传动链和传动带为标准件，而曲轴和连接杆却未标准化。Not all 表示部分否定，可译为：并非所有的，fastener 指坚固件，如螺栓、螺钉等，crankshaft and connecting rod 指曲轴和连（接）杆。

Exercises

Ⅰ. 将下列短语和句子译成中文

1. component, a chain connecting, reliability of machine element, life expectancy of a complete machine, fastener, connecting rod

2. Sometimes certain elements are associated in pairs, such as nuts and bolts or keys and shafts.

3. The most common example of a machine element is a gear, which, fundamentally, is a combination of the wheel and the lever to form a toothed wheel.

Ⅱ. 根据课文填空

1. However simple, any machine is a combination of individual components generally referred to _____ machine elements or parts.

2. Sometimes certain elements are associated in pairs, such as nuts and _____ or keys and shafts.

3. In other instances, a group of elements is combined to form a _____, such as bearings, couplings, and clutches.

4. The most common example of a machine element is a gear, _____, fundamentally, is a combination of the wheel and the lever to form a toothed wheel.

5. The rotation of this gear on a hub or shaft drives other gears which may rotate faster or slower, depending upon the _____ of teeth on the basic wheels.

6. The wheel is fastened to the _____ with a key, and the shaft is joined to other shafts with couplings.

7. The individual reliability of machine elements becomes the basis for estimating the overall life _____ of a complete machine.

8. Testing and practical experience have established the most suitable _____ for common structural and mechanical parts.

9. Not all machine parts in use are standardized.

10. In the automotive industry only fasteners, bearings, bushings, chains, and belts are standardized, crankshafts and connecting rods are not _____.

Ⅲ. 将下列句子译成英语

1. 有时某些零件是成对的关系，如螺母和螺栓。
2. 将轮子用花键固定在轴上，轴与另一个轴之间用联轴器联结。
3. 单个机械零件的可靠性是估计整机全寿命的根据。

Lesson 3 Power Steering System

The cars today are larger and heavier than earlier ones; the tyres are wider, further apart and inflated to lower pressures. In addition, the trend of development has been to place more than half of the weight on the front wheels, especially the weight of the engine, which itself is larger and heavier than in the early days.

To make cars easier to steer, the gear ratio in the steering box at the end of the steering column is changed so that turning the wheel requires less torque. (1) But this increases the number of turns of the steering wheel required on modern cars without power steering compared to 2.5 or 3 turns for cars built before 1940. Modern cars with power steering only require about three turns. Power assisted steering was first developed in the 1920s; one of the first devices was developed by an engineer at Pierce Arrow, an American maker of luxury cars.⁽²⁾ The Cadillac division of General Motors was going to offer power steering as optional equipment on some models in the early 1930s, but the Depression interfered with the development. During World War II power steering was fitted to military vehicles; in 1952 Chrysler began offering it, and it is now standard equipment on many of the biggest American cars.

Electric devices were tried, but power steering today is always hydraulic with oil pressure of perhaps 1000psi (70 kg/cm^2) maintained by a pump driven by the engine of the car. The system is a servomechanism, or servo loop, which makes a correction to compensate for the torque applied to the steering wheel by the driver⁽³⁾. It consists of an actuator and a control valve. The actuator is a hydraulic cylinder with a piston, or ram, which is free to travel in either direction from the center. The function of the control valve is to respond to the torque from the steering wheel by actuating smaller valves at each end of the cylinder. The system is designed to assist the steering linkage rather than replace it, and it does not do all the work of steering, but leaves some of it for the driver. Thus if the hydraulics fail, the car can still be steered, though with greater effort, and at all times the feel of the road is mechanically transmitted from the front wheels to the hands of the driver on the steering wheel, which is an essential element of safe driving.⁽⁴⁾ The power steering makes a positive contribution to safe driving in that if the driver hits a small obstacle on the road or has a flat tyre at speed, the power unit makes it easier to keep the car under control.⁽⁵⁾ Many large cars fitted with wide, stiff radial ply tyres would be nearly impossible to steer at parking speed without power steering.⁽⁶⁾

Hydrostatic systems, designed for off-the-road vehicles, are different from this because they dispense with the steering column and the steering box, and the steering wheel and the steered wheels are connected only by hydraulic tubes or hoses.

The power steering system includes a reservoir to hold the oil. Oil pressure is always provided when the engine is running, but when the system is at rest, that is, when the steering wheel is not turned, equal pressure is available to each side of the piston in the actuator so that it does not move.

There are basically two types of power steering systems: those which have the control valve, usually a rotary one, located within the steering box, and those in which the valve is integrated with the actuator when it is an axial spool valve.

New Words and Phrases

(1) steering box   转向箱
(2) steering column   转向杆
(3) power steering   动力转向
(4) power assisted steering   动力助力转向
(5) luxury   ['lʌkʃəri]   n. 华贵
(6) General Motors   通用汽车公司（美国）
(7) Cadillac   ['kædilæk]   n. 凯迪拉克（著名汽车品牌）

（8）division　［di'viʒən］　n. 部门
（9）depression　［di'preʃən］　n. 沮丧，低沉，不景气
（10）military vehicle　军用车辆
（11）Chrysler　［'kraislə］　n. 克莱斯勒公司
（12）servomechanism　［ˌsəːvəu'mekənizəm］　n. 自动驾驶装置，伺服机构，跟踪器
（13）servo loop　伺服环路，伺服回路
（14）correction　［kə'rekʃən］　n. 改正，修正
（15）actuator　［'æktjueitə］　n. 激励者，传动装置
（16）actuate　［'æktjueit］　v. 开动，促使
（17）ram　［ræm］　n. 柱塞，随机存储器
（18）obstacle　［'ɔbstəkl］　n. 障碍，障碍物
（19）radial ply tyre　径向网层轮胎
（20）off-the-road vehicle　越野车
（21）dispense　［dis'pens］　v. 分发，分配
（22）hose　［həuz］　n. 液压软管
（23）reservoir　［'rezəvwɑː］　n. 水库，蓄水箱，油箱
（24）spool valve　随动阀，伺服阀
（25）interfere with...　干涉……
（26）compensate for...　补偿……
（27）make a positive contribution to...　对……作出了积极贡献

Notes

（1）To make cars easier to steer, the gear ratio in the steering box at the end of the steering column is changed so that turning the wheel requires less torque.

为使汽车容易转向，改变了转向杆末端转向箱的传动比，结果只需较小的扭矩就可以转动方向盘。to make cars easier to steer 不定式作目的状语，make sb./sth. + adj.。这里的 the wheel 是指方向盘，而不是车轮。

（2）Power assisted steering was first developed in the 1920s; one of the first devices was developed by an engineer at Pierce Arrow, an American maker of luxury cars.

动力转向装置在20世纪20年代首次研制出来；最初的装置之一是由美国豪华汽车制造商皮尔斯·埃罗汽车厂的一位工程师研制出来的。Pierce Arrow 与 an American maker of luxury cars 是同位语，皮尔斯·埃罗是美国豪华汽车制造商。

（3）The system is a servomechanism, or servo loop, which makes a correction to compensate for the torque applied to the steering wheel by the driver.

该系统叫作伺服机构或伺服回路，其作用是进行调整以补偿驾驶员施加于转向盘的扭矩。which 引导非限定性定语从句。correction = adjustment；compensate for... 补偿……；the steering wheel 方向盘。

（4）Thus if the hydraulics fail, the car can still be steered, though with greater effort, and at all times the feel of the road is mechanically transmitted from the front wheels to the hands of the driver on the steering wheel, which is an essential element of safe driving.

因此，如果液压系统失灵，尽管司机费些力，汽车仍可开动，而且对路面的感觉始终可由汽车前轮机械地传到驾驶员握着方向盘的双手。这是安全驾驶的一个重要因素。if the hydraulics fail = if the hydraulics has failure/defect; though with greater effort = though with greater effort made by driver; an essential element of safe driving 译为"安全驾驶的重要因素"。

(5) The power steering makes a positive contribution to safe driving in that if the driver hits a small obstacle on the road or has a flattyre at speed, the power unit makes it easier to keep the car under control.

动力转向装置对安全驾驶作出的另一个有益贡献在于：如果驾驶员碰到路面上的一个小障碍物或在快速行驶中轮胎泄气，该动力转向装置使汽车更容易保持控制。make a positive contribution to... 对……作出了积极的贡献; in that = because = due to 由于，因为; have a flat tyre 指轮胎爆胎泄气; under control 在控制之中。

(6) Many large cars fitted with wide, stiff radial ply tyres would be nearly impossible to steer at parking speed without power steering.

许多安装了宽而坚固的径向网层轮胎的大型汽车，如果没有动力转向装置，当汽车减速慢行时，几乎不能对汽车进行转向操作。fitted with = equipped with，过去分词短语修饰主语 large cars; without power steering 译为"如果没有动力转向装置"。

Exercises

Ⅰ. 根据课文填空

The cars today are larger and ___1___ than earlier ones. But power steering today is always ___2___ with oil pressure of perhaps 1000 psi (70 kg/cm^2) maintained by a pump ___3___ by the engine of the car. The system is a servomechanism, or ___4___, which makes a correction to compensate ___5___ the torque applied to the steering wheel by the driver. It consists ___6___ an actuator and a control valve. The actuator is a hydraulic cylinder ___7___ a piston, or ram, which is free to travel in either direction from the center. The function of the control valve is to respond ___8___ the torque from the steering wheel by actuating smaller valves at each end of the cylinder. The system is designed to assist the steering linkage rather ___9___ replace it, and it does not do all the work of steering, but leaves some of it for the driver. Thus if the hydraulics fails, the car can still be steered, ___10___ with greater effort, and at all times the feel of the road is mechanically transmitted from the front wheels to the hands of the driver on the steering wheel, which is an essential element of safe driving.

Ⅱ. 将下列短文译成中文

Hydrostatic systems, designed for off-the-road vehicles, are different from this because they dispense with the steering column and the steering box, and the steering wheel and the steered wheels are connected only by hydraulic tubes or hoses.

The power steering system includes a reservoir to hold the oil. Oil pressure is always provided when the engine is running, but when the system is at rest that is when the steering wheel is not turned, equal pressure is available to each side of the piston in the actuator, so that it does not move.

Ⅲ. 将下列句子译成英文

1. 为使汽车容易转向，改变了转向杆末端转向箱的传动比，结果只需较小的扭矩就可以转动方向盘。
2. 在第二次世界大战期间，动力转向装置曾装在军用车辆上。
3. 如果没有动力转向装置，当汽车减速慢行时，几乎不能对汽车进行转向操作。
4. 如果液压系统失灵，尽管司机费些力，汽车仍可开动。
5. 现今的汽车比早期的汽车大得多也重得多。

Lesson 4　Brake System

Brake is a device used to slow or stop the motion of a vehicle or machine. Brakes are most commonly used to control or stop motor vehicles, trains, bicycles, and rotating devices such as shafts and motors. Some brakes also act as locking devices. An example is the parking brake of an automobile. Most brakes operate by pressing a stationary brake shoe against a moving wheel or other rotating objects.[1] This creates friction, which slows or stops the rotary motion. Brake shoes are made in a variety of sizes and shapes; as they must be highly resistant to heat and wear, they usually contain asbestos or similar material.[2]

Braking is an energy-wasting process. For example, when a brake shoe is pressed against a rotating wheel, friction serves to convert the mechanical energy of moving wheel into heat.[3] The heat released to the surrounding air is wasting energy.

One of the simplest types of brakes is the block brake, which consists of a wooden or metal block that serves as the brake shoe. The block is usually curved to fit the outer rim of the wheel. When the brake is actuated, the block presses against the rotating wheel, producing a braking effect. Double block brakes use two blocks connected by linkage and mounted on opposite sides of the wheel. A common use of block brakes is on locomotives and railway cars.

The band brake is a simple but effective brake that is used on machinery for hoists and elevators in construction equipment and to control the movements of gears in automatic transmissions. A typical band brake consists of a flexible band of metal or other material fitted around the rotating device so that the band may be tightened against the device to slow or stop it. Brakes used in automobiles, trucks, motorcycles and most other motor vehicles are usually either drum or disk tape. Many automobiles use both types with disks at the front wheels and drums at the rear.

In the drum brake or internal expending brake, the mechanism is enclosed in a heavy metal drum that is attached to and rotates with the wheel. Within the drum (but not connected to it) are two curved brake shoes and their operating mechanism. When the driver steps on the brake pedal, the brake shoes are forced outward and press against the drums inner surface.[4] The drum brake's enclosed design keeps the mechanism relatively free of dirt and grit. Because of the design, however, heat generated during fast or repeated stops can not escape quickly enough to prevent fading or loss of brake power. Drum brakes are also affected by moisture.

The disk brake used on motor vehicles and on many airplane wheels is the caliper type instead of a drum. There is a heavy metal disk to which the wheel is attached.[5] A clamp-like caliper assembly is mounted at the rim of the disk but does not turn with the disk. Braking takes place when small brake shoes inside the caliper grip the disk from both sides. Fading does not ordinarily occur with disk brakes because the disk is exposed to the air and can dissipate heat rapidly. Dirt and water rarely cause problems because they tend to be wiped away each time the shoes press against the rotating disk.

New Words and Phrases

(1) brake [breik] n. 制动,刹车；v. 制动
(2) parking brake 停车制动
(3) stationary brake shoe 静止制动蹄
(4) asbestos [æz'bestɔs] n. 石棉
(5) surrounding [sə'raundiŋ] adj. 周围的；n. 环境
(6) block brake 块式制动器
(7) rim [rim] n. 轮缘，轮边
(8) locomotive ['ləukə,məutiv] n. 机车，火车头
(9) band brake 带式制动
(10) hoist [hɔist] n. 提升，升起
(11) elevator ['eliveitə] n. 电梯，升降机
(12) brake pedal 制动踏板
(13) grit [grit] n. 粗砂；v. 研磨
(14) moisture ['mɔistʃə] n. 潮湿
(15) caliper type 钳盘制动式
(16) clamp-like [klæmplaik] adj. 像夹子一样的
(17) grip [grip] v. 抓住，紧握
(18) dissipate ['disipeit] v. 驱散
(19) be exposed to... 暴露于……
(20) wipe away 擦去，扫去
(21) convert... into... 改变……到……

Notes

(1) Most brakes operate by pressing a stationary brake shoe against a moving wheel or other rotating objects.

多数制动器的制动是将相对静止的制动蹄紧压于运动轮或者其他旋转体上。brake shoe 译为"制动蹄"；pressing... against... 将……压在……上。

(2) Brake shoes are made in a variety of sizes and shapes as they must be highly resistant to heat and wear, they usually contain asbestos or similar material.

制动蹄被制成多种不同的大小和形状，由于它们必须要能抗热和耐磨损，所以制动蹄通常含有石棉或类似石棉的材料。a variety of... 多种的；be resistant to... 抵抗……；asbestos 石棉，石棉是一种耐热耐磨的材料。

(3) Braking is an energy-wasting process. For example, when a brake shoe is pressed against a rotating wheel, friction serves to convert the mechanical energy of moving wheel into heat.

制动是一个浪费能量的过程。当一个制动蹄被压紧到旋转轮上时，摩擦作用将运动轮的机械能转化成热能。for example 例如，是插入语；when 引导时间状语从句；这里 serves = acts = makes；convert/change/turn... into... 将……转化为……。

(4) When the driver steps on the brake pedal, the brake shoes are forced outward and press against the drums inner surface.

当驾驶员踩下制动踏板时，制动蹄就被迫向外移动并且紧压在鼓筒内壁上。step on the brake pedal 踩在制动踏板上；press against... 压在……上。

(5) The disk brake used on motor vehicles and on many airplane wheels is the caliper type instead of a drum. There is a heavy metal disk to which the wheel is attached.

用于机动车辆和多数飞机轮子上的盘形制动器是钳盘制动式，而不是轮鼓式，它采用厚重的金属盘，并安装于轮子上面。instead of 而不是；to which the wheel is attached = which the wheel is attached to 是一个定语从句，修饰 a heavy metal disk，指这个厚重的金属盘被安装在轮子上。

Exercises

Ⅰ. 多项选择题

1. Brakes are most commonly used to control or _____ motor vehicles, trains, bicycles, and rotating devices.
   A. stop   B. drive   C. push   D. propel

2. Brake shoes are made in a variety of sizes and shapes, because they must be highly ____ to heat and wear, they usually contain asbestos or similar material.
   A. assistant   B. resistant   C. consistent   D. insistent

3. Friction serves to convert the mechanical energy of moving wheel _____ heat.
   A. with   B. onto   C. to   D. into

4. One of the simplest types of brakes is the block brake, which consists _____ a wooden or metal block that serves as the brake shoe.
   A. of   B. at   C. for   D. on

5. The block presses _____ the rotating wheel, producing a braking effect.
   A. in   B. on   C. against   D. to

6. Brakes used in automobiles, trucks, motorcycles, and most other motor vehicles are usually either ____ or disk tape.
   A. belt   B. drum   C. plate   D. bar

7. When the driver _____ on the brake pedal, the brake shoes are forced outward and

press against the drum's inner surface.

A. presses　　　B. hits　　　C. steps　　　D. paces

8. The disk brake used on motor vehicles and on many airplane wheels is the caliper type ____ of a drum.

A. dozens　　　B. lots　　　C. because　　　D. instead

9. There is a heavy metal disk ____ which the wheel is attached.

A. with　　　B. at　　　C. to　　　D. in

10. Fading does not ordinarily occur with disk brakes, because the disk is ____ to the air and can dissipate heat rapidly.

A. extended　　　B. expanded　　　C. expected　　　D. exposed

Ⅱ. 将下列短语和句子译成英文

1. 制动器，停车制动器，块式制动器，鼓形制动器，盘形制动器，制动蹄，制动踏板。
2. 制动器是一种用于使车辆或机器降低运行速度或停止的装置。
3. 制动是一个浪费能量的过程，摩擦作用将运动轮的机械能转化成热能。
4. 最简单的一种制动器型式是用木块或金属块作为制动蹄的块式制动器。
5. 用于机动车辆和多数飞机轮子上的盘形制动器是钳盘制动式，而不是轮鼓式。

Ⅲ. 将下列短文译成中文

The band brake is a simple but effective brake that is used on machinery for hoists and elevators in construction equipment and to control the movements of gears in automatic transmissions. Brakes used in automobiles, trucks, motorcycles, and most other motor vehicles are usually either drum or disk tape. Many automobiles use both types with disks at the front wheels and drums at the rear.

8.2　Extensive Reading

Lesson 1　Hydraulic Power Transmission

Hydraulic drives are used in preference to mechanical system when power is to be transmitted between points too far apart for chains or belts [1]. High torque at low speed is required; a very compact unit is needed; a smooth transmission and free of vibration is required; easy control of speed and diction is necessary; or output speed must be varied steplessly.

Oil pressure pumps driven by electricity establish an oil flow for energy transmission, which is fed to hydraulic motor or hydraulic cylinder converting it into mechanical energy. The control of the oil flow is by means of valves. The pressurized oil flow produces linear or rotary mechanical motion. The kinetic energy of the oil flow is comparatively low, and therefore the term hydrostatic driver is sometimes used. There is little constructional difference between hydraulic motors and pumps. Any pump may be used as a motor. The quantity of oil flowing at any given time may be varied by means of regulating valves or the use of variable-delivery pumps. [2]

In general terms, hydraulic drives may be divided into rotary and linear types. Rotary drives produce a rotating motion, whilst linear devices in the form of piston and cylinder units produce a reciprocating movement.

All hydraulic motors function broadly is in accordance with the same basic principle. A pressurized fluid is alternately forced into and removed from a chamber. The filling cycle begins with minimum chamber volumes. When the chamber reaches its maximum volume (the maximum capacity), the filling is ended by isolating the chamber from the supply line. The oil is then returned to the oil pump through the return lines and at the same time the next chamber is filled with oil [3].

New Words and Phrases

(1) hydraulic [haiˈdrɔːlik] adj. 液压的
(2) preference [ˈprefərəns] n. 优先选择
(3) compact [kəmˈpækt] adj. 紧凑的，紧密的，简洁的
(4) steplessly [steplisli] adv. 无阶（级）地
(5) oil pressure pump 油泵
(6) hydraulic motor 液压马达
(7) hydraulic cylinder 油缸
(8) valve [vælv] n. 阀
(9) regulating valve 调节阀
(10) relief valve 安全阀
(11) kinetic energy 动能
(12) hydrostatic driver 静压传动装置
(13) variable-delivery pump 变量泵
(14) piston [ˈpistən] n. 活塞
(15) chamber [ˈtʃeimbə] n. 油腔
(16) by means of... 借助于……
(17) be used as... 用作为……
(18) be divided into... 被分为……
(19) in the form of... 以……形式
(20) in accordance with... 与……一致，根据
(21) isolate... from 把……隔开
(22) be filled with... 充满……，装满……

Notes

(1) Hydraulic drives are used in preference to mechanical system when power is to be transmitted between points too far apart for chains or belts.

对于两点之间较远的传动，不适合用传动带和传动链传动的机械系统，可优先考虑采用液压传动。when 引导一个时间状语从句，从句采用被动语态；far apart 远离；chains or belts 链传动或带传动。

(2) The quantity of oil flowing at any given time may be varied by means of regulating valves or the use of variable-delivery pumps.

一定时间的流量可由调节阀或变量泵来控制。at any given time 在给定的时间，过去分词 given 修饰 time；by means of... 借助于……；variable-delivery pumps 变量泵。

(3) When the chamber reaches ... The oil is then returned to the oil pump through the return lines and at the same time the next chamber is filled with oil.

当油腔达到最大容量时，使油腔和进油油路隔开，停止进油，然后油通过回油油路返回到油泵中，同时另一个油腔开始灌油。when 引导时间状语从句；isolate... from 将……隔开；chamber 油腔；return lines 回油油路；at the same time 同时；be filled with... 装满……。

Lesson 2　Diesel Engine

Diesel engine is an internal combustion engine operating on a thermodynamic cycle. In this cycle, the ratio of compression of the air charge is sufficiently high to ignite the fuel subsequently injected into the combustion chamber. (1) The engine differs essentially from the prevalent mixture engine. In the latter, an explosive mixture of air and gas is made externally to the engine cylinder, compressed and ignited by an electric spark. The diesel engine utilizes a wider variety of fuels with a higher thermal efficiency and consequent economic advantage under many service applications. The true diesel engine, as projected by R. Diesel and represented in most low speed engines, such as about 300 rpm, uses a fuel injection system. In this system the injection rate is delayed and controlled to maintain constant pressure during combustion. Adaptation of the injection principle to a higher speed, such as 1,000 ~ 2,000 rpm, has necessitated departure from the constant pressure specification because the time available for fuel injection is so short (milliseconds). Combustion proceeds with little regard to the constant pressure specification. High peak pressures may be developed. Yet non volatile fuels are burned to advantage in these engines. Such kinds of engines can not be strictly identified as true diesels but properly should be called commercial diesels (2). Usually all such engines are classified as diesels.

Identifying alternative features of diesel engine types includes: 1. two cycle or four cycle operation; 2. horizontal or vertical piston movement; 3. single or multiple cylinder; 4. large (5,000 hp) or small (50 hp); 5. cylinders in line, opposed, V or radial; 6. single acting or double acting; 7. high (1,000 ~ 2,000 rpm), low (100 ~ 300 rpm), or medium speed; 8. constant speed or variable speed; 9. reversible or nonreversible; 10. air injection or solid injection; 11. turbocharged or unturbocharged; 12. single or multiple fuel.

Maximum diesel engine sizes (5,000 kW) are smaller than steam turbines (1,000,000 kW) and hydraulic turbines (300,000 kW). Diesel engines give high intrinsic and actual thermal efficiency (20% - 40%). Control of engine output is by regulation of the fuel supplied but without variation of the air supply. Supercharging increases cylinder weight charge and consequently power output for a given cylinder size and engine speed (3). With two cycle constructions scavenging air is delivered by crankcase compression, front end compression, or separate rotary, reciprocating or centrifugal blowers. The cylinder may be without valves but with complete control of admission of scavenging air and release of spent gases in a two port combustion.

New Words and Phrases

(1) thermodynamic [,θə:məudai'næmik] *adj.* 热力学的
(2) sufficiently [sə'fiʃəntli] *adv.* 充分地，十分地
(3) ignite [ig'nait] *v.* 点火
(4) combustion chamber 燃烧室
(5) essentially [i'senʃəli] *adv.* 本质上
(6) prevalent ['prevələnt] *adj.* 普遍的，流行的
(7) thermal efficiency 热效率
(8) delayed [di'leid] *adj.* 延时的
(9) constant ['kɔnstənt] *adj.* 不变的；*n.* 恒量
(10) nonvolatile [nɔn'vɔlətail] *adj.* 不易挥发的
(11) strictly ['striktli] *adv.* 严格地
(12) alternative [ɔ:l'tə:nətiv] *adj.* 二选一的，可选择的
(13) horizontal ['hɔri'zɔntəl] *adj.* 水平的，地平线的
(14) vertical ['və:tikəl] *adj.* 垂直的
(15) multiple ['mʌltipl] *adj.* 多样的，多倍的
(16) radial ['reidiəl] *adj.* 光线的，放射的，半径的，星形的
(17) reversible [ri'və:səbl] *adj.* 可逆的
(18) turbocharged ['tə:bəutʃɑ:dʒd] *adj.* 涡轮增压的
(19) steam turbine 蒸汽轮机
(20) hydraulic turbine 水轮机
(21) intrinsic [in'trinsik] *adj.* 固有的，内在的，本质的
(22) supercharging ['sju:pə,tʃɑ:dʒiŋ] *adj.* 增压的
(23) scavenging ['skævindʒiŋ] *n.* 净化
(24) crankcase ['kræŋk,keis] *n.* 曲轴箱
(25) rotary ['rəutəri] *adj.* 旋转的
(26) reciprocating [ri'siprəkeitiŋ] *adj.* 往复的，来回的
(27) centrifugal blower 离心式鼓风机
(28) be injected into… 被注入到……
(29) differ…from… 与……不同

Notes

(1) Diesel engine is an internal combustion engine operating on a thermodynamic cycle. In this cycle, the ratio of compression of the air charge is sufficiently high to ignite the fuel

subsequently injected into the combustion chamber.

柴油机是靠热力循环运转的一种内燃机。在热力循环中，吸入的空气的压缩比要高到足以点燃随后喷入燃烧室的燃料。operating on a thermodynamic cycle 分词短语修饰 internal combustion engine 内燃机；ratio of compression 空气压缩比；air charge 吸入的空气；injected into the combustion chamber 过去分词短语修饰 fuel，指喷入燃烧室的燃料。

(2) Such kinds of engines can not be strictly identified as true diesels but properly should be called commercial diesels.

这些发动机严格说来不能认作是真正意义上的柴油机，叫做工业用柴油机更合适些。be strictly identified as... 被严格认为……；but 表示转折，后面省略了主语 such kinds of engines。

(3) Control of engine output is by regulation of the fuel supplied but without variation of the air supply. Supercharging increases cylinder weight charge and consequently power output for a given cylinder size and engine speed.

发动机的输出功率是通过调整输入燃料的多少进行控制的，但并不随着空气的供给量改变。对于给定气缸容积和转速的发动机来说，增压使气缸进气量增加，结果使输出功率增大。engine output = output power of engine；regulation of the fuel supplied 指供给燃料的规律；a given cylinder size and engine speed 对于一个给定气缸容积和转速的发动机而言。

第 9 章　Manufacture Technology for Machinery

9.1　Intensive Reading

Lesson 1　Tolerances and Fits

1. Limits of size and tolerances

It is accepted that it is virtually impossible to manufacture a part without error, or in the rare event of a part without error, it is never also proclaimed to be perfect (because the measuring instruments are subject to errors). [1] It is necessary to indicate the maximum errors permitted. The designer must indicate the largest and smallest sizes that can be permitted. The extreme dimensions are called the limits of size, and the difference between them is called the tolerance.

The method of indicating, on a drawing, the permitted tolerance depends mainly upon manufacturing type, but local preference must also be taken account. [2]

2. Fits

Fits are concerned with the relationship between two parts. Considering that a shaft and hole combination: if the shaft is larger than hole, the condition is said to be of interference, and if smaller than the hole, the condition is said to be of clearance.

In order that the precise condition is ensured, the limits of size of both the shaft and hole must be stipulated.

Fits can be classified as follows: clearance fit, interference fit, and transitional fit. Hole-based system and shaft-based system: In order to obtain a range of degrees of clearance, and the degrees of interference, it is necessary to use a wide variation of hole sizes and shaft sizes. For example, a manufacturing company could be making a number of parts, all of a nominal 25mm diameter, but which are slightly different in actual limits of size, to suit the actual fit required of each pair of parts. This situation could mean that a large number of drills, reamers, gauges, etc. were required.

It is logical that, to reduce this number, a standard hole could be used for each nominal size, and variation of fits be obtained by making a shaft smaller or larger than the hole. [3] This is known as a hole-based system.

New Words and Phrases

(1) tolerance　　['tɔlərəns]　　*n.* 公差

(2) fit　　['fit]　　*n.* 配合

(3) virtually　　['vəːtʃuəli]　　*adj.* 事实上的，实际的

第 9 章 Manufacture Technology for Machinery

(4) rare　　［rɛə］　　*adj.* 稀有的，少见的
(5) error　　［'erə］　　*n.* 误差
(6) proclaim　　［prəu'kleim］　　*vt.* 宣布，宣称，声明，显示
(7) instrument　　［'instrumənt］　　*n.* 仪器，工具
(8) permit　　［pə'mit］　　*vt.* 许可，允许，准许
(9) extreme dimension　　*n.* 极限尺寸
(10) stipulate　　［'stipjuleit］　　*vt.* 规定，保证
(11) clearance fit　　间隙配合
(12) interference fit　　过盈配合
(13) transitional fit　　过渡配合
(14) hole-based system　　基孔制
(15) shaft-based system　　基轴制
(16) nominal　　［'nɔminəl］　　*adj.* 名义上的，公称的
(17) reamer　　［'ri:mə］　　*n.* 钻孔器，铰刀
(18) gauge　　［geidʒ］　　*n.* 标准尺，量规，规格

Notes

(1) It is accepted that it is virtually impossible to manufacture a part without error, or in the rare event of a part without error, it is never also proclaimed to be perfect (because the measuring instruments are subject to errors).

人们普遍认为要制造一个没有误差的零件，实际上是不可能的，或者即使偶然制造一个没有误差的零件，但并不能表明该零件是绝对无误差的（因为测量仪器也存在误差）。It is accepted that…，It 是形式主语，为了使句子平衡使用了这种句子结构，that 引导主语从句，第二个 it 是主语从句形式主语，真正的主语是 to manufacture a part without error，第三个 it 和第二个 it 的句型结构相同，be perfect 表示完美，指无缺陷，measuring instruments 译为：测量仪器（工具），be subject to…… 受……的影响（支配），易于……，在这里译为存在。

(2) The method of indicating, on a drawing, the permitted tolerance depends mainly upon manufacturing type, but local preference must also be taken account.

在图纸上所标注的允许公差取决于所采用的加工类型，但还必须考虑到局部优先的原则。indicating 指在图纸上标注，the permitted tolerance 译为：允许公差，local preference 译为：局部优先，be taken account 译为：应考虑……，采用了被动语态。

(3) It is logical that, to reduce this number, a standard hole could be used for each nominal size, and variation of fit be obtained by making a shaft a smaller or larger than the hole.

从理论上讲，为了减少加工刀具的数量，主要是采用基孔制，基孔制的孔是基准孔，可用于各种公称尺寸，可把轴加工比基准孔小或大，形成不同的配合。to reduce this number 为了减少刀具的数量，this number 指的是刀具的数量，nominal size 公称尺寸，making a shaft smaller or larger than the hole 译为：制造一个比基准孔小的或大的轴。

Exercises

Ⅰ. 将下列短语和句子译成英语

1. 公差、配合、误差、测量仪器、极限尺寸、间隙配合、过渡配合、过盈配合、基孔制、基轴制
2. 设计人员必须标注所允许的最大和最小尺寸。
3. 配合可分为如下三种：间隙配合，过盈配合和过渡配合。

Ⅱ. 根据课文选择填空

1. It is accepted that it is virtually _____ to manufacture a part without error.
   A. possible   B. impossible   C. improper   D. improbably
2. The extreme dimensions are called the limits of size, and the difference between them is called the _____.
   A. tolerance   B. fit   C. upper limit   D. lower limit
3. If the shaft is larger than hole, the condition is said to be of _____.
   A. clearance   B. transition   C. interference   D. error
4. Fits can be classified as _____: clearance fit, interference fit, and transitional fit.
   A. following   B. follows   C. followed   D. below
5. it is necessary to use a wide variation of hole sizes and _____ sizes.
   A. shaft   B. part   C. gear   D. measuring instrument

Ⅲ. 将下列短文译成中文

Fits are concerned with the relationship two parts. Considering that a shaft and hole combination: if the shaft is larger than hole, the condition is said to be of interference, and if smaller than the hole, the condition is said to be of clearance.

It is logical that, to reduce this number, a standard hole could be used for each nominal size, and variation of fits be obtained by making a shaft smaller or larger than the hole. This is known as a hole-based system.

Lesson 2　Heat Treatment of Steel

We can alter the characteristics of steel in various ways. In the first place, steel which contains very little carbon will be milder than steel which contains a higher percentage of carbon, up to the limit of about 2 percent.[(1)] Secondly, we can heat the steel above a certain critical temperature, and then allow it to cool at different rates. At this critical temperature, changes begin to take place in the molecular structure of the metal. In the process known as annealing, we heat the steel above the critical temperature and permit it to cool very slowly. This causes the metal to become softer than before, and much easier to machine. Annealing has a second advantage. It helps to relieve any internal stresses which exist in the metal. These stresses are liable to occur through hammering or working the metal, or through rapid cooling. Metal which we cause to cool rapidly contracts more rapidly on the outside than on the inside. This produces unequal contractions, which may give rise to distortion or cracking.[(2)] Metal which cools slowly are less liable to have these internal stresses than metal which cools quickly.

On the other hand, we can make steel harder by rapid cooling. We heat it up beyond the critical temperature, and then quench it in water or some other liquid. The rapid temperature drop fixes the structural change in the steel which occurred at the critical temperature, and makes steel very hard. But a bar of this hardened steel is more liable to fracture than normal steel. We therefore heat it again to a temperature below the critical temperature, and cool it slowly. This treatment is called tempering. It helps to relieve the internal stresses, and makes the steel less brittle than before. The properties of tempered steel enable us to use it in the manufacture of tools which need fairly hard steel. High carbon steel is harder than tempered steel, but it is much more difficult to work.(3)

These heat treatments take place during the various shaping operations. We can obtain bars and sheets of steel by rolling the metal through huge rollers in a rolling mill.(4) The roll pressures must be much greater for cold rolling than for hot rolling, but cold rolling enables operators to produce rolls of great accuracy and uniformity, and with a better surface finish. Other shaping operations include drawing into wire, casting in moulds, and forging.(5)

New Words and Phrases

(1) alter ['ɔːltə] v. 改变
(2) carbon ['kɑːbən] n. 碳
(3) critical temperature 临界温度
(4) molecular structure 分子结构
(5) anneal [ə'niːl] v. (使)退火, n. 热处理
(6) brittle ['britl] adj. 易碎的，脆弱的
(7) contraction [kən'trækʃən] n. 收缩
(8) distortion [dis'tɔːʃən] n. 变形，失真
(9) cracking ['krækiŋ] n. 破裂
(10) quench [kwentʃ] v. 淬火，熄灭
(11) fracture ['fræktʃə] v./n. 破裂
(12) tempering ['tempəriŋ] v. 回火
(13) rolling ['rəuliŋ] n. 碾压，轧制
(14) surface finish 表面光洁度（也叫粗糙度，roughness）
(15) casting ['kɑːstiŋ] n. 铸造，铸件
(16) forging ['fɔːdʒiŋ] n. 锻造
(17) take place 发生
(18) give rise to 产生，引起

Notes

(1) In the first place, steel which contains very little carbon will be milder than steel which contains a higher percentage of carbon, up to the limit of about 2 percent.

首先，含碳量极低的钢比含碳百分比较高的钢软，钢的含碳量最高不超过2%左右。in the first place，首先，which 引导一个限定性定语从句，修饰 steel，be milder than…，比……更加柔韧，相当于 be of temper than…。

(2) This produces unequal contractions, which may give rise to distortion or cracking.

从而产生不均匀的收缩，就可能引起变形或破裂。which 引导一个非限定性定语从句，give rise to 引起，发生。

(3) High carbon steel is harder than tempered steel, but it is much more difficult to work.

高碳钢比回火钢硬，但加工高碳钢却困难得多。tempered steel 指经过回火调质处理后的钢，to work 相当于 to machine。

(4) We can obtain bars and sheets of steel by rolling the metal through huge rollers in a rolling mill.

我们可以在轧钢厂里使用巨大轧机将钢轧制成型钢和板钢。bars and sheets of steel 指型钢和板钢，即：型材和板材，roller 指轧机，a rolling mill 指轧钢厂。

(5) Other shaping operations include drawing into wire, casting in moulds, and forging.

其他成型加工方法还有拉丝、铸造和锻造。shaping operation 指成型加工，draw into wire，译为：拉成丝，casting 铸造，forging 锻造。

Exercises

Ⅰ. 将下列短语和句子译成中文

1. heat treatment, critical temperature, the molecular structure of the metal, annealing, internal stress, distortion, quench, tempering, surface finish, shaping operation.

2. Metal which cools slowly are less liable to have these internal stresses than metal which cools quickly.

3. It helps to relieve the internal stresses, and makes the steel less brittle than before.

4. We therefore heat it again to a temperature below the critical temperature, and cool it slowly.

5. These heat treatments take place during the various shaping operations.

Ⅱ. 根据课文填空

We can alter the characteristics of steel in various ___1___ . In the first place, steel ___2___ contains very little carbon will be milder than steel which contains a higher percentage of carbon, up to the limit of about 2 percent. In the process known ___3___ annealing, we heat the steel ___4___ the critical temperature and permit it to ___5___ very slowly. This causes the metal to become ___6___ than before, and much easier to ___7___ .

On the other hand, we can make steel ___8___ by rapid cooling. We heat it up beyond the ___9___ temperature, and then quench it in ___10___ or some other liquid. The rapid temperature drop fixes the structural change in the steel which occurred at the critical temperature, and makes steel very hard.

Ⅲ. 将下列句子译成英文

1. 我们把钢加热到临界温度以上，再让它慢慢冷却。

2. 这就使金属变得比热处理之前软，因而更易于机械加工。
3. 高碳钢比回火钢硬。

Lesson 3 Welding

There are a number of methods of joining metal articles together, depending on the type of metal and the strength of the joint which is required. Soldering gives a satisfactory joint for light articles of steel, copper or brass, but the strength of a soldered joint is less than that of a joint which is brazed, riveted or welded. [1] These methods of joining metal are normally adopted for strong permanent joints.

The simplest method of welding two pieces of metal together is known as pressure welding. The ends of metal are heated to a white heat for iron; the welding temperature should be about 1300℃ in a flame. At this temperature the metal becomes plastic. The ends are then pressed or hammered together, and the joint is smoothed off. [2] Care must be taken to ensure that the surfaces are thoroughly clean first, for dirt will weaken the weld. Moreover, the heating of iron or steel to a high temperature causes oxidation and a film of oxide is formed on the heated surfaces. For this reason, a flux is applied to the heated metal. At welding heat, the flux melts, and the oxide particles are dissolved in it together with any other impurities, which may be present. The metal surfaces are pressed together, and the flux is squeezed out from the centre of the weld. A number of different types of weld may be used, but for a v-shaped weld should normally be employed. [3] It is rather stronger than thick bars of metal, the ordinary butt weld.

The heat for fusion welding is generated in several ways, depending on the sort of metal, which is being welded and on its shape. An extremely hot flame can be produced from an oxyacetylene torch. For certain welds an electric arc is used. In this method, an electric current is passed across two electrodes, and the metal surfaces are placed between them. The electrodes are sometimes made of carbon, but more frequently they are metallic. The work itself constitutes one of them and the other is an insulated filler rod. An arc is struck between the two, and the heat, which is generated, melts the metal at the weld. A different method is usually employed for welding sheets or plates of metal together. This is known as spot welding. Two sheets or plates are placed together with a slight overlap, and a current is passed between the electrodes. At welding temperature, a strong pressure is applied to the metal sheets. The oxide film, and any impurities which are trapped between the sheets, are squeezed out, and the weld is made.

New Words and Phrases

(1) welding   ['weldiŋ]   n. 焊接，焊缝；adj. 焊接的
(2) metal article   金属件
(3) soldering   ['sɔldəriŋ]   n. 软钎焊，软焊
(4) brass   [brɑːs]   n. 黄铜
(5) pressure welding   加压（压力）焊，压接
(6) fusion welding   熔焊，熔焊接

(7) spot welding　点焊（接）

(8) gas welding　气焊

(9) rivet　['rivit]　n. 铆钉；v. 铆接

(10) flux　[flʌks]　n. 助焊剂；v. 熔化

(11) oxidation　[ˌɔksi'deiʃən]　n. 氧化

(12) oxide　['ɔksaid]　n. 氧化物

(13) impurity　[im'pjuərəti]　n. 杂质，不纯

(14) squeeze　[skwi:z]　v. 挤，压

(15) v-shaped　['vi:ʃeipt]　adj. V形的

(16) butt　[bʌt]　n. 平接（缝）

(17) butt weld　对头（缝）焊接

(18) acetylene　[ə'setili:n]　n. 乙炔，电石气

(19) oxyacetylene　[ˌɔksiə'setili:n]　adj. 氧乙炔的

(20) oxyacetylene torch　氧乙炔焊接，气焊

(21) electric arc　电弧

(22) electrode　[i'lektrəud]　n. 电极，电焊条

(23) filler　['filə]　n. 填充物（剂），填料

(24) filler rod　焊条

(25) overlap　['əuvəlæp]　n.（部分）重叠，搭接（部分）

(26) be squeezed out　（被）榨出，挤（压）出

Notes

(1) Soldering gives a satisfactory joint for light articles of steel, copper or brass, but the strength of a soldered joint is less than that of a joint which is brazed, riveted or welded.

锡焊焊接薄钢件、薄铜件或薄黄铜件，焊接效果很好，但其强度比铜焊、铆接或焊接要低得多。light articles（薄件），a joint（一条焊缝），less than 比……少（低），which 引导定语从句，修饰 a joint。

(2) At this temperature the metal becomes plastic. The ends are then pressed or hammered together, and the joint is smoothed off.

在这种高温下，金属变成塑性体。然后，再把接头强压在一起或锤压在一起，最后把焊缝磨光。表示温度前的介词用 at，ends 表示金属两头，hammer 这里作动词用，译为用锤子打，the joint is smoothed off（焊缝磨光）。

(3) A number of different types of weld may be used, but for a v-shaped weld should normally be employed.

焊接的形式可以多种多样，但通常应采用 V 形焊缝。A number of 后跟可数名词，employed 相当于 used。

Exercises

Ⅰ. 根据课文填空

There are a number of methods of joining metal articles together, depending ___1___ the type of metal and the strength of the joint which is required. Soldering gives a satisfactory joint for light articles of steel, copper or brass, but the strength of a soldered joint is less __2__ that of a joint which is brazed, riveted or welded.

The simplest method of welding two pieces of metal together is known __3__ pressure welding the welding temperature should be about 1300℃ in a flame. __4__ this temperature the metal becomes plastic. For this reason, a flux is applied to the heated metal. At welding heat, the flux melts, and the oxide particles are __5__ in it together with any other impurities, which may be present. The metal surfaces are __6__ together, and the flux is squeezed __7__ from the centre of the weld.

The heat for fusion welding is generated in several ways, depending on the sort of metal, __8__ is being welded and on its shape. A different method is usually __9__ for welding sheets or plates of metal together. This is known as spot __10__.

Ⅱ. 将下列句子译成中文

1. There are a number of methods of joining metal articles together, depending on the type of metal and the strength of the joint which is required.

2. In this method, an electric current is passed across two electrodes, and the metal surfaces are placed between them.

3. A different method is usually employed for welding sheets or plates of metal together; this is known as spot welding.

Ⅲ. 将下列句子译成英文

1. 焊接两片金属最简单的方法称为压焊。
2. 可采用许多形式的焊接方法，但 V 型焊是用得最普遍的。
3. 几种方法可产生焊接的热量，根据不同种类的金属而异。

Lesson 4 Machine Tools

Most of the mechanical operations are commonly performed on five basic machine tools:

The drill press;

The lathe;

The shaper or planer;

The milling machine;

The grinder.

Drilling

Drilling is performed with a rotating tool called a drill. Most drilling in metal is done with a twist drill. The machine used for drilling is called a drill press. Operations, such as reaming and tapping, are also classified as drilling. [(1)] Reaming consists of removing a small amount of metal from a hole already drilled. Tapping is the process of cutting a thread inside a hole so that a cap screw or blot may be threaded into it.

Turning and Boring

The lathe is commonly called the father of the entire machine tool family. For turning operations, the lathe uses a single point cutting tool, which removes metal as it travels past the revolving workpiece. Turning operations are required to make many different cylindrical shapes, such as axes, gear blanks, pulleys, and threaded shafts. Boring operations are performed to enlarge, finish, and accurately locate holes.

Milling

Milling removes metal with a revolving, multiple cutting edge tools called milling cutter. Milling cutters are made in many styles and sizes. Some have as few as two cutting edges and others have 30 or more[2]. Milling can produce flat or angled surfaces, grooves, slots, gear teeth, and other profiles, depending on the shape of the cutters being used.

Shaping and Planning

Shaping and planning produce flat surfaces with a single point cutting tool. In shaping, the cutting tool on a shaper reciprocates or moves back and forth while the work is fed automatically towards the tool.[3] In planning, the workpiece is attached to a worktable that reciprocates past the cutting tool.[4] The cutting tool is automatically fed into the workpiece a small amount on each stroke.

Grinding

Grinding makes use of abrasive particles to do the cutting. Grinding operations may be classified as precision or nonprecision, depending on the purpose. Precision grinding is concerned with grinding to close tolerances and very smooth finish[5]. Non precision grinding involves the removal of metal where accuracy is not important.

New Words and phrases

(1) drill   [dril]   *n.* 钻床，钻头
(2) machine tool   机床
(3) twist drill   麻花钻，螺旋钻
(4) lathe   [leið]   *n.* 车床
(5) shaper   ['ʃeipə]   *n.* 牛头刨床
(6) planer   ['pleinə]   *n.* 龙门刨床
(7) mill   [mil]   *n.* 铣床
(8) grinder   ['graində]   *n.* 磨床
(9) ream   [ri:m]   *v.* 铰孔
(10) tap   [tæp]   *v.* 攻丝
(11) thread   [θred]   *n.* 螺纹

第 9 章　Manufacture Technology for Machinery

(12) boring operation　钻孔
(13) pulley　　['puli]　　n. 滑轮
(14) shaft　　[ʃæft]　　n. 螺杆，轴
(15) bore　　[bɔː]　　v. 镗削，钻孔
(16) groove　　[gruːv]　　n. 槽口
(17) slot　　[slɔt]　　n. 缝隙
(18) profile　　['prəufail]　　n. 轮廓，外形
(19) abrasive particle　磨削粒（剂）
(20) workpiece　　['wəːkpiːs]　　n. 工件
(21) worktable　　['wəːk,teibl]　　n. 工作台
(22) be classified as...　将……分为
(23) consist of...　由……组成
(24) be attached to...　附在，安装在……上，
(25) back and forth　前后，来回
(26) be concerned with...　与……联系，有关

Notes

(1) The machine used for drilling is called a drill press. Operations, such as reaming and tapping, are also classified as drilling.

用于钻孔的机器叫做"钻床"，铰孔和攻丝也归类于钻孔。过去分词短语 used for drilling 修饰主语 machine, drill press（钻床），reaming and tapping（铰孔和攻丝）。

(2) Milling cutters are made in many styles and sizes. Some have as few as two cutting edges and others have 30 or more.

铣刀制成不同的式样和尺寸。有些铣刀仅有两个刃口，而有些铣刀有多达30个或更多的刃口。in many styles and sizes（许多样式和尺寸），as...as（与……一样），few 表示否定，cutting edges（刀刃），as few as two cutting edges（仅有两个刀刃）。

(3) In shaping, the cutting tool on a shaper reciprocates or moves back and forth while the work is fed automatically towards the tool.

在成形刨削操作中，当工件被自动推向刀具时，成型刨床上的刀具作往复或前后移动。cutting tool（刀具），back and forth（来回往复）相当于 to and fro，while 引导时间定语从句。

(4) In planning, the workpiece is attached to a worktable that reciprocates past the cutting tool.

在刨削加工时，工件固定在一个工作台上，工作台上的刀具可作来回运动。be attached to..., （附到……上），这里指固定在工作台上。

(5) Precision grinding is concerned with grinding to close tolerances and very smooth finish.

精磨应用于接近于公差限和非常光滑的磨削。be concerned with, 与……联系，有关，close tolerances 表示接近公差限的尺寸，finish（磨光）。

Exercises

Ⅰ. 根据课文填空

Drilling is performed __1__ a rotating tool called a drill. Most drilling in metal is done with a twist drill. The machine used for drilling is __2__ a drill press. Operations, such as reaming and tapping, are also classified as drilling. Reaming consists of removing a small amount of metal __3__ a hole already drilled. Tapping is the process of cutting a thread inside a hole so __4__ a cap screw or blot may be threaded into it.

The lathe is commonly called the __5__ of the entire machine tool family. For turning operations, the lathe uses a single point cutting tool, which removes metal as it travels past the revolving workpiece.

Shaping and planning produce flat surfaces with a single point cutting tool. In shaping, the cutting tool on a shaper reciprocates or moves back and forth while the work is fed automatically towards the tool. In __6__, the workpiece is attached __7__ a worktable that reciprocates past the cutting tool. The cutting tool is automatically __8__ into the workpiece a small amount on each stroke.

Grinding makes use __9__ abrasive particles to do the cutting. Grinding operations may be classified as precision or nonprecision, depending on the purpose. Precision grinding is concerned __10__ grinding to close tolerances and very smooth finish.

Ⅱ. 将下列短语或句子译成中文

1. drill press, planer, grinder, cutting edge, tolerance, cutting tool
2. Milling can produce flat or angled surfaces, grooves, slots, gear teeth, and other profiles, depending on the shape of the cutters being used.
3. Nonprecision grinding involves the removal of metal where accuracy is not important.

Ⅲ. 将下列句子译成英文

1. 大多数的机加工主要是由五种基本的机床来完成。
2. 车床一般被称为整个机床加工设备家庭成员中之父。
3. 磨削加工是利用研磨颗粒来切削金属,磨削加工可分为精磨和粗磨。

9.2 Extensive Reading

Lesson 1 Material Properties

The properties of material may be divided into the following four groups: Physical properties, Chemical properties, Mechanical properties, and Manufacturing properties.

Physical properties include color, density, melting point, freezing point, specific heat, heat of fusion, thermal conductivity, thermal expansion, electrical conductivity, magnetic property, and so on.

Of the chemical properties, corrosion resistance plays an important role in the choice of materials and generally includes resistance to chemical or electrochemical attack.[1] Corrosion resistance can also be important during the manufacturing process, because it can influence the formation of surface films affecting friction and lubrication, and thermal and electrical conductivity.[2]

Mechanical properties generally include the reaction of a material to mechanical loadings. In the majority of cases, it is the mechanical properties with which the engineer is principally concerned with material selection, because to evaluate their performance in terms of the desired functions he or she needs to know how materials would react to the design loading.

The manufacturing or technological properties of a material, which describe the suitability of the material for a particular process, are very complex and can generally not be assessed by a single number.[3]

To evaluate these properties, various testing methods have been developed to describe the machineability, formability, drawability, castability, and so on, of a material.[4]

New words and phrases

(1) mechanical [miˈkænikəl] adj. 机械的
(2) manufacture [ˌmænjuˈfæktʃə] v. 制造，加工
(3) density [ˈdensəti] n. 密度
(4) specific heat 比热
(5) thermal conductivity 热传导性
(6) thermal expansion 热膨胀
(7) electrical conductivity 电传导性
(8) fusion [ˈfjuːʒən] n. 熔化，熔解
(9) conductivity [ˌkɔndʌkˈtiviti] n. 传导性
(10) magnetic [mægˈnetik] adj. 磁的，有磁性的，有吸引力的
(11) corrosion [kəˈrəuʒən] n. 侵蚀，腐蚀
(12) electrochemical [iˌlektrəuˈkemikəl] adj. 电化学的
(13) suitability [suːtəˈbiliti] n. 适宜性，适当
(14) friction [ˈfrikʃən] n. 磨擦
(15) lubrication [ˌluːbriˈkeiʃən] n. 润滑
(16) technological [ˌteknəˈlɔdʒikəl] adj. 工艺的
(17) assess [əˈses] v. 估定，评定
(18) electrochemical [iˌlektrəuˈkemikəl] adj. 电化学的
(19) film [film] n. 薄膜
(20) machineability [məˌʃiːnəˈbiliti] n. 加工性
(21) formability [fɔːməˈbiliti] n. 可锻性，可成型
(22) drawability [ˌdrɔːəˈbiləti] n. 可延伸性
(23) castability [ˌkɑːstəˈbiləti] n. 锻造性
(24) be divided into... 将……分成……

(25) play an important role in... 在……方面起重要作用
(26) in the majority of cases 在多数情况下
(27) in terms of 根据，依据，在……方面

Notes

(1) Of the chemical properties, corrosion resistance plays an important role in the choice of materials and generally includes resistance to chemical or electrochemical attack.

材料的化学性能中的抗腐蚀性能，通常包括抗化学、电化学腐蚀，在材料性能的选择中起着重要作用。corrosion resistance 译为：抗腐蚀性，play an important role in... 在……方面起重要作用，这是两个并列句，由 and 连接，公共的主语是 corrosion resistance; resistance to chemical or electrochemical attack 译为：抗化学或电化学腐蚀，这里的 attack 指 corrosion。

(2) Corrosion resistance can also be important during the manufacturing process, because it can influence the formation of surface films affecting friction and lubrication, and thermal and electrical conductivity.

抗腐蚀性能在生产过程中也很重要，由于在材料表面形成薄膜，而薄膜影响材料的摩擦与润滑及其导热和导电性能。affecting friction and lubrication, and thermal and electrical conductivity 是分词短语修饰 surface films，thermal and electrical conductivity 译为：导热和导电性能。

(3) The manufacturing or technological properties of a material, which describe the suitability of the material for a particular process, are very complex and can generally not be assessed by a single number.

材料的加工性能，或工艺性，反映了对一个特定工艺过程材料的适应性，工艺性是十分复杂的且通常不能用单纯的数值来评价。which 引导一个非限定性定语从句，修饰 technological properties of a material。

(4) To evaluate these properties, various testing methods have been developed to describe the machineability, formability, drawability, castability, and so on, of a material.

为了评价这些性能，产生了很多测试方法，用来描述材料的可加工性能、可成型性、可延伸性和可锻造性等。machineability, formability, drawability, castability 可分别译为：可加工性、可成型性、可延伸性和可锻造性。

Lesson 2 Iron and Steel

The earth contains a large number of metals which are useful to man. One of the most important of these is iron. Modern industry needs considerable quantities of this metal, either in the form of iron or in the form of steel. A certain number of non-ferrous metals, including aluminum and zinc, are also important but even today the majority of our engineering products are of iron or steel.[1] Moreover, iron possesses magnetic properties, which have made the development of electrical power possible.[2]

The iron ore which we find in the earth is not pure. It contains some impurities which we must remove by smelting. The process of smelting consists of heating the ore in a blast furnace with coke and limestone, and reducing it to metal. Blasts of hot air enter the furnace from the bottom and provide the oxygen which is necessary for the reduction of ore.(3) The ore becomes molten, and its oxide combines with carbon from the coke. The nonmetallic constituents of the ore combine with the limestone to form a liquid slag. This floats on top of the molten iron, and passes out of the furnace through a tap. The metal which remains is pig-iron.

We can melt this down again in another furnace—a cupola with more coke and limestone, and tap it out into a ladle or directly into moulds. This is cast iron. Cast iron does not have the strength of steel. It is brittle and may fracture under tension. But it possesses certain properties which make it very useful in the manufacture of machinery. In the molten state it is very fluid, and therefore it is easy to cast it into intricate shapes. Also it is easy to machine it. Cast iron contains small proportions of other substances. These nonmetallic constituents of cast iron include carbon, silicon and sulphur, and the presence of these substances affects the behaviour of the metal. Iron which contains a negligible quantity of carbon, for example wrought iron, behaves differently from iron which contains a lot of carbon.(4)

The carbon in cast iron is present partly as free graphite and partly as a chemical combination of iron and carbon, which we call cementite. This is a very hard substance, and it makes the iron hard too. However, iron can only hold about 1.5% of cementite. Any carbon content above that percentage is present in the form of a flaky graphite. Steel contains no free graphite, and its carbon content ranges from almost nothing to 1.5%. We make wire and tubing from mild steel with a very low carbon content, and drills and cutting tools from high carbon steel.

New Words and phrases

(1) considerable　　[kən'sidərəbl]　　*adj.* 相当大（多）的，提炼
(2) non-ferrous　　['nʌn'ferəs]　　*adj.* 非铁的
(3) non-ferrous metal　　有色金属
(4) aluminum　　[ə'lju:minəm]　　*n.* 铝
(5) zinc　　[ziŋk]　　*n.* 锌
(6) magnetic property　　磁性
(7) iron ore　　铁矿石
(8) smelt　　[smelt]　　*v.* 熔（冶，精）炼
(9) limestone　　[laimstəun]　　*n.* 石灰石
(10) coke　　[kuk]　　*n.* 焦炭
(11) reduce　　[ri'dju:s]　　*v.* （使）还原（脱氧），提炼
(12) reduction　　[ri'dʌkʃən]　　*n.* 还原（法，作用）
(13) nonmetallic　　[,nɔnmi'tælik]　　*adj.* 非金属的
(14) constituent　　[kən'stitjuənt]　　*n.* 要素，成分
(15) silicon　　['silikən]　　*n.* 硅
(16) sulphur　　['sʌlfə]　　*n.* 硫

(17) slag   [slæg]   n. （炉，铁，矿）渣
(18) tap   [tæp]   n. 开关，龙头，排［放］出孔
(19) pig iron   n. 生铁，铣铁
(20) cupola   ['kjuːpələ]   n. 冲天［化铁，熔铁］炉
(21) ladle   [leidl]   n. 铁［钢］水包
(22) brittle   ['britl]   adj. 脆的，易碎的
(23) tension   ['tenʃən]   n. 张［拉］力
(24) intricate   ['intrikət]   adj. 复杂的
(25) negligible   ['neglidʒəbl]   adj. 可忽略的
(26) Wrought   [rɔːt]   adj. 锻的，可锻的
(27) wrought iron   n. 熟［锻］铁
(28) graphite   ['græfait]   n. 石墨
(29) free graphite   游离石墨
(30) cementite   [si'mentait]   n. 渗碳体
(31) flaky   ['fleiki]   adj. （薄）片状的
(32) tubing   ['tjuːbiŋ]   n. 管，管道
(33) mild   [maild]   adj. 软的，低碳的；温和的，轻微的
(34) mild steel   低碳钢

Notes

(1) A certain number of non-ferrous metals, including aluminum and zinc, are also important but even today the majority of our engineering products are of iron or steel.

虽然某些有色金属，包括铝和锌，也很重要，但即使在今天，大多数工业产品仍是用铁或钢制造的。even 在句子中加强语气，译为：甚至，即使，the majority of..., 大多数……，engineering products 指工业产品。

(2) Moreover, iron possesses magnetic properties, which have made the development of electrical power possible.

而且，铁具有磁性。因而使电力的发展成为可能。possesses = has，译为：具有，magnetic property，译为：磁性，which 引导非限定性定语从句，修饰 magnetic property，句子中的 made the development of electrical power possible 结构，相当于 make pron. /n. adj. 结构。

(3) Blasts of hot air enter the furnace from the bottom and provide the oxygen which is necessary for the reduction of ore.

热风从高炉底部吹入高炉内，以供给铁矿石进行还原反应所需的氧气。blasts of hot air 指热风（空气），which 引导一个定语从句，修饰 the oxygen, the reduction of ore 译为：铁矿石的还原反应。

(4) Iron which contains a negligible quantity of carbon, for example wrought iron, behaves differently from iron which contains a lot of carbon.

含碳量极少的铁，例如：熟铁，在性能上同含碳量高的生铁不同。which 引导一个定语从句修饰主语 iron，a negligible quantity of... 译为：极少量的……，wrought iron 译为：熟铁，谓语 behave，指性能的表现，iron which contains a lot of carbon 译为：含碳量高的铁。

第 10 章　Control Technology

10.1　Intensive Reading

Lesson 1　Introduction to Control Engineering

Whenever energy is to be used purposefully, some form of control is necessary. In recent times there has been a considerable advance made in the art of automatic control. The art is, however, quite old, stemming back to about 1790 when James Watt invented the centrifugal governor to control the speed of his steam engines. He found that while in many applications an engine speed independent of load torque was necessary, in practice when a load was applied the speed fell and when the load was removed the speed increased.

In a simple centrifugal governor system, variations in engine speed are detected and used to control the pressure of the steam entering the engine. Under steady conditions the moment of the weight of the metal spheres balances that due to the centrifugal force and the steam valve opening is just sufficient to maintain the engine speed at the required level. [1] When an extra load torque is applied to the engine, its speed will tend to fall, the centrifugal force will decrease and the metal spheres will tend to fall slightly. Their height controls the opening of the steam valve which now opens further to allow a greater steam pressure on the engine. The speed thus tends to rise, counteracting the original tendency for the speed to fall. If the extra load is removed, the reverse process takes place, the metal spheres tend to rise slightly, so tending to close the steam valve and counteracting any tendency for the speed to rise. [2]

It is obviously that without the governor the speed would fall considerably on land. However, in a correctly designed system with a governor the fall in speed would be very much less. An undesirable feature which accompanies a system which has been designed to be very sensitive to speed changes is the tendency to "hunt" or oscillate about the final speed. The real problem in the synthesis of all systems of this type is to prevent excessive oscillation but at the same time produce good "regulation". Regulation is defined as the percentage change in controlled quantity on load relative to the value of the controlled under condition of zero load. Regulators form an important class of control system, their object generally being to keep some physical quantity constant (e.g. speed, voltage, liquid level, humidity, etc.) regardless of load variation. A good regulator has only very small regulation.

The 1914—1918 war caused military engineers to realize that to win wars it is necessary to position heavy masses (e.g. ships and guns) precisely and quickly. [3] Classic work was performed by N. Minorsky in the USA in the early 1920s on the automatic steering of ships and the automatic positioning of guns on board ships. In 1934 the word "servomechanism" (derived from the Latin) was used in the literature for the first time by H. L. Hazen. He defined a servomechanism as "a power amplifying device in which the amplifier element driving the output is actuated by the difference between the input to the servo and its output". This definition can be applied to a wide variety of "feedback control systems". More recently it has been suggested that the term "servomechanism" or "servo" be restricted to a feedback control system in which the controlled variable is mechanical position. [4]

The automatic control of various large-scale industrial processes, as encountered in the manufacture and treatment of chemicals, food and metals, has emerged during the last thirty years as an extremely important part of the general field of control engineering. [5] In the initial stages of development it was scarcely realized that the theory of process control was intimately related to the theory of servomechanisms and regulators. Even nowadays complete academic design of process control systems is virtually impossible owing to our poor understanding of the dynamics of processes. In much of the theory introduced in this book, servomechanisms and regulators are used as examples to illustrate the methods of analysis. These methods are, however, often applicable to process control systems, which will be themselves introduced separately.

New words and phrases

(1) purposefully   ['pə:pəsfuli]   adv. 有意图地，有目的地
(2) independent...of   不受……支配的，与……无关的
(3) sphere   [sfiə]   n. 球，球体
(4) extra   ['ekstrə]   adj. 额外的，临时的
(5) counteract   [ˌkauntə'rækt]   v. 抵消，抵制，阻碍
(6) be sensitive to...   对……敏感
(7) oscillate   ['ɔsileit]   n. 振荡，振动，摆动
(8) relative to...   与……相关
(9) humidity   [hju:'midəti]   n. 湿气，湿度
(10) steer   [stiə]   v. 掌舵，驾驶
(11) servomechanism   [ˌsə:vəu'mekənizəm]   n. 伺服机构，随动系统
(12) intimately   ['intimitli]   adv. 密切地，直接地
(13) owe to...   归功于……
(14) dynamics   [dai'næmiks]   n. 动态，动力学
(15) be applied to...   被应用于……

Notes to the Text

(1) Under steady conditions the moment of the weight of the metal spheres balances that due to the centrifugal force... to maintain the engine speed at the required level.
在稳定条件下，由于离心力的作用和蒸汽阀的开度刚好足够维持发动机转速所要求的

水平，瞬间与金属摆球重量平衡。due to = because of，is just sufficient to maintain（刚好足以维持）at the required level（以所需要的量）。

（2）If the extra load is removed, the reverse process takes place, ... to close the steam valve and counteracting any tendency for the speed to rise.

如果额外的负载被去除，将发生相反的过程，金属球要轻微上升，蒸汽阀倾向于关闭，抵消了一些速度增加的倾向。if 引导条件状语从句，takes place（产生，发生），tend to rise slightly（有稍微上升趋势）。

（3）The 1914—1918 war caused military engineers to realize that to win wars it is necessary to position heavy masses (e.g. ships and guns) precisely and quickly.

1914—1918 年战争促使军队工程师意识到为了赢得战争胜利需要准确而迅速地使重型装备（例如船只和枪炮）机动。不定式 to realize 表示目的，that 引导宾语从句，从句中 it 是形式主语，真实主语是 to position heavy masses (e.g. ships and guns) precisely and quickly，position 作动词，译为定位、驻扎，副词词组 precisely and quickly 修饰 position。

（4）More recently it has been suggested that the term "servomechanism" or "servo" be restricted to a feedback control system in which the controlled variable is mechanical position.

最近更多人提议伺服机构和伺服受到反馈控制系统的机械位置变量的限制。it has been suggested that...（有人建议……），that 引导是主语从句，suggest 后面的从句用虚拟语气，be 动词用原型，be restricted to...（限制于……）。

（5）The automatic control of... has emerged during the last thirty years as an extremely important part of the general field of control engineering.

在过去的 30 年里，控制工程通用领域中的一个极其重要的部分，诸如化工、食品加工、金属加工等各种各样的大规模的工业过程控制已经出现。the automatic control 作主语，has emerged 作谓语，large-scale（大规模的），as an extremely important part of...（作为重要的部分）。

Exercises

Ⅰ. 根据课文填空

1. When James Watt _____ the centrifugal governor to control the speed of his steam engines.

2. When a load was applied the speed fell and when the load was removed the speed _____.

3. In a simple centrifugal governor system, variations in engine speed are _____ and used to control the pressure of the steam entering the engine.

4. The steam valve opening is just sufficient to maintain the engine speed _____ the required level.

5. The centrifugal force will _____ and the metal spheres will tend to fall slightly.

6. If the extra load is _____, the reverse process takes place; the metal spheres tend to rise slightly.

7. It is obviously _____ without the governor the speed would fall considerably on land.

8. The 1914—1918 war caused military engineers to realize that to win wars it is _____ to position heavy masses (e. g. ships and guns) precisely and quickly.

9. The automatic control of various _____ industrial processes has emerged during the last thirty years as an extremely important part of the general field of control engineering.

10. In the initial _____ of development it was scarcely realized that the theory of process control was intimately related to the theory of servomechanisms and regulators.

Ⅱ. 将下列短语和句子译成中文

1. steam engine, servomechanisms, centrifugal force, torque, feedback control system, dynamics.

2. He defined a servomechanism as "a power amplifying device in which the amplifier element driving the output is actuated by the difference between the input to the servo and its output".

3. If the extra load is removed, the reverse process takes place; the metal spheres tend to rise slightly.

Ⅲ. 将下列句子译成英文

1. 由于离心力的存在，金属球刚好足以维持发动机转速所需要的水平。

2. 显然，去除载荷发动机的转速会上升很快。

3. 在研究的初期很少有人认识到控制理论的重要性。

Lesson 2　Applications of Automatic Control

Although the scope of automatic control is virtually unlimited, we will limit this discussion to examples which are commonplace in modern industry.

Servomechanisms

Although a servomechanism is not a control application, this device is commonplace in automatic control. A servomechanism, or 'servo' for short, is a closed-loop control system in which the controlled variable is mechanical position or motion. It is designed so that the output will quickly and precisely respond to a change in the input command. Thus we may think of a servomechanism as a following device.

Another form of servomechanism in which the rate of change or velocity of the output is controlled is known as a rate or velocity servomechanism.

Process Control

Process control is a term applied to the control of variables in a manufacturing process. Chemical plants, oil refineries, food processing plants, blast furnaces, and steel mill are examples of production processes to which automatic control is applied. Process control is concerned with maintaining at a desired value such process variables as temperature, pressure, flow rate, liquid level, viscosity, density, and composition.

Much current work in process control involves extending the use of the digital computer to provide direct digital control (DDC) of the process variables. In direct digital control the computer calculates the values of the manipulated variables directly from the values of the set points and the measurements of the process variables. The decisions of the computer are applied to digital actuators in the process. Since the computer duplicates the analog controller action, these conventional controllers are no longer needed.

Power Generation

The electric power industry is primarily concerned with energy conversion and distribution. Large modern power plants which may exceed several hundred megawatts of generation require complex control systems to account for the interrelationship of the many variables and provide optimum power production. [1] Control of power generation may be generally regarded as an application of process control, and it is common to have as many as 100 manipulated variables under computer control. [2]

Automatic control has also been extensively applied to the distribution of electric power. Power systems are commonly made up of a number of generating plants. As load requirements fluctuate, the generation and transmission of power is controlled to achieve minimum cost of system operation. In addition, most large power systems are interconnected with each other, and the flow of power between systems is controlled.

Numerical Control

There are rainy manufacturing operations such as boring, drilling, milling, and welding which must be performed with high precision on a repetitive basis. Numerical control (NC) is a system that uses predetermined instructions called a program to control a sequence of such operations. [3] The instructions to accomplish a desired operation are coded and stored on some medium such as punched paper tape, magnetic tape, or punched cards. These instructions are usually stored in the form of numbers-hence the name numerical control. The instructions identify what tool is to be used, in what way (e.g. cutting speed), and the path of the tool movement (position, direction, velocity, etc.).

Transportation

To provide mass transportation systems for modern urban areas, large, complex control systems are needed. Several automatic transportation systems now in operation have high-speed trains running at several-minute intervals. Automatic control is necessary to maintain a constant flow of trains and to provide comfortable acceleration and braking at station stops.

Aircraft flight control is another important application in the transportation field. This has been proven to be one of the most complex control applications due to the wide range of system parameters and the interaction between controls. Aircraft control systems are frequently adaptive in nature; that is, the operation adapts itself to the surrounding conditions. For example, since the behavior of an aircraft may differ radically at low and high altitudes the control system must be modified as a function of altitude.

Ship-steering and roll-stabilization controls are similar to flight control but generally require far higher powers and involve lower speeds of response.(4)

New words and phrases

(1) scope　　[skəup]　　n. 范围，显示器
(2) commonplace　　['kɔmənpleis]　　adj. 平常的
(3) servomechanism　　[,sə:vəu'mekənizəm]　　n. 伺服机构，伺服机械
(4) closed-loop　　['kləuzdlu:p]　　n. 闭合回路；闭合环路，闭环
(5) respond　　[ri'spɔnd]　　v. 响应，起反应，回答，应答
(6) viscosity　　[vi'skɔsəti]　　n. 黏度，黏性
(7) manipulate　　[mə'nipjuleit]　　v. 操作；操纵，控制，处理
(8) measurement　　['meʒəmənt]　　n. 测量，度量；测量结果，度量制
(9) actuator　　['æktjueitə]　　n. 启动器，制动器，执行器，传动装置
(10) fluctuate　　['flʌktjueit]　　v. 波动，起伏
(11) following device　　随动装置
(12) punched paper tape　　穿孔纸带
(13) punched card　　穿孔卡片
(14) ship-steering　　船舶转向

Notes to the Text

(1) Large modern power plants which may exceed... of the many variables and provide optimum power production.

发电量可能超过几百兆瓦的现代化大型电厂需要复杂的控制系统来说明许多变量之间的相互关系，并提供最佳的电能。which 引导定语从句，修饰 power plants，不定式 to account for... 表示目的状语，有说明、计算之意。

(2) Control of power generation may be generally regarded... as many as 100 manipulated variables under computer control.

发电厂的控制一般被认为是一种过程控制的应用，而且通常有多达100个控制变量受计算机控制。be generally regarded as...（一般被认为……），as... as...（与……一样）as many as + 可数名词，as much as + 不可数名词，可译为"多达……"，under computer control（在计算机控制之下）。

(3) Numerical Control (NC) is a system that uses predetermined instructions called a program to control a sequence of such operations.

数字控制是一个系统，该系统使用的是称为程序的预定指令来控制一系列运行。that 引导同位语从句，called a program 是过去分词短语作 instructions 的后置定语，不定式短语 to control a sequence of such operations 作目的状语。

(4) Ship-steering and roll-stabilization controls are similar to flight control but generally require far higher powers and involve lower speeds of response.

船舶转向和摇摆稳定性控制与飞行控制相似，但是一般需要更高的功率和低速响应。ship-steering（船舶转向的），are similar to...（与……相似），far +形容词比较级，表示程度加强了。

Exercises

Ⅰ. 根据课文完形填空

A servomechanism, or 'servo' for short, is a __1__ control system in which the controlled variable is mechanical __2__ or motion. It is designed so __3__ the output will quickly and precisely respond __4__ a change in the input command. Thus we may think of a servomechanism as a following device.

Automatic control has also been extensively applied to the __5__ of electric power. Power systems are commonly made __6__ of a number of generating plants. As load requirements fluctuate, the generation and transmission of power is controlled to achieve __7__ cost of system operation. In addition, most large power systems are __8__ with each other, and the flow of power between systems is controlled.

Aircraft flight control is __9__ important application in the transportation field. This has been proven to be one __10__ the most complex control applications due to the wide range of system parameters and the interaction between controls.

1. A. opened-loop　　B. closed-loop　　C. automatic　　D. digital
2. A. position　　　　B. direction　　　C. point　　　　D. force
3. A. as　　　　　　　B. that　　　　　 C. than　　　　 D. to
4. A. in　　　　　　　B. at　　　　　　 C. to　　　　　 D. of
5. A. delivery　　　　B. transportation　C. transition　 D. distribution
6. A. down　　　　　　B. with　　　　　 C. up　　　　　 D. at
7. A. maximum　　　　 B. tiny　　　　　 C. much　　　　 D. minimum
8. A. interconnected　B. connected　　　C. interchanged D. interacted
9. A. one　　　　　　 B. other　　　　　C. the　　　　　D. another
10. A. in　　　　　　 B. of　　　　　　 C. at　　　　　 D. to

Ⅱ. 将下列句子译成中文

1. Although the scope of automatic control is virtually unlimited, we will limit this discussion to examples which are commonplace in modern industry.
2. Automatic control has also been extensively applied to the distribution of electric power.
3. Automatic control is necessary to maintain a constant flow of trains and to provide comfortable acceleration and braking at station stops.

Ⅲ. 将下列句子译成英文

1. 伺服机构是一个闭环控制系统，系统中的控制变量是机械位置和运动。
2. 船舶转向的控制与飞行控制相似。
3. 电力系统通常由许多发电厂组成。

Lesson 3 Programmable Controllers

In the 1960s, electromechanical devices were the order of the day as far as control was concerned. These devices, commonly known as relays, were being used by the thousands to control many sequential-type manufacturing processes and stand-alone machines. Many of these relays were in use in the transportation industry, more specifically, the automotive industry. These relays used hundreds of wires and their interconnections to affect a control solution. The performance of a relay was basically reliable—at least as a single device. But the common applications for relay panels called for 300 to 500 or more relays, and the reliability and maintenance issues associated with supporting these panels became a very great challenge. Cost became another issue, for in spite of the low cost of the relay itself, the installed cost of the panel could be quite high. The total cost including purchased parts, wiring, and installation labor, could range from \$30 ~ \$50 per relay. To make matters worse, the constantly changing needs of a process called for recurring modifications of a control panel. With relays, this was a costly prospect, as it was accomplished by a major rewiring effort on the panel. In addition, these changes were sometimes poorly documented, causing a second-shift maintenance nightmare months later. In light of this, it was not uncommon to discard an entire control panel in favor of a new one with the appropriate components wired in a manner suited for the new process.[1] Add to this the unpredictable, and potentially high, cost of maintaining these systems as on high-volume motor vehicle production lines, and it became clear that something was needed to improve the control process—to make it more reliable, easier to troubleshoot, and more adaptable to changing control needs.[2]

That something, in the late 1960s, was the first programmable controller. This first "revolutionary" system was developed as a specific response to the needs of the major automotive manufacturers in the United States. These early controllers, or Programmable Logic Controllers (PLC), represented the first systems that (1) could be used on the factory floor, (2) could have there "logic" change without extensive rewiring or component changes, and (3) were easy to diagnose and repair when problems occurred. It is interesting to observe the progress that has been made in the past 15 years in the programmable controller area[3]. The pioneer products of the late 1960s must have been confusing and frightening to a great number of people. For example, what happened to the hardwired and electromechanical devices that maintenance personnel were used to repairing with hand tools? They were replaced with "computers" disguised as electronics designed to replace relays. Even the programming tools were designed to appear as relay equivalent presentations. We have the opportunity now to examine the promise, in retrospect, what the programmable controller brought manufacturing?

All programmable controllers consist of the basic functional blocks shown in Figure 10.1. We will examine each block to understand the relationship to the control system. First we looked at the center, as it is the heart of the system. It consists of a microprocessor, logic memory for the storage of the actual control logic, storage or variable memory for use with data that will

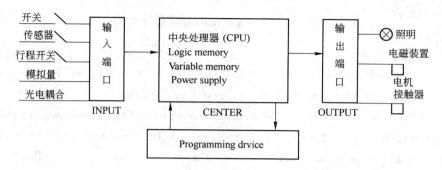

Figure 10.1

ordinarily change as a function of the control program execution, and a power supply to provide electrical power for the processor and memory. Next comes the I/O block. This function takes the control level signals for the CPU and converts them to voltage and current levels suitable for connection with factory grade sensors and actuators.⁽⁴⁾ The I/O type can range from digital, analog, or a variety of special purpose "smart" I/O which are dedicated to a certain application task. The programmer is normally used only to initially configure and program a system and is not required for the system to operate. It is also used in troubleshooting a system, and can prove to be a valuable tool in pinpointing the exact cause of a problem. The field devices shown here represent the various sensors and actuators connected to the I/O. These are the arms, legs, eyes, and ears of the system, including pushbuttons, limit switches, proximity switches, photosensors, thermocouples, position sensing devices, and bar code reader as input; and pilot light, display devices, motor starters, DC and AC drivers, solenoids, and printers as outputs.

New words and phrases

(1) heritage   ['heritidʒ]   n. 继承物，遗产，天性
(2) electromechanical   [i,lektrəumi'kænikəl]   adj. 机电的，电机学的
(3) sequential   [si'kwenʃəl]   adj. 有顺序的，连接的
(4) recur   [ri'kə:]   v. 循环，在，重新
(5) troubleshoot   ['trʌblʃu:t]   v. 故障排除
(6) retrospect   ['retrəuspekt]   n. 回想，追溯
(7) actuator   ['æktjueitə]   n. 调节器，执行机构
(8) solenoid   ['səulənɔid]   n. 螺线管，电磁线圈

Notes to the Text

（1）In light of this, it was not uncommon to discard an entire control panel in favor of a new one with the appropriate components wired in a manner suited for the new process.

按照这样来考虑，丢弃整个旧的控制面板，同意使用一个适合的新的控制过程方式相匹配的接线元件的控制面板，也是很常见的事情了。in light of = according to/in accordance with（根据，依照），it 是形式主语，不定式短语 to discard an entire control panel... 为真

正的主语，双重否定 not uncommon 意为肯定，discard = throw out，in favor of = agree with （同意，赞成），with 表示具有，过去分词短语 suited for the new process 作后置定语，修饰 manner。

(2) It became clear that something was needed to improve the control process—to make it more reliable, easier to troubleshoot, and more adaptable to changing control needs.

越来越清楚地认识到要使系统更可靠，更容易排除故障，更适合不断变化的控制过程需要，就必须改进控制过程。that something was needed to... 是主语从句，need 后跟不定式，to troubleshoot（排除故障）。

(3) It is interesting to observe the progress that has been made in the past 15 years in the programmable controller area.

观察可编程控制器在最近15年取得的进步是很有趣的事情。It is interesting...（有趣的是），be interested（感到有趣），that 是定语从句，修饰 progress。

(4) This function takes the control level signals for the CPU and converts them to voltage and current levels suitable for connection with factory grade sensors and actuators.

它的功能是为 CPU 提供控制水平信号，并把它们转化为适合于连接工厂级别的传感器和执行机构的标准电压和电流。converts... to (into)（把……转化……），suitable for （适合于），connection with...（与……连接）。

Exercises

Ⅰ. 根据课文填空

The performance of a relay was basically reliable—at least __1__ a single device. But the common applications for relay panels called __2__ 300 to 500 or more relays, and the reliability and maintenance issues associated with __3__ these panels became a very great challenge. Cost became another __4__ , for in spite of the low cost of the relay itself, the installed cost of the panel could be quite high. The total cost including purchased parts, wiring, and installation labor, could range __5__ $30 ~ $50 per relay. To make matters worse, the constantly changing needs of a process called for recurring modifications of a control panel. With relays, this was a costly prospect, as it was accomplished by a major rewiring effort on the panel. In __6__ , these changes were sometimes poorly documented, causing a second-shift maintenance nightmare months later. In light __7__ this, it was not uncommon to discard an entire control panel __8__ favor of a new one with the appropriate components wired in a manner suited for the new process.

That something, in the late 1960s, was the first __9__ controller. This first "revolutionary" system was developed as a specific response to the needs of the major automotive __10__ in the United States.

Ⅱ. 将下列短文译成中文

Many of these relays were in use in the transportation industry, more specifically, the automotive industry. These relays used hundreds of wires and their interconnections to affect a control solution.

All programmable controllers consist of the basic functional blocks. We will examine each block to understand the relationship to the control system. First we looked at the center, as it is the heart of the system. It consists of a microprocessor.

Ⅲ. 将下列短语和句子译成英文

1. 可编程控制器，中央处理单元，微处理器，继电器，可编程逻辑控制器，热电偶，传感器

2. 在 20 世纪 60 年代的后期，发明了第一个可编程控制器，这是汽车工业在控制领域的第一场革命。

3. 20 世纪 60 年代后期的首批产品可能使许多人感到迷惑和恐惧。

Lesson 4 Adaptive Control Systems

An adaptive control system is one whose parameters are automatically adjusted to compensate for corresponding variations in the properties of the process.[1] The system is, in a word, "adapted" to the needs of the process. Naturally there must be some criteria on which to base an adaptive program. To specify a value for the controlled variable (i.e. the set point) is not enough—adaption is not required to meet this specification. Some "objective function" of the controlled variable must be specified in addition. It is this function that determines the particular form of adaption required.

The objective function for a given process may be the damping of the controlled variable. In essence, there are then two loops, one operating on the controlled variable, the other on its damping. Because damping identifies the dynamic loop gain, this system is designated as a dynamic adaptive system.

It is also possible to stipulate an objective function of the steady-state gain of the process. A control system designed to this specification is then steady-state adaptive.

There is, in practice, so little resemblance between these two systems that their classification under a single title "adaptive" has led to, much confusion.[2]

A second distinction is to be made, this not on the objective function, but rather on the mechanism through which adaption is introduced, if enough is known on a process that parameter adjustments can be related to the variables which cause its properties to change, adoption may be programmed. However, if it is necessary to base parameter manipulation upon the measured value of the objective function, adaption is effected by means of a feedback loop. This is known as a self adaptive system.

Dynamic Adaptive Systems

The prime function of dynamic adaptive systems is to give a control loop a consistent degree of stability. Dynamic loop gain is then the objective function of the controlled variable being regulated; its value is to be specified.

The property of the process most susceptible to change is gain. In some cases the steady state gain changes, which is usually termed nonlinearity. Other processes exhibit a variable period, which reflects upon their dynamic gain. But by whichever mechanism loop stability is affected, it can always be restored by suitable adjustment of controller gain. (This assumes that the desired degree of damping could be achieved in the first place, which rules out limit cycling.)

Many cases of variable process gain have already been cited. In generally, attempt is made to compensate for these conditions by the introduction of selected nonlinear functions into the control system. For example, the characteristic of a control valve is customarily chosen with this purpose in mind. But compensation in this way can fall short for several reasons.

(1) The source of the gain variation lies in outside the loop, and hence is not identified by controller input or output.

(2) The required compensation is a combined function of several variables.

(3) The gain of the process varies with time.

The Steady state Adaptive Problem

Where the dynamic adaptive system controls the dynamic gain of a loop, its counterpart seeks a constant steady-state process gain. This implies, of course, that the steady-state process gain is variable and that one particular value is most desirable.

Consider the example of a combustion control system whose fuel-air ratio is to be set for the highest efficiency. Excess fuel or air will both reduce efficiency. The true controlled variable is efficient, while the true manipulated variable is the fuel air ratio. The desired steady state gain in this instance is $dc/dm = 0$. The system is to be operated at the point where either an increase or decrease in ratio decreases efficiency. This is a special case of steady-state adaption known as "optimizing". A gain other than zero may reasonably be stipulated, however.

Where the value of the manipulated variable which satisfies the objective function is known relative to conditions prevailing within the process, the adaption may be easily programmed. As an example, the optimum fuel-air ratio may be known for various conditions of air flow and temperature. The control system may then be designed to adapt the ratio to air flow and temperature much in the way that the controller settings are changed, as a function of flow in the example of dynamic adaptation.[3]

New words and phrases

(1) adaptation　　[ˌədæpˈteiʃən]　　n. 适合，适应，适应性控制
(2) designate　　[ˈdezigneit]　　vt. 指明，称为，标志
(3) stipulate　　[ˈstipjuleit]　　vt. 规定，保证
(4) confusion　　[kənˈfjuːʒən]　　n. 混乱，混淆
(5) prevail　　[priˈveil]　　vi. 流行，经常发生
(6) fall short　　未能满足，不能达到

Notes to the Text

(1) An adaptive control system is one whose parameters are automatically adjusted to compensate for corresponding variations in the properties of the process.

适应性控制系统是一种能自动调整其参数以补偿与过程特性相应变化的系统。whose parameters are automatically adjusted 是定语从句，不定式 to compensate for... 表示目的，译为"以弥补……"

(2) There is, in practice, so little resemblance between these two systems that their classification under a single title "adaptive" has led to, much confusion.

实际上，这两种系统之间几乎不存在相似，它们在单一名称"适应性"之下的分类已经引起了许多混淆。in practice（实际上）相当于 in fact, indeed, virtually, actually；little resemblance 表示否定，so...that...（如此……以至），under a single title（在一个名称下），lead to（导致）。

(3) The control system may then be designed to adapt the ratio to air flow and temperature much in the way that the controller settings are changed, as a function of flow in the example of dynamic adaptation.

用改变控制器设定值的方法来设计控制系统，使燃油-空气比适应于空气流量与温度的变化，作为动态适应系统例子中的一个流量函数。不定式 to adapt 表示目的，译为"适应于、使……适应"，ratio to...（对……的比率），that 引导定语从句，修饰 way，as 这里表示作为。

Exercises

Ⅰ. 根据课文填空

1. An adaptive control system is one _____ parameters are automatically adjusted to compensate for corresponding variations in the properties of the process.

2. To specify a value for the controlled variable is not enough—adaption is not required to _____ this specification.

3. It is this function _____ determines the particular form of adaption required.

4. There is, in practice, _____ little resemblance between these two systems that their classification under a single title "adaptive" has led to, much confusion.

5. Adaption is effected by means of a feedback loop. This is known as a _____.

6. The prime function of dynamic adaptive systems is to give a _____ a consistent degree of stability.

7. The characteristic of a control valve is customarily chosen _____ this purpose in mind.

8. Consider the example of a combustion control system whose fuel-air ratio is to be _____ for the highest efficiency.

9. Where the value of the manipulated variable _____ satisfies the objective function is known relative to conditions prevailing within the process.

10. The control system may then be designed to adapt the ratio _____ air flow and

temperature much in the way that the controller settings are changed.

Ⅱ. 将下列短文译成中文

The objective function for a given process may be the damping of the controlled variable. In essence, there are then two loops, one operating on the controlled variable, the other on its damping. Because damping identifies the dynamic loop gain, this system is designated as a dynamic adaptive system.

Ⅲ. 将下列短文译成英文

规定过程稳态增益的目标函数也是可能的，设计满足系统要求的控制系统是稳态适应系统。事实上两个系统之间是完全不一样，以至在一个名称为"适应性"的条件下的分类会引起很多混乱。

10.2　Extensive Reading

Lesson 1　Closed-loop Control System

It is well known that there are three basic components in a closed-loop control system.[1] They are:

1. The Error Detector. This is a device which receives the low-power input signal and the output signal which may be of different physical natures, converts them into a common physical quantity for the purposes of subtraction, performs the subtraction, and gives out a low-power error signal of the correct physical nature to actuate the controller.[2] The error detector will usually contain "transducers"; these are devices which convert signals of one physical form into another.

2. The Controller. This is an amplifier which receives the low-power error signal, together with power from an external source. A controlled amount of power (of the correct physical nature) is then supplied to the output element.

3. The Output Element. It provides the load with power of the correct physical nature in accordance with the signal received from the controller.[3]

Other devices such as gear-boxes and "compensating" devices are often featured in control systems, but these can usually be considered to form part of one of the other elements.

New words and phrases

(1) closed loop control system　闭环控制系统
(2) transducer　[trænz'djuːsə]　n. 传感器，变频器，变换器
(3) amplifier　['æmplifaiə]　n. 扩音器，放大器
(4) compensate　['kɔmpenseit]　v. 偿还，付报酬

Notes to the Text

(1) It is well known that there are three basic components in a closed-loop control system.

众所周知，在闭环控制系统中有三个基本元件。It is well known that...译为"众所周知……"

(2) This is a device which receives the low-power input signal...and gives out a low-power error signal of the correct physical nature to actuate the controller.

这是一个能接受低功率输入信号和输出信号的装置，这些信号可能具有不同的物理性质。为了降低误差，将他们转换成普通的物理量，该设备能减少误差，输出能改正其物理性质的低功率误差信号来驱动控制器。which receives...是定语从句，修饰 device，which may be of...是定语从句，修饰 input signal and the output signal，for the purposes of...（为了……目的），gives out（发出），physical nature（物理性质），to actuate 相当于 to drive。

(3) It provides the load with power of the correct physical nature in accordance with the signal received from the controller.

提供与控制器输出信号一致的恰当的物理特性能量加载。provide...with...（用……提供给……），in accordance with...（与……一致）。

Lesson 2　Digital Control Systems

In a digital control system, a central processor makes the required calculations sequentially for a number of control loops. The result of a calculation may be used to drive a control valve directly or to set the set point of an analog controller. The former arrangement is known as direct digital control (DDC), and the latter as set point control (SPC).[1] The control algorithms solved by the computer are the same in either case. But the decision whether to use a computer for DOC or SPC is sufficiently important for us to examine the benefits and limitations of each in some detail.

DDC or SPC

Figure 10.2 shows two ways of implementing DDC. The upper loop is provided with a digital-manual station (HIC) for manual back-up. Should the computer fail, the last valve position is held and the HIC is placed in a manual mode.[2] A light identifies the station as being in manual to attract the operator's attention. Should the operator transfer the station to manual, a logic signal is sent to the computer to report his action. When the station again returns to digital control, the computer "initializes" data stored in memory, so that automatic control can proceed bumplessly, starting at the last valve position when in manual. In the event of computer failure, all loops normally under its control must be tended by the operation. There could be as many as 100 of more, depending on the installation. Some may be sufficiently critical for manual control to be unacceptable. For these, analog backup may be chosen, as shown in the lower loop of Figure 10.2. In the event of computer failure, an analog controller takes over regulation of the loop. However, some consideration must be given to the set point of the analog controller, or an undesirable bump may result upon transfer to analog.[3]

One practice is to transfer to manual upon computer failure and leave the subsequent switch to analog control to the discretion of the operator. Another practice is to cause the analog

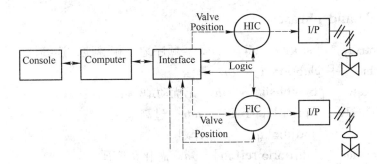

Figure 10.2 Direct digital control can be implemented with manual
Backup (above) or analog backup (below)

controller's set point to track its measurement, so that there can be no deviation at the time of transfer. Alternately, the analog set point could track the digital set point, to eliminate the possibility of initiating analog control at an undesirable set point developed during a transient condition.

In the case of analog backup, two controllers have been installed (the computer plus the analog controller) although only one is in use at any given time. Consequently analog backup is prohibitively expensive except for extreme circumstances. To justify that system, the computer must be able to control the process much better than the analog controller. In actual practice, this is not likely to be the case.

If the digital computer is asked simply to duplicate the analog control function, it will not perform it as well, because the act of sampling introduces phase lag into the loop according to Eq. $\Phi_\Delta = -180\Delta t/\tau_0$. If the scan period is much shorter than the loop period, this contribution may be negligible, and therefore digital control may be justified for slower loops. However, for fast loops like flow and liquid level, even a 1s sample interval may produce a noticeable deterioration in response. Yet these loops constitute the majority of loops in a typical chemical plant or petroleum refinery. To operate most of the loops at sample intervals of 1s or less loads the computer excessively; it is better reserved for complicated tasks involving extensive calculations that can be performed at less frequent intervals.

Flow and liquid level are best regulated by analog control. A flow controller can be directed by a computer, using set point control. The configuration for SPC is identical to the lower loop in Figure 10.2 except that the computer outputs are set point rather than valve position to the FIC (flow-indicating controller). The flow controller is always controlling; a computer failure simply stops the set point from being updated. The set point may be generated by a feedback algorithm or any one of a variety of calculations based on production scheduling, feed forward control, etc. The operator may place the FIC in manual, in automatic with local set point, or in automatic with computer-driven set point. Whenever the operator returns to this last condition, the computer initializes its stored data to avoid bumping the set point the operator has introduced.

New words and phrases

(1) sequentially　　［siˈkwenʃəli］　　*adv.* 顺序地，相继地，连续地
(2) algorithm　　［ˈælgəriðəm］　　*n.* 算法
(3) bumplessly　　［bʌmplisli］　　*adv.* 无扰动地
(4) prohibitively　　［prəuˈhibitivli］　　*adv.* 过高
(5) scheduling　　［ˈʃədjuːəliŋ］　　*n.* 计划
(6) deterioration　　［diˌtiəriəˈreiʃən］　　*n.* 恶化，变质

Notes to the Text

(1) The former arrangement is known as direct digital control (DDC), and the latter as set point control (SPC).

前一种方案称为直接数字控制（DDC），后者称为设定值控制（SPC）。the former... the latter... 经常成对出现，译为"前者……，后者……"，is known as...（叫做，称作）。

(2) Should the computer fail, the last valve position is held and the HIC is placed in a manual mode.

如果计算机出了故障，阀门就保持在最后位置上，而 HIC 放在手动模式。Should the computer fail 是一倒装句，是 if 引导的虚拟条件句，省略了 if 后 should 提前，完整的句子是 If the computer should fail。

(3) In the event of computer failure, an analog controller takes over regulation of the loop. However, some consideration must be given to the set point of the analog controller, or an undesirable bump may result upon transfer to analog.

在计算机出故障的情况下，模拟控制器承担回路调节。然而，必须考虑模拟控制器的预定点，否则，不希望的扰动可能会影响切换到模拟状态。

第 11 章 Computer Technologies for the Design and Manufacture of Machinery

11.1 Intensive Reading

Lesson 1 CAD (Computer-aided Design) Technology

In the broadest sense, Computer-aided Design (CAD) refers to any application of a computer to the solution to design problems; the engineer may communicate with the computer in many forms, either via the visual display screen, keyboard, graph plotter or many more machine interfaces [1]. They can ask a question and receive an answer from the computer in a matter of seconds. More specifically, CAD is a technique in which the engineer and a computer work together as a team, utilizing the best characteristics of each.

In the past, the conventional tools of the engineer in his/her role as a designer have been drawing boards and instruments, calculators and technical data sheets. More recently, the advent of the computer caused major changes in industry. The first real progress in the use of computers in the manufacturing process came in the late 1950s with the introduction of numerical controlled (NC), and later computer numerical controlled (CNC), machine tools. Data supplied to the machines, on tape, controlled the motions of the tools that produced the parts of an assembly. There was no direct link to the designer other than drawings and tables of values.

An important change came with the introduction of CAD in the early 1960s. CAD allowed the designer to interact graphically with the computer, and enables the engineer to test a design idea and to rapidly see its effects; the design idea can then be modified and reassessed. The process being repeated until a good design is achieved. Following each iteration, the design, solution hopefully improves. Therefore, the more cycles that can be carried out within the financial, material and time constraints, the better the result should be [2].

The computer can be exploited to speed up and improve the accuracy of the design process. It will perform large numbers of complicated calculations in a very short space of time and will produce results, which are accurate and reliable [3]. This foregoing feature of the computer proves invaluable in its role as a design aid; some designs could simply not be performed by man in a reasonable time.

The computer is capable of holding vast quantities of information on permanent media such as magnetic disc or temporarily in immediate access store [4]. It is therefore possible to represent the details of an engineering drawing or the shape of a car body in digital form and store this digital information in memory. This data can then be retrieved from memory, rapidly converted and displayed on a VDU graphics screen, or alternatively, plotted onto paper using a graph plotter.

Besides, the designer can quickly and easily update or amend any part of the drawing. The drawing data can then be written back to memory in its updated form.

CAD has many roles to play in the world of engineering, such as: the application of computer systems to the production of engineering drawings; the use of finite element techniques to solve stress and thermal problems on complex components; the analysis of mechanisms and linkages, plus a host of additional engineering applications.

New Words and phrases

(1) refer ［ri'fə:］ v. 涉及，谈及，意指
　　refer to 意指，是……
(2) via ［'vaiə］ prep. 经，由，通过
(3) keyboard ［'ki:bɔ:d］ n. 计算机键盘
(4) graph plotter 绘图仪
(5) interface ［'intəfeis］ n. 计算机接口
(6) specifically ［spi'sifikəli］ adv. 明确地，确切地
(7) utilize ［'ju:tilaiz］ v. 利用，使用
(8) conventional ［kən'venʃənəl］ adj. 常规的，习惯的
(9) link ［liŋk］ v. 连接，联合
(10) exploit ［'eksplɔit］ vt. 开发，利用
(11) accuracy ［'ækjurəsi］ n. 正确性，精确度
(12) perform ［pə'fɔ:m］ v. 执行，做
(13) foregoing ［'fɔ:gəuiŋ］ adj. 在前的，前述的
(14) invaluable ［in'væljuəbl］ adj. 无价的，价值无法估计的
(15) permanent ［'pə:mənənt］ adj. 永久性的
(16) temporarily ［'tempərərili］ adv. 临时地，暂时地
(17) access ［'ækses］ n. 访问，存储
(18) VDU ［ˌvi: di:'ju:］ n. 视频显示装置
(19) finite element 有限元
(20) communicate with… 与……交流，与……通信
(21) receive…from… 从……得到
(22) link to… 把……连接到……

Notes

(1) In the broadest sense, Computer-aided Design (CAD) refers to any application of… either via the visual display screen, keyboard, graph plotter or many more machine interfaces.

从广义上讲，计算机辅助设计（CAD）是指计算机在解决设计问题中的应用。工程技术人员可以借助于可视显示屏幕、键盘、绘图仪和人机接口等诸多方式与计算机通信。In the broadest sense 从广义上讲，refers to… 意指，提到，communicate with… 与……通

第 11 章　Computer Technologies for the Design and Manufacture of Machinery　·159·

信，in many forms 用许多形式，either…or 既……也……，via = through/by，graph plotter 绘图仪。

（2）Therefore, the more cycles that can be carried out within the financial, material and time constraints, the better the result should be.

因此，在时间、材料和资金允许的条件下所执行的设计循环次数越多，设计效果就越好。the more…the better…越多越好，within…在……之内。

（3）It will perform large numbers of complicated calculations in a very short space of time and will produce results, which are accurate and reliable.

它能够在短时间内完成大量的、复杂的计算并得出准确和可靠的结果。perform 相当于 do/conduct/make，larger numbers of + 可数名词，译为许多，这里 space = interval，which 引导非限定性定语从句，修饰 results。

（4）The computer is capable of holding vast quantities of information on permanent media such as magnetic disc or temporarily in immediate access store.

计算机可在诸如磁盘的永久性介质上保存大量的信息，或者临时存储在直接存储器上。is capable of…能够……，holding 这里相当于 storing 保存，vast quantities of + 不可数名词，译为大量的。

Exercises

Ⅰ．根据课文填空

In the broadest sense, Computer-aided Design (CAD) refers ___1___ any application of a computer to the solution of design problems, the engineer may communicate ___2___ the computer in many forms, either via the visual display screen, keyboard, graph plotter ___3___ many more machine interfaces. They can ask a question and receive an ___4___ from the computer in a matter of seconds. More specifically, CAD is a technique in which the engineer and a computer work together as a team, utilizing the best characteristics of each.

In the past, the conventional tools of the engineer in his/her role as a designer have been ___5___ boards and instruments, calculators and technical data sheets. More recently, the advent of the computer caused major changes in industry. The first real progress in the use of computers in the manufacturing process came in the late 1950s ___6___ the introduction of numerical controlled (NC), and later computer numerical controlled (CNC), machine tools. Data supplied to the machines, on tape, controlled the motions of the tools ___7___ produced the parts of an assembly. There was no direct link to the designer other than drawings and tables of values.

An important change came with the introduction of CAD in the ___8___ 1960s. CAD allowed the designer to interact graphically with the computer, and enables the engineer to test a design idea and to rapidly see its effects; the design idea can then be ___9___ and reassessed. The process being repeated ___10___ a good design is achieved.

Ⅱ．将下列短语和句子译成英文

1．计算机辅助设计，显示屏幕，键盘、绘图仪，磁盘，图形，存储器，视频显示器，有限元技术

2. 在广义上讲，计算机辅助设计（CAD）指的是计算机在解决设计问题中的应用。

3. 20世纪60年代初随着计算机辅助设计的引入产生了一场重大变革。

4. 过去，工程技术人员设计时所使用的传统工具是制图板、制图仪、计算器和技术数据图纸。

5. 工程技术人员能够检验一个设计思想，并很快地查看到设计效果，然后对其进行修改和重新评价。

Ⅲ．将下列短文译成中文

CAD has many roles to play in the world of engineering, such as: the application of computer systems to the production of engineering drawings; the use of finite element techniques to solve stress and thermal problems on complex components; the analysis of mechanisms and linkages, plus a host of additional engineering applications.

Lesson 2　CAPP (Computer Aided Process Planning) Technology

Computer Aided Process Planning (CAPP) can be defined as the functions which use computers to assist the work of process planners. The levels of assistance depend on the different strategies employed to implement the system. Lower level strategies only use computers for storage and retrieval of the data for the process plans which will be constructed manually by process planners, as well as for supplying the data, which will be used in the planner's new work. In comparison with lower level strategies, higher-level strategies use computers to automatically generate process plans for some work pieces of simple geometrical shapes. Sometimes a process planner is required to input the data needed or to modify plans which do not fit specific production requirements well[1]. The highest-level strategy, which is the ultimate goal of CAPP, generates process plans by computer, which may replace process planners, when the knowledge and expertise of process planning and working experience have been incorporated into the computer programs[2]. The database in a CAPP system based on the highest level strategy will be directly integrated with conjunctive systems, e.g. CAD and CAM. CAPP has been recognized as playing a key role in CIMS (Computer Integrated Manufacturing System)[3].

More than 20 years have elapsed since the use of computers to assist process planning was first proposed. Tremendous efforts have been made in the development of CAPP systems. For the time being, the research interests for development of CAPP systems are focused on intelligent and integrated process planning systems. For increasing the intelligence of CAPP systems, some new concepts, such as neural networks, fuzzy logic, and machine learning have been explored for the new generation of CAPP systems[4]. For increasing the integrability of CAPP system, feature based design, the roles of features, integrating process planning with scheduling, and integrating process planning with manufacturing resources planning have been focused on. This phenomenon is entitled concurrent or simultaneous engineering.

Since a process plan determines the methods, machines, sequences, fixturing, and tools required in the fabrication and assembly of components, it is easy to see that process planning is one of the basic tasks to be performed in manufacturing systems[5]. The task of carrying out the difficult and detailed process plans has traditionally been done by workers with a vast knowledge and understanding of the manufacturing process [6]. Many of these skilled workers, now considered process planners, are either retired or close to retirement, with no qualified young process planners to take their place. An increasing shortage of process planners has been created. With the high pressure of serious' competition in the world market, integrated production has been pursued as a way for companies to survive and succeed. Automated process planning systems have been recognized as playing a key role in CIMS. It is for reasons such as these that many companies look for computer aided process systems [7].

New words and phrases

(1) CAPP (Computer Aided Process Planning)　计算机辅助工艺设计
(2) interactive　[ˌintərˈæktiv]　adj. 交互式的
(3) retrieval　[riˈtriːvəl]　n. 取回，恢复，修补，检索
(4) manually　[ˈmænjuəli]　adv. 手动，手工，人力
(5) generate　[ˈdʒenəreit]　v. 产生，发生
(6) geometrical shape　几何形状
(7) specific　[spiˈsifik]　adj. 明确的，详细的
(8) ultimate　[ˈʌltimət]　adj. 最后的，最终的
(9) CIMS (Computer Integrated Manufacturing System)　计算机集成制造系统
(10) elapse　[iˈlæps]　v. (时间) 流逝，消逝
(11) tremendous　[triˈmendəs]　adj. 极大的，具大的
(12) neural network　神经网络
(13) fuzzy logic　模糊逻辑
(14) machine learning　学习机器
(15) integrability　[ˌintigrəˈbiləti]　n. 整体性，集成性，可积分性
(16) fixturing　[ˈfikstəriŋ]　n. 夹具
(17) fabrication　[fæbriˈkeiʃən]　n. 制作，构成，装配
(18) pursue　[pəˈsju]　v. 追求
(19) phenomenon　[fiˈnɔminən]　n. 现象
(20) concurrent　[kənˈkʌrənt]　adj. 并发的，协作的
(21) simultaneous　[ˌsiməlˈteiniəs]　adj. 同时的，同时发生的
(22) be defined as　将……定义为
(23) depend on...　依靠，依赖
(24) in comparison with...　与……比较
(25) be incorporated into...　合并……一体，集成……一体
(26) be integrated with...　与……结合，与……一体
(27) carry out　执行，贯彻
(28) take one's place　接替，取代
(29) be recognized as...　被……承认

(30) shortage of… 缺乏……
(31) play a key role 起重要作用

Notes

(1) Sometimes a process planner is required to input the data needed or to modify plans which do not fit specific production requirements well.

有时工艺员需要输入所需数据和调整那些不适合某些具体产品要求的工艺流程。主句采用被动式，翻译时可采用主动式，which 引导定语从句，修饰 plans，do not fit = do not meet，不适合，不满足。

(2) The highest-level strategy, which is the ultimate goal of CAPP, generates process plans by computer, which may replace process planners, when the knowledge and expertise of process planning and working experience have been incorporated into the computer programs.

最高水平决策是 CAPP 的最高追求，即当工艺知识、专门技术和工作经验被融合在计算机程序中时，用计算机代替工艺员制作生成工艺流程。全句主语是 The highest-level strategy，可简化为 The highest-level strategy generates process plans by computer. 两个 which 都是引导非限定性定语从句，修饰各自前面的词，when 引导一个时间状语从句，翻译时可将状语译在前面。expertise 指工艺方面的技术，be incorporated into…结合到……。

(3) The database in a CAPP system based on the highest level strategy will be directly integrated with conjunctive systems, e. g. CAD and CAM. CAPP has been recognized as playing a key role in CIMS (Computer Integrated Manufacturing System).

最高水平决策的 CAPP 系统数据库将直接集成在相关系统中，如 CAD 和 CAM 系统中，CAPP 被认为在 CIMS（计算机集成制造系统）中起关键作用。based on…基于……，以……为基础，be directly integrated with…直接与……集成，be recognized as…被承认是……，playing a key role in…在……方面起重要作用，CIMS 指计算机集成制造系统。

(4) For increasing the intelligence of CAPP systems, some new concepts, such as neural networks, fuzzy logic, and machine learning have been explored for the new generation of CAPP systems.

为提高 CAPP 系统的智能化程度，一些新概念，如神经网络，模糊逻辑学和学习机器在新生代 CAPP 系统中被探索开发。neural networks, fuzzy logic, and machine learning 是控制技术中产生的新方法，学习机器是最近统计学科和计算机学科的交叉学科，利用这些新技术改善 CAPP 系统。

(5) Since a process plan determines the methods, machines, sequences, fixturing, and tools required in the fabrication and assembly of components, it is easy to see that process planning is one of the basic tasks to be performed in manufacturing systems.

由于工艺流程决定了在制造和装配零件时所需的方法、机器、顺序、工装和刀具，不难看出编制工艺流程是制造系统要执行的基本任务之一。Since 这里表示原因，引导原因状语从句，it 是主句的形式主语，真正的主语是后面的不定式 to see，that 引导的句子是动词 see 的宾语，to be performed = to be made，不定式的被动式。

(6) The task of carrying out the difficult and detailed process plans has traditionally been

done by workers with a vast knowledge and understanding of the manufacturing process.

传统上推行任务的困难和详细工艺过程制定由精通制造工艺的操作工人来解决。carrying out 执行，workers with a vast knowledge and understanding of the manufacturing process 译为具有大量制造工艺知识和技能的工人。介词 with 表示具有。

（7）It is for reasons such as these that many companies look for computer aided process systems.

这就是许多公司关注计算机辅助工艺设计系统的原因。It 是形式主语，that 引导主语从句。

Exercises

Ⅰ. 选择题

1. _____ can be defined as the functions which use computers to assist the work of process planners.
   A. CAD　　　　B. CAM　　　　C. CAE　　　　D. CAPP

2. Higher-level strategies use computers to automatically generate process _____ for some work pieces of simple geometrical shapes.
   A. diagram　　　B. plans　　　C. form　　　D. flowchart

3. When the knowledge and expertise of process planning and working experience have been incorporated _____ the computer programs.
   A. into　　　　B. in　　　　C. to　　　　D. of

4. CAPP has been recognized _____ playing a key role in ClMS (Computer Integrated Manufacturing System).
   A. of　　　　B. as　　　　C. for　　　　D. with

5. More than 20 years have _____ since the use of computers to assist process planning was first proposed.
   A. walked　　　B. flown　　　C. elapsed　　　D. spent

6. Tremendous efforts have been _____ in the development of CAPP systems.
   A. made　　　B. got　　　C. put　　　D. set

7. Since a process plan determines the methods, machines, sequences, fixturing, and tools required in the fabrication and assembly of _____.
   A. parts　　　B. framework　　　C. components　　　D. system

8. It is easy to see _____ process planning is one of the basic tasks to be performed in manufacturing systems.
   A. what　　　B. where　　　C. which　　　D. that

9. Many of these skilled workers, now considered process planners, are either retired _____ close to retirement.
   A. too　　　B. and　　　C. nor　　　D. or

10. Automated process planning systems have been recognized as _____ a key role in CIMS.

  A. taking   B. playing   C. performing   D. acting

Ⅱ. 将下列句子译成英文

1. CAPP 被认为在 CIMS（计算机集成制造系统）中起关键作用。

2. 为提高 CAPP 系统的智能化程度，一些新概念，如神经网络，模糊逻辑学和学习机器在新生代 CAPP 系统中被探索开发。

3. 计算机辅助工艺设计是计算机协助工艺员完成工艺流程功能。

4. 该现象有资格说是并行工程。

5. 自动化的工艺流程系统已经被认为是 CIMS 中至关重要的部分。

Ⅲ. 将下列短文译成中文

  More than 20 years have elapsed since the use of computers to assist process planning was first proposed. Tremendous efforts have been made in the development of CAPP systems. For the time being, the research interests for development of CAPP systems are focused on intelligent and integrated process planning systems.

Lesson 3 Dynamic Simulation Technique for the Design of Machine

  1. Introduction

  The general motives for "Virtual Prototyping" are probably familiar to all engineers: Stricter legal requirements (e.g. with regard to exhaust emissions and sound) and tougher customer demands (e.g. with regard to performance and handling) lead to more advanced, complex systems, which are harder to be optimized with traditional methods [1]. Development will cost more and need more time, in contrast to this; increased competition demands lower development cost and shorter project times.

  Cases have recently been published where complete machines were simulated for evaluation of the simulation technique itself, sub-systems, comfort-related aspects, or durability. This paper too, will deal with dynamic simulation of complete machines, but for analysis and optimization of overall performance and related aspects. The focus will be on wheel loaders with hydrodynamic transmissions, but most findings will be also applicable to other off-road machinery [2].

  2. Design Process and Visualization

  The aim of the present project is evolution of the current product development process, rather than revolution by means of design science. The research question is therefore how to augment the existing design process with dynamic simulation. As mentioned before, the focus is on analysis and optimization of overall performance and related aspects.

  The revised design process has to fulfill the following non-optional targets: Lead to development of compared with today. Saved resources (time, money, and people) can then be spent on optimizing one or all of the aspects mentioned in the first item in the list.

  (1) products of at least equal high performance, efficiency, and operate ability;

  (2) with increased robustness;

  (3) in a shorter time;

  (4) at a lower development cost.

In an earlier project, a valuable lesson has been learned, speed matters when it comes to iterations, especially in the concept phase. When Volvo's old loading unit calculation program was to be replaced by a more modem version, this was done with a proprietary simulation system, which was based on a multi-body system (MBS) and a modem database[3]. The development was done in-house. This new simulation system has been proved to be more flexible, more accurate, and especially more efficient for the user, except for some pre-study engineers[4]. Since the new system obtains results by multi-body simulation, rather than calculation of hard-coded explicit equations, one run takes a couple of seconds longer than with the old program. Brute-force optimizations of the old type are no longer time efficient. If this had been known before, i.e. if it had been included in the project targets, one could have developed a special downscaled version, that was less accurate but faster.

However, one example can be given, a critical phase in a so-called 'short loader cycle' is when the machine, coming backwards with a full bucket, changes direction towards the load receiver. During that time, there is a close interaction between the main subsystems.

(1) In order to reverse the machine, the operator lowers the engine speed (otherwise the gear shifting will be jerky and the transmission couplings might wear out prematurely). Less torque is available at lower speeds. Additionally, the engine response is worse at lower speeds, mainly due to inertia of the turbocharger.

(2) When switching gears from reverse to forward, the loader is still rolling backwards. This forces an abrupt change of rotational direction of the torque converter's turbine wheel, thus greatly increasing the slip, which leads to a sudden increase in torque demand from the engine.

(3) Some operators do not stop lifting the loading unit while reversing, thus requiting high oil flow throughout the whole process. The oil flow is proportional to the hydraulic pump's displacement and shaft speed, and the load-sensing pumps can be assumed to be directly connected to the engine crankshaft[5]. Thus, at lower engine speeds and high demand of oil flow, the displacement goes towards maximum. The amount of torque that a pump demands of the engine is proportional to its displacement and hydraulic pressure. Since the loader's bucket is full and due to the loading unit's geometry, hydraulic pressure is high. With displacement at maximum, this also leads to an increased torque demand.

3. Conclusions

This paper presented the joint research by Volvo Wheel Loaders and Linktoping University on simulation of complete machines for analysis and optimization of overall performance. The motivation on the side of the industrial partner is to develop products of equally high performance, efficiency and operate ability, but with more robustness regarding these aspects, in a shorter time and at a lower total development cost. A revised product development process (with regard to the research topic) has been proposed. Examples of areas for future research have also been presented.

New words and phrases

(1) motive   ['məutiv]   n. 动机，目的

(2) virtual prototyping　虚拟原型机，虚拟样机
(3) optimize　['ɔptimaiz]　v. 使优化
(4) complete machine　整机
(5) wheel loader　轮式装载机
(6) sub-system　['sʌbsistəm]　n. 子系统
(7) dynamic simulation　动态仿真
(8) augment　[ɔːg'ment]　v. 增加，增大
(9) fulfill　[ful'fil]　v. 实现，完成
(10) robustness　[rəu'bʌstnis]　n. 强壮，健壮，耐用
(11) iteration　[,itə'reiʃən]　n. 反复
(12) Volvo　['vɔlvəu]　沃尔沃公司（国际著名的汽车和工程机械公司，总部位于瑞典）
(13) proprietary　[prəu'praiətəri]　adj. 所有的，私人所有的
(14) in-house　['in'haus]　adj. 内部的
(15) flexible　['fleksibl]　adj. 灵活的，柔性的
(16) accurate　['ækjurət]　adj. 精确的
(17) pre-study engineer　预研工程师
(18) explicit　[ik'splisit]　adj. 外在的，清楚的，直接的
(19) equation　[i'kweiʒən]　n. 方程式，等式，反应式
(20) brute-force optimization　受力优化
(21) downscaled　['daun,skeil]　adj. 减少规模的，小的
(22) critical phase　临界阶段
(23) full bucket　满斗
(24) interaction　[,intər'ækʃən]　n. 交（相）互作用
(25) jerky　['dʒəːki]　adj. 急拉的，急动的，不平稳的
(26) prematurely　[,priːmə'tjuəli]　adv. 过早地，早熟地
(27) inertia　[i'nəːʃiə]　n. 惯性，惯量
(28) abrupt change　突然变化
(29) turbine wheel　涡轮
(30) slip　[slip]　n. 滑倒
(31) throughout　[θruː'aut]　adv. 全部地，彻底地
(32) assume　[ə'sjuːm]　v. 假定，设想
(33) crankshaft　['kræŋk,ʃɑːft]　n. 机轴
(34) motivation　[,məuti'veiʃən]　n. 动机
(35) be probably familiar to...　也许熟悉……
(36) with regard to...　关于……
(37) in contrast to...　与……相反，与……形成对比
(38) deal with...　处理，对付
(39) by means of...　借助……依靠……

(40) As mentioned before　如前面所述，正如前面提到的
(41) be replaced by…　由……取代
(42) except for…　除……以外
(43) a couple of…　几个
(44) wear out　磨损
(45) due to…　由于
(46) be proportional to…　与……成比例

Notes

(1) The general motives for "Virtual Prototyping" are probably familiar to all engineers: Stricter legal requirements (e.g. with regard to exhaust emissions and sound) and…lead to more advanced, complex systems, which are harder to be optimized with traditional methods.

可能所有的工程师都熟悉虚拟样机技术的应用目的。如今严格的法律法规（例如有关废气排放和噪声方面的）和苛刻的用户需求（例如有关设备性能和操作方面的）都需要更为先进、复杂系统的技术支持，用传统的方法很难优化。virtual prototyping 指虚拟样机技术，即在计算机环境下对整机进行动力学和运动学仿真，sth. be familiar to sb. 某事为某人所熟悉，with regard to…关于……，which 引导非限定性从句，修饰 complex systems，这里 with = by，使用。

(2) The focus will be on wheel loaders with hydrodynamic transmissions, but most findings will be also applicable to other off-road machinery.

本文所讨论的主要焦点是液压驱动的轮式装载机，所得到的结果也适用于其他越野机械。most findings 指大多数的研究结果，off-road machinery = full terrain machinery，越野机械，也指全地形机械。

(3) When Volvo's old loading unit calculation program was to be replaced by a more modern version, this was done with a proprietary simulation system, which was based on a multi-body system (MBS) and a modem database.

当 Volvo 公司的旧装载计算程序被认为高级的程序替代后，上述工作就可以用独有的仿真系统完成，这些系统是在多种系统和现代数据库的基础上发展起来的。Volvo 是一家国际著名的专业从事工程建设机械和车辆的制造商，总部位于瑞典，loading unit = loader，不定式被动语态 to be replaced by…被……取代，modem version = modem calculation program，which 引导非限定性定语从句，based on…基于……，multi-body system (MBS) 多体系统，是一种计算机仿真系统。

(4) This new simulation system has been proved to be more flexible, more accurate, and especially more efficient for the user, except for some pre-study engineers.

现在人们已经证明，这种新的仿真系统对用户来说，适应性、精度和效率都比较高，但对于那些进行预测性研究的工程师来说，其优越性并没有显现出来。句子采用完成被动式，for the user 对用户而言，except for 除外，except for some pre-study engineers 意指对于一些预研工程师而言并不是前文所述的事实情况。

(5) The oil flow is proportional to the hydraulic pump's displacement and shaft speed, and

the load-sensing pumps can be assumed to be directly connected to the engine crankshaft.

我们假定载荷传感泵与发动机的机轴直接相连，通常发动机的油量是和液压泵的排液量及发动机的机轴转速成一定比例的。句子后部的假设条件句翻译时可先译，is proportional to...与……成比例，the hydraulic pump's displacement 指液压泵每分钟的排量，load-sensing pumps 载荷传感泵，be directly connected to...直接连接到……。

Exercises

Ⅰ. 根据课文填空

This paper too, will deal __1__ dynamic simulation of complete machines, but for analysis and optimization of overall performance and __2__ aspects. The focus will be __3__ wheel loaders with hydrodynamic transmissions, but most findings will be also applicable to other off-road __4__.

The aim of the present project is evolution of the current product development process, rather than revolution __5__ means of design science. The research question is therefore how to augment the existing design process with dynamic __6__. As mentioned before, the focus is on analysis and optimization of overall performance and related aspects.

Some operators do not stop lifting the loading __7__ while reversing, thus requiting high oil flow throughout the whole process. The oil flow is proportional __8__ the hydraulic pump's displacement and shaft speed, and the load-sensing pumps can be assumed to be directly connected __9__ the engine crankshaft. Thus, __10__ lower engine speeds and high demand of oil flow, the displacement goes towards maximum.

Ⅱ. 将下列短文译成英文

如果我们采用传统的设计方法来满足这些要求，将会花费较多的研制费用和时间，但竞争日益激烈的市场则要求降低研制费用和缩短研制周期。

现在人们已经证明，这种新的仿真系统对用户来说，适应性、精度和效率都比较高，但对于那些进行预研工程师来说，其优越性并没有显现出来。

Ⅲ. 将下列句子译成中文

1. The motivation on the side of the industrial partner is to develop products of equally high performance, efficiency and operate ability.

2. When switching gears from reverse to forward, the loader is still rolling backwards.

3. Less torque is available at lower speeds. Additionally, the engine response is worse at lower speeds, mainly due to inertia of the turbocharger.

4. In an earlier project, a valuable lesson has been learned, especially in the concept phase.

5. The general motives for "Virtual Prototyping" are probably familiar to all engineers.

Lesson 4 Virtual Reality

Virtual reality is a system that enables one or more users to move and react in a computer-simulated environment. Various types of devices allow users to sense and manipulate virtual objects much as they would feel real objects. This natural style of interaction gives participants the feeling of being immersed in the simulated world. virtual world is created by mathematical models and computer programs.

Virtual reality simulations differ from other computer simulations in that they require special interface devices that transmit the sights, sounds, and sensations of the simulated world to the user.[1] These devices also record and send the speech and movements of the participants to the simulation program.

In the future, your office may be less like a cubicle and more like the Holodeck on "Star Trek". Computer scientists are already experimenting with the technology, called tele immersion that will allow us to peer into the offices of colleagues hundreds of miles away and make us feel as if we were sharing the same physical space.[2]

Computer scientists at several universities working on a project called the National Tele Immersion Initiative have demonstrated a prototype system that enables a scientist working at his desk in hill to see his distant colleagues on two screens mounted at right angles to his desk. It gives him the illusion of looking through windows into offices on the other side. And unlike video conferencing, tele immersion provides life size 3D images.

In the prototype system, each researcher is surrounded by a bank of digital cameras that monitor his movements from a variety of angles.[3] The researchers also wear head mounted tracking gear and polarized glasses similar to those used to view 3D movies. When a researcher moves own head, view of his coworks shifts accordingly. If he leans forward, for example, his colleagues appear closer, even though they are hundreds of miles away.

To make the system work, powerful computers must convert digital images of each participant into data that are transmitted via the Internet, and then reconstructed into images projected on the screens.[4] So far, the movement is jerky because today's computers cannot transmit data fast enough.

The scientists hope that tele immersion will open up a host of other applications[5]: for example, patients in areas could "visit" medical specialists in far away cities.

New words and phrases

(1) virtual reality　虚拟现实

(2) manipulate　[mə'nipjuleit]　v. 操作，操纵

(3) cubicle　['kju:bikl]　n. 小卧室

(4) Star Trek　星际旅行（电影名）

(5) holodeck　n. 全息驾驶舱，holo 表示"全的"、"全息的"等意思

(6) tele immersion　远程投入（沉浸），远程参与

(7) prototype system　原型（样机）系统

(8) video conferencing　n. 视频会议

(9) coworker　['kəuˌwə:kə]　n. 合作者，同事

(10) in that　由于

(11) peer into...　窥视

（12）a host of 一大群，许多
（13）convert...into... 将……转化……
（14）a bank of 一系列；一排，一束

Notes

（1）Virtual reality simulations differ from in that they require special interface devices that transmit the sights, sounds, and sensations of the simulated world to the user.

虚拟现实仿真与其他计算机仿真的不同之处在于它需要特殊的接口设备把对虚拟世界的视觉、声音及感觉传递给用户。differ from（与……不同），in that（由于）相当于because，引导原因状语从句，they 指 virtual reality simulations，that 引导定语从句，修饰 devices。

（2）Computer scientists are already experimenting with of colleagues hundreds of miles away and make us feel as if we were sharing the same physical space.

计算机科学家正在做远程沉浸技术的实验。这项技术让我们在几百英里外看到同事的办公室，好像我们与他们正处于同一个物理空间一样。are already experimenting with...（正在用……做实验），called tele immersion 是过去分词短语作后置定语，修饰 technology，that 引导定语从句，修饰 tele immersion，allow 常跟不定式，allow sb to do（允许某人做什么），peer into（窥视），hundreds of miles away（几百英里外），as if（好像），用虚拟语气，从句中 be 动词用 were。

（3）In the prototype system, each researcher is surrounded by a bank of digital cameras that monitor his movements from a variety of angles.

在这个原型系统中，每个研究人员身边都有一排从不同角度监视他运动的数字照相机。be surrounded by...，（被……包围），a bank of（许多，一排），that 引导定语从句，修饰 cameras。

（4）To make the system work, powerful computers must convert digital images and then reconstructed into images projected on the screens.

为了使系统运行，高性能计算机把每个参与者的数字图像处理成数据，并在因特网上进行传输，然后重建图像并投影到屏幕上。不定式 to make 为了表示目的，convert...into...（将……转化……），that 引导定语从句，修饰 data，via 相当于 through/by，projected on...（投影在……）。

（5）The scientists hope that tele immersion will open up a host of other applications.

科学家希望远程沉浸技术能开发出大量的其他应用。that 引导宾语从句，作 hope 的宾语，open up（开启，开发）这里相当于 develop/exploit，a host of = many（许多）。

Exercises

Ⅰ. 根据课文填空

Virtual reality is a system that enables one or more users to move and react in a __1__ environment. Various types of devices allow users to sense and manipulate __2__ objects much as they would feel real objects. This natural style of interaction gives participants the feeling of being

3 in the simulated world. Virtual world is created by mathematical 4 and computer programs.

Virtual reality simulations differ from other computer simulations 5 that they require special interface devices that transmit the sights, sounds, and 6 of the simulated world to the user.

In the 7 system, each researcher is surrounded by a bank 8 digital cameras that monitor his movements from a variety of angles. The researchers also wear head mounted tracking gear and polarized glasses 9 to those used to view 3D movies. When a researcher moves own head, view of his coworks shifts accordingly. If he leans forward, for example, his colleagues appear closer; even 10 they are hundreds of miles away.

Ⅱ. 将下列短语和句子译成中文

1. Virtual Reality, simulation, tele immersion, video conferencing, prototype system, head-mounted monitor.

2. The researchers also wear head mounted tracking gear and polarized glasses similar to those used to view 3D movies.

3. This natural style of interaction gives participants the feeling of being immersed in the simulated world.

Ⅲ. 将下列短文译成英文

虚拟现实仿真与其他计算机仿真的不同之处在于它需要特殊的接口设备，这种设备把虚拟世界的视觉、声音及感觉传递给用户。同时这些设备也记录参与者的语言和动作并发送给计算机仿真程序。

11.2　Extensive Reading

Lesson 1　The Five Phases of Software Development

The development of a large software package can be broken down into five phases:

1. Establishing the Requirements

During the initial phase, the software experts and their customers exchange various documents and conduct a series of meetings in an attempt to develop a complete, consistent, unambiguous set of program specifications. These specifications are intended to serve as a basis for common agreement among all the parties concerned as to what the software product is supposed to accomplish when it becomes operational. [1]

2. Designing the Routine

In the second phase the programmers and the design engineers determine what types of hardware units will be used, what coding languages will be employed, and how the various subtasks will be carried out by the professional staff. [2] During this phase, program flowcharts and other visual aids are used in structuring and outlining the content of the component parts of the overall software package.

3. Coding the Commands

Once the design phase has been completed, the commands are coded in the appropriate language. We often regard the coding phase as being the primary assignment of the professional programmer, but actually, coding typically consumes only about one sixth of the programmer's time and effort.[3]

4. Testing the Program

The first few versions of the program are invariably riddled with errors. Some of these errors can be detected automatically by the computer; others must be located and corrected by running a series of test cases—simple runs of which the correct answers are known in advance. In general a test case will exercise only a small portion of the completed program; hence, large numbers of them are needed if we are reasonably certain that the programs as a whole are essentially error free. In practice it is usually impossible to "prove" that a particular program has been completely debugged. Indeed, many have been found to contain errors long after they have been declared operational. The first FORTRAN translation routine, for example, was found to contain several coding errors 18 months after it was officially released.

5. Operating and Maintaining the Program

When the program has been debugged, it can be operated on a routine basis. However, this is not the end of the programming efforts. Because of the subsequent discovery of changing requirement and various types of discrepancies, most programs must be maintained on a continuous basis. When we talk about "maintaining" a program we are referring to the periodic changes necessary to meet these important needs. Program maintenance is often regarded as a rather unglamorous occupation. However, it provides employment for perhaps 60 percent of all the professional programmers now working in the United States.

New words and phrases

(1) phase [feiz] n. 阶段，相位
(2) consistent [kən'sistənt] adj. 一致的
(3) program specifications 程序设计规范
(4) unambiguous [ˌʌnæm'bigjuəs] adj. 明确的，清楚的
(5) employ [im'plɔi] v. 使用，雇用
(6) subtask ['sʌbtɑːsk] n. 子任务
(7) flowchart ['fləuˌtʃɑːt] n. 程序图，流程图
(8) component [kəm'pəunənt] n. 组成，成分，adj. 组成的，构成的
(9) appropriate [ə'prəuprieit] adj. 适当的
(10) assignment [ə'sainmənt] n. 任务，作业
(11) detect [di'tekt] v. 发现
(12) FORTRAN ['fɔːtræn] n. 一种计算机编程语言
(13) essentially [i'senʃəli] adv. 主要地，本质上
(14) debug [diː'bʌg] v. 调试；n. 调试工具

(15) release [ri'li:s] n. /v. 释放，解除，发布，发表
(16) subsequent ['sʌbsikwənt] adj. 后来的
(17) discrepancy [dis'krepənsi] n. 差异，差别
(18) periodic [ˌpiəri'ɔdik] adj. 定期的，周期的
(19) unglamorous [ʌn'glæmərəs] adj. 乏味的，无味的
(20) occupation [ˌɔkju'peiʃən] n. 职业
(21) serve as 作为，用于
(22) in advance 事先，提前
(23) in practice 实际上

Notes

(1) These specifications are intended to serve as is supposed to accomplish when it becomes operational.

目的是使这些设计规范可作为开发程序的各方共同遵守协议的基础，在运行过程时作为软件产品开发必须完成的工作内容。specifications 指设计规范、规格，to serve as（作为……之用），concerned as to 相当 be concerned about/as to（有关的），what 引导介词 to 的宾语从句，be supposed to（必需的），when 引导时间状语从句。

(2) In the second phase the programmers and the design engineers determine what types of… and how the various subtasks will be carried out by the professional staff.

在第二个阶段，程序员和设计工程师要决定使用什么样的硬件设备，采用什么样的编程语言及专业人员，如何来实现子任务。phase（阶段，时期），由两个 what 引导和一个 how 引导的三个并列的宾语从句作 determine 的宾语，从句都采用被动语态，subtasks（子任务），前缀 sub-表示子、次、下之意，be carried out by…（被……执行），professional staff 在这里指设计人员。

(3) We often regard the coding phase as being the primary assignment of the professional programmer, but actually, coding typically consumes only about one sixth of the programmer's time and effort.

我们往往把编程阶段看作是专业程序员的基本任务，而事实上，编程工作大约只占程序员六分之一的时间和精力。Regard…as…（把……看作……），actually 相当于 virtually，effort（努力）在这里译为"精力"。

Lesson 2 Database Technologies

Many computer applications require that data be stored for subsequent processing. Simple storing the data is not enough, however. A typical computer system, even a small one, can have dozens of disks and tapes, each holding data for dozens of different applications. For any given application, one and only one set of data will do. We must be able to store, locate, and retrieve the specific data needed by a given program. That is the concern of data management.

There are problems with traditional data management. Many result from viewing applications independently. For example, consider payroll, most organizations prepare their payrolls by computer because using a machine instead of a small army of clerks saves money. Thus, the firm develops a payroll program to process a payroll file. Inventory, accounts receivable, accounts payable, and general ledger analysis are similar applications, so the firm develops an inventory program, an inventory file, an accounts receivable program, an accounts receivable file, and so on. (1) Each program is independent, and each processes its own independent data file.

Why this is a problem? For one thing, different applications often need the same data elements. For example, schools generate both bills and student grade reports. Viewing the applications independently, the billing program reads a file of billing data, and the grade report program reads an independent file of grade data. The outputs of both programs are mailed to each student's home; thus, student names and addresses must be redundantly recorded on both files. What happens when a student moves? Unless both files are updated, one will be wrong. Redundant data are difficult to maintain.

A subtler problem is data dependency. Each access method has its own rules for storing and retrieving data, and certain "tricks of the trade" can significantly improve the efficiency of a given program. (2) Because the motivation for using the computer is saving money, the programmer is often tempted to save even more by taking advantage of these efficiencies. Thus, the program's logic becomes dependent upon the physical structure of the data. When a program's logic is tied to its physical data structure, changing that structure will almost certainly require changing the program. (3) As a result, program's using traditional access methods can be difficult to maintain.

The solution to both problems is often organizing the data as a single, integrated database. The task of controlling access to all the data can then be concentrated in a centralized database management system.

How does the use of a centralized database solve the data redundancy problems. All data are collected and stored in a single place; consequently, there is one and only one copy of any given data element. When the value of an element changes the single database copy is corrected. Any program requiring access to this data element gets the same value, because there is only one value.

How does a database help to solve the data dependency problem? Since the responsibility for accessing the physical data rests with the database management system, the programmer can ignore the physical data structure. (4) As a result, programs tend to be much less dependent upon their data, and are generally much easier to maintain. Expectatively the trend toward database management is to continue.

New words and phrases

(1) retrieve [ri'tri:v] v. 检索
(2) payroll ['peirəul] n. 工资单（表）
(3) inventory ['invəntəri] n. 产品目录，存货
(4) ledger ['ledʒə] n. 分类账
(5) redundant [ri'dʌndənt] adj. 冗余的，多余的

(6) subtler ['sʌtl] adj. 微微的；隐约的，模模糊糊的
(7) update [ʌp'deit] v. 更新
(8) tricks of the trade 行业技巧
(9) centralized ['sentrəlaizd] adj. 集中的，中央集权的
(10) centralized database management system 中央数据库管理系统
(11) shielding ['ʃi:ldiŋ] adj. 屏蔽的，防护层的
(12) administrator [əd'ministreitə] n. 管理员，行政人员
(13) schema ['ski:mə] n. 计划，方案
(14) mapping ['mæpiŋ] v. 映射
(15) logical view 逻辑视图
(16) layout ['leiaut] n. 布局，版面，格式
(17) accuracy ['ækjurəsi] n. 精确度
(18) competition [,kɔmpi'tiʃən] n. 竞争
(19) feedback ['fi:dbæk] n. 反馈
(20) formidable ['fɔ:midəbl] adj. 艰难的，令人敬畏的
(21) decision-making [di'siʒən,meikiŋ] adj. 决策的
(22) be concerned about 关心
(23) be tempted + to v. 受到诱惑
(24) take advantage of 利用
(25) rest with 取决于，由……负责，归于……

Notes

(1) Inventory, accounts receivable, accounts payable, and general ledger analysis are similar applications, so the firm develops an inventory program, an inventory file, an accounts receivable program, an accounts receivable file, and so on.

存货清单、收入账、支出账和一般分类账分析的应用都与工资单相类似，于是，公司又开发了清单程序、清单文件、收入账程序、收入账文件等等。inventory, accounts receivable, accounts payable, and general ledger 分别指存货清单、收入账、支出账和一般分类账。

(2) Each access method has its own rules for storing and retrieving data, and certain "tricks of the trade" can significantly improve the efficiency of a given program.

为了存贮和检索数据，每种存取方法都有自己的规律，某些数据管理技巧能够极大地改善一个给定程序的效率。certain "tricks of the trade" 指某些数据管理技巧，trade 指用户与计算机进行数据交换；a given program 译成：一个给定的程序。

(3) When a program's logic is tied to its physical data structure, changing that structure will almost certainly require changing the program.

当程序的逻辑结构受到它的物理数据结构的约束时，改变数据结构肯定需要改变程序。be tied to…译为：受到……的约束，主句的主语是分词短语 changing that structure。

(4) How does a database help to solve the data dependency problem? Since the

responsibility for accessing the physical data rests with the database management system, the programmer can ignore the physical data structure.

  数据库又是如何协助解决数据依赖性问题呢？由于数据库管理系统负责存取物理数据，因此，程序员就可不考虑物理数据结构。Since 引导一个原因状语从句，responsibility for 译为：职责，任务；accessing the physical data 译为：访问物理数据；rest with 取决于，由…负责；database management system 译为：数据库管理系统，physical data structure 译为：物理数据结构。

第12章 Information and Network Technology

12.1 Intensive Reading

Lesson 1 GPS

1. Introduction

Global Positioning System (GPS) is a space-based radio navigation system, consisting of 24 satellites and ground support. GPS provides users with accurate information about their position and velocity, as well as the time, anywhere in the world and all weather conditions.

2. History and Development

GPS was initiated in 1973. By creating a system that overcame the limitations of many existing navigation systems, GPS became attractive to a wide range of users. GPS has been successful in classical navigation applications, and because it can use small, inexpensive equipment, GPS has also been used in many new applications.

3. How to Work

GPS determines location by computing the difference between the time a signal is sent and the time it is received. [1] GPS satellites carry atomic clocks that provide extremely accurate time. The time information is placed in codes broadcasted by the satellites so that a receiver can continuously determine the time of signal broadcasted. The signal contains data that a receiver uses to compute the locations of the satellites and to make other adjustments needed for accurate positioning. The receiver uses the difference between the time of signal reception and the time of broadcast to compute the distance, or range from the receiver to the satellite. The receiver must account for propagation delays, or decreases in the signal's speed caused by the ionosphere and troposphere. [2] With information about the ranges to three satellites and location of the satellite when the signal was sent, receiver can compute its own three-dimensional position.

An atomic clock synchronized to GPS is required to compute ranges from these three signals. [3] However, by taking a measurement from a fourth satellite, the receiver avoids the need for an atomic clock. Thus the receiver uses the fourth satellite to compute latitude, longitude, altitude, and time.

New words and phrases

(1) GPS (global positioning system)   全球定位系统
(2) radio navigation   无线电导航

(3) satellite ['sætəlait] n. 卫星
(4) accurate ['ækjurət] adj. 正确的
(5) velocity [vi'lɔsəti] n. 速度，速率
(6) initiate [i'niʃieit] v. 创始，开始
(7) overcome [,əuvə'kʌm] v. 战胜，克服
(8) propagation [,prɔpə'geiʃən] n.（电磁波）传播
(9) ionosphere [ai'ɔnə,sfiə] n. 电离层
(10) troposphere ['trɔpəusfiə] n. 对流层
(11) three-dimensional ['θri:di'menʃənəl] adj. 三维的，立体的
(12) synchronize ['siŋkrənaiz] vt. 同步
(13) latitude ['lætitju:d] n. 纬度
(14) longitude ['lɔndʒitju:d] n. 经度
(15) altitude ['æltitju:d] n.（海拔）高度
(16) consist of… 由……组成
(17) provide…with… 提供……
(18) a wide range of… 广泛的……
(19) account for… 计算，说明，占……

Notes

(1) GPS determines location by computing the difference between the time a signal is sent and the time it is received.

GPS 的工作原理是通过计算信号发送与接收的时间差来定位。difference between…and…，两者之间的差异（区别），the time a signal is sent 指信号发送的时间，and 连接两个并列句，the time it is received 指信号接收的时间，it 指 a signal。

(2) The receiver must account for propagation delays, or decreases in the signal's speed caused by the ionosphere and troposphere.

接收机还应考虑电离层和对流层造成传输延迟或信号传播速度衰减的影响。account for 这里的意思是解释，计算，说明，可译为：考虑；caused by the ionosphere and troposphere 译为：电离层和对流层造成的影响。

(3) An atomic clock synchronized to GPS is required to compute ranges from these three signals.

为通过三种不同卫星信号来定位，原子钟必须与 GPS 同步。to compute ranges from these three signals 是一个目的状语在翻译时往往先译，主句为被动语态，翻译时译成主动语态。

Exercises

I. 将下列术语和句子译成中文

1. GPS, radio navigation system, atomic clock, receiver, three-dimensional position, latitude, longitude, altitude

2. Global Positioning System (GPS) is a space-based radio navigation system, consisting of 24 satellites and ground support.

3. By creating a system that overcame the limitations of many existing navigation systems, GPS became attractive to a wide range of users.

4. The time information is placed in codes broadcasted by the satellites so that a receiver can continuously determine the time of signal broadcasted.

5. However, by taking a measurement from a fourth satellite, the receiver avoids the need for an atomic clock.

Ⅱ. 根据课文填空

1. Global Positioning System (GPS) is a space-based radio navigation system, consisting of 24 _____ and ground support.

2. GPS was initiated in 1973. By creating a system that overcame the limitations of many existing _____.

3. GPS became attractive to a wide range _____ users.

4. GPS determines location by computing the _____ between the time a signal is sent and the time it is received.

5. The time information is placed in codes broadcasted by the satellites so _____ a receiver can continuously determine the time of signal broadcasted.

6. The receiver uses the difference between the time of signal reception and the broadcast time to compute the distance, or range _____ the receiver to satellite.

7. The signal contains data that a receiver uses to compute the _____ of the satellites and to make other adjustments needed for accurate positioning.

8. The receiver must account _____ propagation delays, or decreases in the signal's speed caused by the ionosphere and troposphere.

9. when the signal was _____, receiver can compute its own three-dimensional position.

10. Thus the receiver uses four satellites to compute latitude, _____, altitude, and time.

Ⅲ. 将下列句子译成英语

1. 全球定位系统由24颗卫星和地面机站组成。
2. 全球定位系统能为用户提供其精确的位置信息。
3. 全球定位系统成为了广大用户的青睐。
4. 接收机通过信号接收与信号传播的时间差来计算距离。
5. 接收机通过第四颗卫星计算出经度、纬度、海拔高度以及时间。

Lesson 2　Electronic Mail

The most widely used tool on the internet is electronic mail, or E-mail. E-mail is used to send written messages between individuals or groups of individuals, often geographically separated by large distances. [1] E-mail messages are generally sent and received by mail servers—computers that are dedicated to processing and directing E-mail. Once a server has received a message, it will direct the message to the specific computer that the E-mail is addressed to.(2) To send E-mail, the process is reversed. In a very convenient and inexpensive way to transmit messages, E-mail has dramatically affected scientific, personal, and business communications.

E-mail is the basis of much organized exchange between groups of individuals. List servers, for example, make it possible to address a list of subscribers either in one-way communication, as in keeping interested people up-to-date on a product, or two-way communication, as in online discussion groups.(3)

Another use of E-mail is Usenet, in which discussions on a particular subject are grouped together into newsgroups. There are thousands of newsgroups covering an extremely wide range of subjects. Messages to a newsgroup are not posted directly to the user, but are accessible in the form of an ordered list on a dedicated local news server. The networking of these servers makes such discussions available worldwide. Associated software not only enables users to choose messages which they want to read, but also replies to them by posting messages to the newsgroup.(4)

New Words and Phrases

(1) individual　　[ˌindiˈvidjuəl]　n. 个人，个体
(2) geographical　　[dʒiəˈgræfikəl]　adj. 地理的，地域的
(3) inexpensive　　[ˈiniksˈpensiv]　adj. 不贵的，廉价的
(4) up-to-date　　[ˈʌptəˈdeit]　adj. 当代的，现代的，最新的
(5) accessible　　[əkˈsesəbl]　adj. 可接近的，可进入的，可到达的
(6) two-way　　[ˈtuːˈwei]　adj. 双向的
(7) dedicated　　[ˈdedikeitid]　adj. 专注的，献身的
(8) available　　[əˈveiləbl]　adj. 可得到的，可利用的
(9) dramatically　　[drəˈmætikəli]　adv. 引人注目的，非常大的
(10) subscriber　　[səbˈskraibə]　n. 订户
(11) Usenet　　[juːznet]　n. 世界新闻网络系统
(12) post　　[pəust]　n. 邮件；v. 邮递
(13) worldwide　　[ˈwəːldˌwaid]　adj. 全世界的，世界范围的
(14) an extremely wide range of　　非常广泛的

Notes

(1) E-mail is used to send written messages between individuals or groups of individuals, often geographically separated by large distances.

电子邮件常用来在地理位置很远的个人之间或团体之间发送信息。often geographically separated by large distances = often spatially separated by long distances，指远距离或空间距离较远的两者之间的通讯。

(2) Once a server has received a message, it will direct the message to the specific computer that the E-mail is addressed to.

第 12 章　Information and Network Technology

服务器一收到信息，就把该信息传送到邮件应到达的特定计算机上去。Once，一旦，引导一个条件从句，that the E-mail is addressed to 是一个定语从句，修饰 the specific computer。

（3）List servers, for example, make it possible to address a list of subscribers either in one-way communication, as in keeping interested people up-to-date on a product, or two-way communication, as in online discussion groups.

例如：数据服务器使寻找订户清单成为可能，既可以用单向通信，以保持人们对最新产品的感兴趣，也可以在线讨论中进行双向通信。List server 指用于数据或货物清单管理的服务器，在句中作主语，make it possible 译为：使之成为可能，it 指不定式短语：to address a list of subscriber，寻找订户清单，one（two）-way communication，译为：单（双）向通讯，up-to-date 最新的，新式的，online discussion 译为：在线讨论。

（4）Associated software not only enables users to choose messages which hey want to read, but also replies to them by posting messages to the newsgroup.

相关软件不仅使用户可以选择他们想读的信息，而且可以通过将信息发送到新闻组的方式加以回复。not only…but also，不仅，而且；which hey want to read 是一个定语从句，修饰 messages。

Exercises

Ⅰ．将下列术语与句子译成英语

1. 电子邮件、世界新闻网络系统、互联网、万维网、企业内联网、网址、数据库、服务器、客户端
2. 电子邮件常用来于远距离个人之间或团体之间发送信息。
3. 这些服务器的联网使全世界范围内的用户均可参与这种讨论。

Ⅱ．根据课文选择填空

1. E-mail messages are generally sent and received by _____.
   A. mail servers　　B. database　　C. client　　D. relay station

2. A very convenient and _____ way to transmit messages, E-mail has dramatically affected scientific, personal, and business communications.
   A. expensive　　B. speed　　C. inexpensive　　D. effective

3. List servers, for example, make it possible to address a list of subscribers either in one-way communication, as in keeping interested people up-to-date on a product, _____ two-way communication, as in online discussion groups.
   A. nor　　B. or　　C. and　　D. with

4. Another use of E-mail is Usenet, _____ discussions on a particular subject are grouped together into newsgroups.
   A. which　　B. in which　　C. that　　D. on which

5. Messages to a newsgroup are not posted directly to the user, but are accessible in the _____ of an ordered list on a dedicated local news server.
   A. model　　B. size　　C. format　　D. form

Ⅲ. 下列短文译成中文

Once a server has received a message, it will direct the message to the specific computer that the E-mail is addressed to. To send E-mail, the process is reversed. In a very convenient and inexpensive way to transmit messages, E-mail has dramatically affected scientific, personal, and business communications.

Lesson 3　Network Security Problems

Any one who is responsible for the security of a trusted network will be concerned when connecting it to a distrusted network. In the case of connections to the internet, this concern may be based largely on anecdotal evidence gleaned from widespread media coverage of security breaches. A closer inspection of the facts and statistics behind, some of the media coverage will, however, only serve to deepen that concern. For example, the US National Computer Security Agency (NCSA) asserts that most attacks to computer systems go undetected and unreported, citing attacks made against 9000 Department of Defense computers by the US Defense Information Systems Agency (DISA). These attacks had an 88 percent success rate and went undetected by more than 95 percent of the target organizations. Only 5 percent of that detected an attack, a mere 22 sites, reacted to it.

It is noteworthy that these sites belong to the US Department of Defense (DOD) and were not commercial sites, which may give security less priority than the DOD. (1)

NCSA also quoted the FBI as reporting that in more than 80 percent of FBI investigated computer crimes, unauthorized access was gained through the Internet.

Putting a value on the damage done by such attacks is difficult but a 1995 survey conducted by Ernst & Young, a New York based accounting firm, reported that one third of businesses connected to the Internet reported up to 100 000 USD in financial loss over a two-year period due to malicious acts by computer users outside the firm. (2) A little more than two percent of connected companies reported losses of more than 1M USD.

There is amazement in the computer security industry at the level of ignorance to the problem. To understand the risks often involves a steep learning curve and they have few real parallels in everyday life, for example nobody worries that a burglar will be able to trick their front door into opening by posting cryptic messages through the letterbox. When there is a good "hacker" story to report the press goes into frenzy, but the general level of awareness is still surprisingly low. For example the Sunday Times which prides itself on providing accurate coverage of IT issues published an article recently that claimed that most businesses worry too much about Internet security. (3) The article goes on to explain that encryption is all that is needed to be completely secure. The article focuses purely on privacy of communication and completely misses the possibility of an attack originating from the Internet.

Despite fears about security, organizations are increasingly coming to regard a presence on the Internet as an important part of their strategic planning. (4) Security concerns will not be allowed to prevent organizations from exploiting the commercial opportunities the Internet is perceived to offer. As a result, organizations have to find ways to manage the security issue. This ties growth in the Internet security market directly to growth in the Internet. The compound annual growth rate of the Internet firewall market between 1995 and 2000 is projected to be 174% driven by rapid growth of both the Internet, and Intranets. The most significant trend driving this growth is the rapid and aggressive deployment of World Wide Web servers for both Internet and Intranet use. Unit shipments of web server software are expected to grow from 127 000 units in 1995 to just more than 5 million units in 2000. Although the IT industry has traditionally enjoyed rapid development, this level of growth is unprecedented.

It is difficult to separate figures for the European or UK's firewall markets from the world wide statistics quoted in the literature. 1996 may see similar levels of activity in Europe and the UK to those seen in the USA in 1995. A 1995 survey of government agencies and Fortune 500 companies conducted by the Computer Security Institute found that while 78% of respondents used the Internet, 39% did not have a firewall. Similarly 40% of the audience at a February 1996 NSCA conference devoted to firewalls and Internet security did not have a firewall. Given that approximately 40% of the Fortune 500 companies using the Internet have still to install a firewall and that the Internet continues to double annually, it is little surprise that the security auditing business is booming. [5] Organizations are finding that they do not have the in-house skills or knowledge necessary to assess either the current situation or the potential risks, and are wrestling with what level of security they require. [6]

New words and phrases

(1) anecdotal [,ænik'dəutəl] *adj.* 轶事的，轶话的
(2) widespread ['waid'spred] *adj.* 广泛传播的
(3) glean [gli:n] *v.* 收集
(4) media coverage 媒体报道
(5) NCSA *n.* 美国国家计算机安全局
(6) DISA *n.* 美国国防部信息系统局
(7) DOD *n.* 美国国防部
(8) FBI *n.* 美国联邦调查局
(9) Sunday Times *n.* 星期日时报
(10) Intranet ['intrənet] *n.* 企业内部局域网
(11) hacker ['hækə] *n.* 黑客，
(12) firewall ['faiəwɔ:l] *n.* 防火墙.
(13) encryption [in'kripʃən] *n.* 加密，编码
(14) belong to… 属于……
(15) due to… 由于……
(16) be driven by… 受……驱动（使）
(17) regard…as… 把……当作……，认为是……
(18) prevent from… 阻止（碍）……

(19) be wrestling with… 对……热衷，与……格斗（较劲）

Notes

(1) It is noteworthy that these sites belong to the US Department of Defense (DOD) and were not commercial sites, which may give security less priority than the DOD.

值得注意的是，这些网站属于美国国防部，而不是商业网站，商业网站的安全级别低于美国国防部的网站。

It 是形式主语，that 引导主语从句，It is noteworthy that…，译为值得注意的是……，belong to…，属于……，the US Department of Defense 指美国国防部，which 引导一个非限定性定语从句，修饰 sites，less priority than…，低于……优先权。

(2) Putting a value on the damage done by such attacks is difficult, but a 1995 survey conducted by Ernst & Young, a New York based accounting firm, reported that one third of businesses connected to the Internet reported up to 100 000 USD in financial loss over a two-year period due to malicious acts by computer users outside the firm.

这些攻击造成的损失是难以估量的，Ernst&Young 1995 年的调查显示，一个纽约的会计公司，由于公司外计算机用户的恶意操作，三分之一的交易连接在互联网上，两年内财政损失超过 100 000 美元。

本句的主要语言特点是过去分词短语作定语修饰前面的名词。如：done by…，修饰 damage，conducted by …，修饰 survey；Putting a value on the damage done by such attacks 是 is 的主语，译为：这些攻击造成的损失，a New York based accounting firm，译为：一个纽约的会计公司，作为 reported 的主语，that 引导一个宾语从句，due to malicious acts，由于恶意操作。

(3) For example the Sunday Times which prides itself on providing accurate coverage of IT issues published an article recently that claimed that most businesses don't worry too much about Internet security.

例如，以准确报道 IT 主题而自诩的《星期日时报》最近发表一篇文章声称，大多数商家并不太担忧互联网的安全问题。

这是一个比较复杂的句子，该复合句可简化为一个简单句：the Sunday Times published an article recently. 由 which 引导一个定语从句，修饰 the Sunday Times，这是一个报道信息技术产业的报刊，第一个 that 引导一个定语从句，修饰 an article，第二个 that 引导的是动词 claimed 的宾语从句。

(4) Despite fears about security, organizations are increasingly coming to regard a presence on the Internet as an important part of their strategic planning.

尽管对安全问题有所恐惧，但还是有许多组织把进入互联网作为它们战略计划的一个重要组成部分。

句中 Despite，相当于 in spite of，organizations 指公司或企业等单位，regard…as…，译为：将（把）……看作为……。

(5) Given that approximately 40% of the Fortune 500 companies using the Internet have still to install a firewall and that the Internet continues to double annually, it is little surprise that

the security auditing business is booming.

假如财富 500 强中使用互联网的公司中约 40% 将不得不安装防火墙，而且互联网将持续每年翻番增长的话，人们对安全检查业务将会爆炸性增长的事实感到不足为奇了。

句中 given that…，表示：假如，引导一个条件从句，approximately 相当于 about，大约，the Fortune 500 companies，指世界财富 500 强企业，using the Internet 是一个分词短语，后置定语，修饰 companies，it is little surprise that…，that 引导主语从句，译为：不足为奇。

(6) Organizations are finding that they do not have the in-house skills or knowledge necessary to assess either the current situation or the potential risks, and are wrestling with what level of security they require.

组织发现现在他们缺乏必要的内部技术和知识来评估目前所处的状态或潜在的风险，对于它们所需要的安全级别也在不断地探索中。

句中的 to assess either the current situation or the potential risks 是不定式短语，作目的状语，译为：评估目前所处的状态或潜在的风险，be wrestling with…，对……热忱，有积极性，意指对……研究和探索。

Exercises

Ⅰ. 将下列术语和句子译成中文

1. the US National Computer Security Agency (NCSA), the US Defense Information Systems Agency (DISA), FBI, IT, letterbox, hacker, firewall, World Wide Web server

2. NCSA also quoted the FBI as reporting that in more than 80 percent of FBI investigated computer crimes, unauthorized access was gained through the Internet.

3. The article focuses purely on privacy of communication and completely misses the possibility of an attack originating from the Internet.

4. Security concerns will not be allowed to prevent organizations from exploiting the commercial opportunities the Internet is perceived to offer.

5. It is difficult to separate figures for the European or UK's firewall markets from the world wide statistics quoted in the literature.

Ⅱ. 根据课文填空

It is noteworthy __1__ these sites belong to the US Department of Defense (DOD) and were not commercial sites, __2__ may give security less priority __3__ the DOD.

NCSA also quoted the FBI as reporting that in more than 80 percent of FBI investigated computer crimes, __4__ access was gained through the Internet.

Security concerns will not be allowed to prevent organizations __5__ exploiting the commercial opportunities the Internet is perceived to offer. __6__ a result organizations have to find ways to manage the security issue. This ties growth in the Internet security market directly to growth in the Internet. The compound annual growth rate of the Internet firewall market between 1995 __7__ 2000 is projected to be 174% driven by rapid growth of both the Internet and __8__. The most significant trend driving this growth is the rapid and aggressive deployment of World Wide __9__ servers for both Internet and Intranet use. Unit shipments of web server software are expected to grow from 127 000 units in 1995 to just more than 5 million ___10___ in 2000. Although the IT industry has traditionally enjoyed rapid development, this level of growth is unprecedented.

Ⅲ. 将下列句子译成英文
1. 黑客攻击的损失难以估价。
2. 假设财富500强中使用互联网的公司中约40%将不得不安装防火墙。
3. 人们对安全检查的业务将会快速发展感到不足为奇了。
4. 国际互联网防火墙市场每年增长率有望达到174%。
5. 很难评估互联网安全的潜在风险。

Lesson 4 Digital Television and Flat Television

Ever since Philo T. Farnsworth put together the first television set in his Indiana, garage in 1927; the basic technological principles for bringing electronic pictures into the home have remained the same. There have been only two major changes in the way that TV sets work: the introduction of color in 1954, and the change from tubes to transistors in the 1970s. Now a thorough change is about to take place, digital television which uses a different method of signal transmission will significantly change the way that future television sets will look and perform.[1]

Tile digital set, already on sale in Europe and planned to be introduced to the United States this fall, is a cross between a computer terminal and a TV set. Although the differences it will bring may not be dramatic, its improved quality will be increasingly appreciated, as zoom effects, stereo sound, and freeze-frame views of live shows become commonplace.[2] Digital TV promises to give viewers a clearer, more consistent picture than has been available so far.

Since the 1950s, nearly all-electronic products have been getting steadily smaller. Calculators now slide into checkbooks, stereo speakers no larger than bricks pack an audio wallop and compact discs have compressed the record industry.[3] Through it all, the beloved television set has remained bulky mainly because one of its primary components, the cathode ray picture tube, has proved difficult, and uneconomical, to shrink. But a recent breakthrough by a small in the US, semiconductor company may hasten the development of large size flat TV, computer and other video screens a goal electronics firms have been eyeing for years.

MRS Technology Inc. has developed a lithographic production system specifically for the high volume manufacture of flat panel, active matrix liquid crystal displays.[4] The Model, 4500 Panel Printer, as the machine is called, can make one inch-thick, color LCD screens up to 18 inches diagonal in size. They weigh only a few pounds and could be hung on a wall like a painting. MRS claims this is the first cost effective manufacturing process of its kind, and that because of it, conventional-size active matrix screens may reach the marketplace in the near future. "The change will not happen overnight", explains William Schneider, vice president of marketing for MRS. But you'll start to see them in about a year and I expect them to take over the market for 10 years. A lot of people have spent a lot of money trying to make this happen.

第 12 章 Information and Network Technology

New words and phrases

(1) digital ['didʒitəl] adj. 数字（式）的
(2) Indiana [ˌindi'ænə] n. 印第安纳（州）
(3) garage ['gɑrɑːdʒ] n. （汽）车库，（飞）机库
(4) fall [fɔːl] n. 秋季
(5) cross [krɔs] n. 十字，交叉，杂交，混合种
(6) dramatic [drə'mætik] adj. 戏剧（性）的；惊人的，奇迹般的
(7) zoom [zuːm] v. n. 图像（电子）放大；变焦距
(8) freeze-frame ['friːz'freim] n. （图像）定格
(9) steadily ['stedili] adv. 不断地，稳定地
(10) slide [slaid] (slid, slid 或 slidden) v. （使）滑，（使）溜
(11) checkbook ['tʃekbuk] n. 支票簿，存折
(12) pack [pæk] v. 填塞，堆积
(13) audio ['ɔːdiəu] adj. 声［音］频的，听觉的
(14) wallop ['wɔləp] n. 乐趣，快感
(15) bulky ['bʌlki] adj. 体积（庞）大的，笨重的
(16) uneconomical ['ʌnˌiːkə'nɔmikəl] adj. 不经济的
(17) shrink [ʃriŋk] v. （使）收缩，缩小
(18) hasten ['heisən] v. （使）加紧；促进，加速
(19) goal [gəul] n. 目的［标］
(20) Inc. = incorporated n. 股份有限公司
(21) panel ['pænl] n. 板，仪表板；小组（委员会）
(22) flat-panel [flæt'pænl] n. 平板
(23) matrix ['meitriks] n. 矩阵
(24) active-matrix ['æktiv'meitriks] n. 有源矩阵
(25) liquid-crystal display （LCD） 液晶显示器
(26) diagonal [dai'ægənəl] adj. 对角线（的）
(27) claim [kleim] v. 要求，索赔；断言
(28) cost-effective ['kɔsti'fektiv] adj. 经济的，划算的，效益的
(29) marketplace ['mɑːkitpleis] n. 市场
(30) overnight [ˌəuvə'nait] adv. 一夜之间，很快地
(31) slide into 溜进……内

Notes

(1) Now a thorough change is about to take place, digital television which uses a different method of signal transmission will significantly change the way that future television sets will look and perform.

现在即将发生一个深刻的变革，这就是数字电视。数字电视利用不同方式进行信号传

输,将会大大改变未来电视机的画面及工作方式。

句中 be about to + V. 表示将来的意思,这里相当于 will + V., take place, 发生, which 引导一个定语从句,修饰 digital television, 由 that 引导的是 way 的同位语从句, future television sets will look and perform, 译为:未来电视机的画面和工作方式。

(2) Although the differences it will bring may not be dramatic, its improved quality will be increasingly appreciated, as zoom effects, stereo sound, and freeze-frame views of live shows become commonplace.

虽然它产生的差异也许不是惊人的,但随着其质量的改进将会使现场直播的变焦效果、立体声以及定格景观等成为平常的事。

Although 引导一个状语从句,句子 it will bring 修饰:the differences,句子 its improved quality will be increasingly appreciated, 意指:数字电视质量的改善带来增值的效果,也就是产生画面质量的提高。freeze-frame views 指直播画面定格。

(3) Calculators now slide into checkbooks, stereo speakers no larger than bricks pack an audio wallop and compact discs have compressed the record industry.

计算器可以放进支票簿内,比砖块还小的立体声扬声器能产生出巨大的音响效果,唱片工业能够生产高密度的唱片。

句中 slide into…, 滑(溜)进……, 指放入, stereo speaker, 立体声扬声器, an audio wallop 指巨大的音响效果, the record industry 指唱片工业, compact discs have compressed the record industry, 意指:唱片工业能够生产高密度的唱片。

(4) MRS Technology Inc. has developed a lithographic production system specifically for the high volume manufacture of flat panel, active matrix liquid crystal displays.

MRS 技术股份有限公司研制出了一种平板印刷系统,该系统专门用于大量制造平板有源矩阵液晶显示器。

a lithographic production system, 译为:一种平板印刷系统, flat panel 是指平板显示器, active matrix liquid crystal displays, 译为:有源矩阵液晶显示器,是 flat panel 的同位语。

Exercises

I. 将下列术语和句子译成英文

1. 数字电视、平板电视、液晶显示器、信号传输、立体声扬声器、显像管、半导体、视频、音频。
2. 电视机的工作方式只发生了两个重大的变化。
3. 数字电视在欧洲已上市,并计划于今年秋季引入美国。
4. 半导体公司可能会加快大尺寸平板电视的研制。
5. 平板电视的重量只有几英磅,可以像油画一样挂在墙壁上。

II. 根据课文选择填空

There have been only two major changes in the way that TV sets work: the ___1___ of color in 1954, and the change from tubes to ___2___ in the 1970s. Now a thorough change is about to take ___3___, digital television ___4___ uses a different method of signal transmission will significantly change the way that future television sets will look and perform.

Tile digital set, already __5__ sale in Europe and planned to be introduced to the United States this fall, is a cross __6__ a computer terminal and a TV set. Although the differences it will bring may not be dramatic, its improved quality will be increasingly appreciated, as zoom effects, stereo sound, and freeze-frame __7__ of live shows become commonplace. Digital TV promises to give viewers a clearer, more consistent picture than has been __8__ so far.

Since the 1950s, nearly all-electronic products have been getting steadily smaller. Calculators now slide __9__ checkbooks, stereo speakers no larger than bricks pack an audio wallop and compact discs have __10__ the record industry.

( ) 1. A. introduction   B. development   C. sale   D. improvement
( ) 2. A. semiconductor   B. transistors   C. LED   D. screen
( ) 3. A. place   B. replace   C. off   D. away
( ) 4. A. in which   B. how   C. which   D. what
( ) 5. A. off   B. by   C. in   D. on
( ) 6. A. from   B. both   C. between   D. in
( ) 7. A. color   B. video   C. sound   D. views
( ) 8. A. possible   B. available   C. visible   D. unstable
( ) 9. A. onto   B. into   C. in   D. off
( ) 10. A. compressive   B. comprised   C. impressed   D. compressed

Ⅲ. 将下列短文译成中文

There have been only two major changes in the waythat TV sets work: the introduction of color in 1954, and the change from tubes to transistors in the 1970s. Now a thorough change is about to take place.

The Model, 4500 Panel Printer, as the machine is called, can make one inch-thick, color LCD screens up to 18 inches diagonal in size. Digital TV promises to give viewers a clearer, more consistent picture than has been available so far.

12.2 Extensive Reading

Lesson 1 The Application of Data Bus Technology

In recent years, the dataBus technology, a combination and integration of computer technology, network communication technology, control technology and conversion technology, has gradually been applied to large-tonnage cranes in China[1]. The application of data Bus technology can realize the transmission of data of engine, gearbox, steering gear and ABS system through data Bus, as well as fulfill the transmission and management of data among torque limiter system, single cylinder extension system, engine system and hydraulic pressure system and all the other transmission parts based on data Bus. The whole work process can be monitored through checkout gear and display unit for reading all kinds of operational status and information at real time [2]. The application of data Bus has simplified the connection of circuits and improved the efficiency and precision of data transmission [3]. Furthermore, it also has many extended functions.

New words and phrases

(1) data bus   数据总线
(2) combination   [ˌkɔmbi'neiʃən]   n. 结合，联合，合并
(3) network communication technology   网络通信技术
(4) conversion   [kən'və:ʃən]   n. 变换，转换
(5) transmission   [trænz'miʃən]   n. 传输，播送，传送
(6) gearbox   ['giəbɔks]   n. 变速箱，齿轮箱
(7) steering gear   转向操纵
(8) ABS system   自动刹车系统
(9) torque limiter system   力矩限制器系统
(10) cylinder   ['silində]   n. 油缸，气缸
(11) extension   [ik'stenʃən]   n. 延长，扩充
(12) monitor   ['mɔnitə]   v. 监视，监控
(13) checkout gear   检测设备，测量装置
(14) display   [ˌdis'plei]   v. 显示
(15) operational status   操作状态，运行情况
(16) simplify   ['simplifai]   v. 简化
(17) circuit   ['sə:kit]   n. 电路
(18) precision   [pri'siʒən]   n. 精度
(19) furthermore   ['fə:ðəmɔ:]   adv. 而且，此外
(20) extend   [ik'stend]   v. 扩充，延伸
(21) based on…   基于……
(22) at real time   实时

Notes

(1) In recent years, the data Bus technology, …, and conversion technology, has gradually been applied to large-tonnage cranes in China.

近年来，中国在大吨位起重机上已开始应用数据总线技术，该技术是计算机技术、网络通信技术、控制技术和转换技术的综合与集成。全句采用了完成被动式结构，主语是 the data Bus technology 总线技术，全句的主体结构是：the data Bus technology has gradually been applied to large-tonnage cranes in China，主语后面是插入语，由几个专业术语短语组成，combination and integration 译为：综合与集成。

(2) The whole work process can be monitored through checkout gear and display unit for reading all kinds of operational status and information at real time.

借助检测装置和显示装置可以对整个行驶和作业过程进行监控，实时显示各种状态和

信息。be monitored through…，译为：通过（借助）……监控，句子采用被动语态，checkout gear and display unit 译为：检测装置和显示装置。

(3) The application of data Bus has simplified the connection of circuits and improved the efficiency and precision of data transmission.

数据总线的应用大大简化了电气线路连接，提高了数据传输效率和精度。data Bus 数据总线技术是一种计算机通信技术，其中：Can、Bus 技术是应用较广的一种总线技术，该句子是由 and 连接的两个并列句，采用完成式，公共的主语是 the application of data Bus，数据总线技术的应用。

Lesson 2　Multimedia Technology

You know you have good reason to own a business strength PC at home. It helps you complete the work chores that otherwise would keep you burning the midnight oil back at the office. But what can you do with your home PC when you are not working? That is where multimedia comes in. It is relatively cheap and easy to add stereo sound, a CDROM drive and Windows to today's work at home PC. What you end up with, though, is something far more revolutionary than just a computer that talks, plays compact discs, and displays pretty pictures.[1] Your multimedia PC—MPC, for short—is the key to discovering books and encyclopedias that bring ideas to life through images and speech, games that match the quality and fun of the best entertainment, and software that unleashes your personal creativity in music, animation, and video.

Multimedia is a computer technology. Its applications involve the integrated processing of various types of data, like sound, images, full motion video, graphics, character data, and etc.. Now, multimedia applications have been developed for traditional uses like customer service, office automation (OA), and computer aided instruction (CAI). In the multimedia environment, we have graphics and text at the same time, we can also add photograph, animation, good-quality sound, and full motion video, development of the technologies make computers much more powerful and much easier to use.

The requirements for a MPC are described in detail in *Microsoft's Multimedia PC Specification Version* 1 0. Here are the key terms of the specifications.

FULL MOTION VIDEO: Full motion video is digitally recorded video played back at the broadcast standard of 30 frames per second, or closes enough to that speed so the video appears smooth rather than jerky.

MIDI: MIDI is short for Musical Intranet Digital Interface, a standard specification developed by music synthesizer manufacturers.[2] The concept of being able to control several instruments from one keyboard has grown into a method for putting musical instruments, tape recorders, VCRs, mixers, and even stage lighting under the control of a single computer.

New words and phrases

(1) multimedia　　[ˌmʌltiˈmiːdiə]　　*adj.* 多媒体的

(2) chore [tʃɔː] n. 任务，杂事
(3) relatively [ˈrelətivli] adv. 相对地
(4) stereo [ˈsteriˌəu] adj. 立体的，立体声的
(5) revolutionary [ˌrevəˈljuːʃənəri] adj. 革命性的
(6) compact disc 光盘
(7) encyclopedia [enˌsaikləuˈpiːdjə] n. 百科全书
(8) unleash [ˌʌnˈliːʃ] v. 解放，发挥
(9) involve [inˈvɔlv] v. 包括，涉及
(10) video [ˈvidiəu] adj. 视频（的）
(11) traditional [trəˈdiʃənəl] adj. 传统的
(12) animation [ˌæniˈmeiʃən] n. 动画
(13) specification [ˌspesifiˈkeiʃən] n. 规范
(14) jerky [ˈdʒəːki] adj. 急动的，不平稳的
(15) synthesizer [ˈsinθisaizə] n. 合成器
(16) keyboard [ˈkiːbɔːd] n. 键盘
(17) mixer [ˈmiksə] n. 混频器，混响器

Notes

(1) What you end up with, though, is something far more revolutionary than just a computer that talks, plays compact discs, and displays pretty pictures.

虽然，你最终得到的收获远比一台仅能说话、能播放光盘和能显示美丽图像的计算机更具有革命性。what 引导主语从句，谓语为 is，end up with（以……告终），far more than...（比……更为），that 引导定语从句，修饰 computer。

(2) MIDI is short for Musical Intranet Digital Interface, a standard specification developed by music synthesizer manufacturers.

MIDI 是乐器数字接口的缩写，它是由音乐合成器制造商开发的标准规范。is short for...（是由……缩短，缩略），a standard specification 由过去分词短语 developed by 来修饰，是 Musical Intranet Digital Interface 的同位语，developed by（由……开发的）。

参考译文及参考答案

第 7 章 机电一体化技术

7.1 精读

1 机电一体化

机电一体化技术并不是什么新事物，它是指把精密机械工程、控制理论、计算机技术和电子技术等领域的最新技术结合起来应用于设计过程中，以创造出功能更强，适应性更好的产品。当然，这也是很多具有超前思想的设计师和工程师多年来一直致力研究的事情。

如图 7.1 所示，机电一体化是一门由机械学、电子学、信息技术多学科融合的学科（不是简单的混合），目标是使工程师完成产品开发，这就是为什么机电一体化技术目前在工业上非常流行的原因。

1969 年 Yasukawa 电气公司的一位日本工程师杜撰出了这个新英文单词 "mechatronics"（机电一体化），来反映机械与电气工程学科的融合。直到 20 世纪 80 年代初期，机电一体化一直是指电气化的机械装置。在 20 世纪 80 年代中期，机电一体化产生了工程学，它是由机械学和电子学组成的边缘学科。现在，机电一体化包括了许多技术，这些技术都是各自领域知名的技术。每项技术仍然是以机械和电子技术的融合作为基础，但现在已包括了更多的技术特别是软件和信息技术。例如，由机械系统和电子系统产生的许多早期机器人已经成为机电一体化技术的核心。

机电一体化一词正式被学术界承认是在 1996 年出版的电气和电子工程师协会和美国机械工程师协会关于"机电一体化"会刊上。在第一期里，作者对机电一体化进行了定义。在承认关于机电一体化方面许多流行的定义后，人们选择了如下的一段收入了学报："机械工程和电子学及智能计算机控制相互促进的综合作用，应用于工业产品的设计和制造过程。"在这部分作者提出了机电一体化范畴至少包括11个方面：

- 建模与设计；
- 系统集成；
- 执行元件和传感器；
- 智能控制；
- 机器人技术；
- 制造加工；
- 运动控制；
- 振动和噪声控制；
- 微电子装置和光电子系统；

- 自动化系统；
- 其他应用。

Keys to the Exercises

I.
1. C 2. B 3. D 4. D 5. B 6. C 7. D 8. B 9. B 10. A

II.
1. 机电一体化是一门由机械学、电子学、信息技术多学科融合的学科（不是简单的混合），目标是使工程师完成产品开发，这就是为什么机电一体化技术目前在工业上非常流行的原因。
2. 在20世纪80年代中期，机电一体化产生了工程学，它是由机械学和电子学组成的边缘学科。
3. 例如，由机械系统和电子系统产生的许多早期机器人已经成为机电一体化的核心。

III.
1. mechatronics, electronics, mechanics, intelligent control, robotics, information technology, scientific term.
2. Mechatronics is the interdisciplinary of mechanics, electronics and information technology.
3. Robot is the evolutional outcome of mechatronics, which includes mechanics, electronics and Intelligent Control technology, etc..
4. Mechatronics has been applying widely to auto industry, mechanical industry and national defense industry.
5. Today, mechatronics has become the key technology of developing robots.

2 机械化和自动化

自从18世纪末工业革命开始，工业机械化进程一直在不断地发展，并且变得越来越复杂。但目前的工业自动化过程较以前的工业自动化过程有很大的不同。20世纪的工业自动化之所以有别于18、19世纪的机械化，是因为机械化仅应用于操纵（执行）机构，而自动化则涉及整个生产单元中的执行和控制两个（核心）部分。尽管不是所有的情况，但在大多数情况下，控制元件依然发挥着强大的力量，机械化已经代替了手工劳动，而自动化代替了脑力劳动。

机械化程度的发展在过去和现在的区别不是很明显，而在一端是具有强大辨别和控制功能的电子计算机，另一端是我们目前所说的"转换机构"正如传输带一样与其他设备简单地连接起来。自动调整机构能够自动调节系统，也就是说，它能在没有人干预和调整的情况下，自动对系统或生产过程进行控制和调节。现代工业技术的核心因素就是当前人们经常提起的反馈（控制），它是以自动调节系统为基础，借助于系统偏差与期望值之间的偏差来控制，可由自动检测、测量、显示和校正方法得到。反馈控制应用于高速运转的大型数字计算机进行复杂运算时，对于输入的复杂问题，计算机通常会一直运行，直到求出与问题匹配的结果。这或许与我们以前熟知的机器有很大的差别。同样的，反馈是我们所熟悉的机械概念。旧式的蒸汽机安装有离心传感器，控制杆上的两个球不停地绕立轴旋转，气压升高，发动机转速变快，旋转控制器速度增加，使立杆上升，关闭阀门，切断蒸汽，从而发动机恢复到合适的速度。

随着工业革命的出现，机械化也随之产生，由于这时的机械化仅局限于单个生产过程。因此，需要使用人工控制每部机器及装卸材料，并把材料从一个地方运到另一个地方。仅仅在很少的情况下，这些生产过程才能够自动地衔接起来，形成连续的产品生产线。

一般而言，从20世纪20年代以来，尽管现代工业已经实现了高度机械化，然而通常机械化的部分还没有联系在一起。机械化的工厂生产了光电灯泡、瓶子和大量生产的产品的元件，这些机械化工厂的自动化程度日益得到了加强。20世纪40年代电子计算机的发展，意味着在机械控制领域内将出现大量比计算机更简单、更廉价的产品。这些装置——机械装置、气动装置、液压装置，在近些年内已有了很大的发展，并将继续发展下去，普通的观点认为这有利于自动控制的发展。当然不仅仅电子设备对目前自动控制的发展举足轻重，无疑在今后自动控制发展方面还继续会发挥不可估量的作用。

Keys to the exercises

I.

1. ever since 2. from 3. in as much as 4. brain 5. without 6. of 7. with 8. to 9. in 10. than

II.

1. 工业革命，机械化和自动化，自我调节系统，反馈，大量生产的产品，液压控制，元件（部件），装载和卸载

2. 现代工业技术的核心因素就是当前人们经常提起的反馈（控制），它是以自动调节系统为基础，借助于系统偏差与期望值之间的偏差来控制，可由自动检测、测量、显示和校正方法得到。

3. 机械化引入工业革命，由于仅局限于单个生产过程。因此，需要使用人工控制每部机器及装卸材料，并把材料从一个地方运到另一个地方。

III.

1. In general, computer technology and information technology have rapidly developed ever since the 1980s.

2. By virtue of the automatic self-regulating system, the quality of products made by this mass-produced line has become higher and higher, and lower and lower in the productive cost.

3. The mechanization, which was introduced with the Industrial Revolution, because it was limited to individual processes, required the employment of human labor to control each machine as well as to load and unload materials and transfer them from one place to another.

4. An automatic mechanism is a system which has a capacity for self-regulate without the need for human adjustment.

5. This robot is fitted with the advanced intelligent control components.

3 数控与自动机器

迄今所叙述的机床自动化的主要不利条件是这项技术的经济性。装备一台进行自动化生产的机床是很费钱的。因此，除非零件的生产量非常大，否则，机床自动化就会因成本过高而变得不可行。非常需要一种在单批量生产中既快速又经济的自动化生产方法。这种方法已经有了，这就是数控机床技术。采用数控技术时，零件的图纸先被转换成穿孔纸带型的指令，经计算机改编后用来控制专用机床进行作业。这样，通用机床——前面已经作了叙述——按照储存在磁带上的信息去加工零件。磁带可以反复用来重复加工相同的零件，也可以储存起来以备后用。而且，可以用其他磁带来"命令"同一部机床加工另外的零件。数控和自动化之间很多性能是一样的。然而，数控技术更灵活，装备机床的花费更少，更换更快，而且停机维修时间更短。

在加工外形轮廓时，数控能够用数学方法将确定的曲线转换成成品，既节省时间，又无需样板，还可提高加工精度。另一个优点看来是能大大节省时间，也就是说不增添设备就能提高生产率。

自动化并不是什么新鲜事。半自动机器已在纺织工业和工程中使用多年。这些机器仅需在工作前安装调试好，加上负荷启动起来就行了。然后，在一段有限的时间内，它们就会自行工作，只需一个操作人员照看它们就够了。人们由这类机器研制出了传输机，它们多数用在汽车制造工业中。在使用这些机器的生产厂家，工件加工中的各个阶段都是在一条机器作业线上的某台全自动机器上完成的。待加工工件是自动装上机器的，从一台机器传送到下一台机器也是自动的。

目前使用的大多数传输机采用电动、气动或液压技术。

虽然利用气动和液压方法进行自动控制已达到很高的效率，但是，近来发展起来的更多的电子技术比起它们来却有许多优点。采用电子控制方法能使控制系统的操作更迅速、更精确而且更灵活。它们还使信息处理成为可能。无论是控制系统本身的内部信息还是来自外部的信息，都可以利用电子技术进行处理。这样，就可以对极其复杂的工序进行自动控制。

Keys to the exercises

I.

1. disadvantage 2. in 3. for 4. unless 5. that 6. by 7. over 8. make 9. and 10. out.

II.

1. 机床主要不利的方面在于加工过程的经济性。用于自动化生产的机床是很费钱的。
2. 然而，数控技术更灵活，加工花费更少，转换更快，而且停机维修时间更短。
3. 目前使用的大多数传输机采用电动、气动或液压技术。
4. 虽然利用气动和液压方法进行自动控制已达到很高的效率。

III.

1. machine tool, numerical control, fully-automatic machine, manufacturer, pneumatic and hydraulic technique, flexible manufacture

2. Numerical control can improve accuracy, decrease machining time, and increase

productive capacity.

3. The control of extremely complex manufacturing processes can be carried out automatically by numerical control.

4. By using numerical control, the blueprint for a part is converted into a computer instruction.

4 计算机集成制造系统（CIMS）

一个计算机集成制造（CIM）系统通常被认为是包含生产系统所有活动的一个系统集成。生产系统囊括产品的计划、设计及控制的制造系统。CIM 旨在将现有的计算机技术结合起来，以对整个生产过程进行管理和控制。许多公司以 CIM 为途径来建设未来的自动化工厂。

与传统的生产模式相比，CIM 的目的是以最低的成本，在最短的时间内将产品设计和材料转化成适销对路的商品。CIM 的起端为产品的设计，终端为该产品的制造。CIM 的应用把设计与制造之间原有的分离结合起来了。

CIM 与传统的加工车间的制造系统的区别在于计算机在制造过程中所起的作用。计算机集成制造系统基本上是由单一集成数据库联结的一个计算机系统网络。由于利用了数据库的信息，CIM 系统能够直接控制生产活动，记录结果并维护正确的数据。CIM 是集设计、制造、运送和财务功能为一体的计算机化系统。

CIM 系统的一个主要组成部分是计算机辅助设计（CAD）系统。凡是利用计算机对工程设计进行开发、分析或修正的一切设计活动都属于 CAD 的范畴。由 CAD 系统完成的设计工作包括：

- 几何建模；
- 工程分析；
- 设计评审与评估；
- 自动绘图。

CIM 系统的另一主要部分是计算机辅助制造（CAM），采用 CAD 系统的一个重要原因是 CAD 系统为产品制造提供了一个数据库。然而，并非所有的 CAD 数据库都能与制造软件兼容。CAM 系统完成的任务有：

- 数控（NC）或计算机数控（CNC）编程；
- 计算机辅助工艺规划（CAPP）；
- 生产计划与安排；
- 刀具与夹具设计。

Keys to the exercises

I.
1. A 2. C 3. D 4. A 5. C 6. C 7. B 8. D 9. A 10. C

II.

1. 计算机集成制造系统，计算机辅助工程，计算机辅助设计，计算机辅助制造，柔性加工系统，计算机辅助工艺规划，计算机数控，几何建模

2. 计算机集成制造是一种先进方法，许多公司正在利用这种技术建造未来的自动化工厂。

3. 计算机集成制造系统主要是一个由单一集成数据库联系在一起的计算机网络。

III.

1. The major purpose of CIMS is to transform product designs and materials into salable goods at a minimum cost in the shortest possible time.

2. Using the information in the database, a CIMS can control manufacturing activities, record results, and maintain accurate.

3. However, not all CAD databases are compatible with manufacturing software.

7.2 泛读

1 柔性制造系统（FMS）

在现代制造系统中，最著名的系统就是柔性制造系统。FMS 的发展始于 20 世纪 60 年代的美国，其设计思想是把生产线的高可靠性和高生产率同数控机床可编程的灵活性相结合，以便能生产更多的零件。在 20 世纪 60 年代后期安装的一个加工飞机传动箱系统至今仍在使用。然而，FMS 直到 20 世纪 70 年代后期和 20 世纪 80 年代初期才开始在全球范围内发展，这些 FMS 系统才卖得出去。

FMS 基本上是一个由自动化、传送带、计算机组成的加工车间。这种系统的布局非常复杂。由于不同零件的加工时间相差很大，就很难将 FMS 与一个集成系统相联结，使得 FMS 通常成为花费昂贵的自动化系统。

FMS 的一些常见特征有夹板更换器、收集铁屑的地下传送系统和将零件送至机器的传送系统。

FMS 系统通常采用能够监控生产的计算机监视零件计数，刀具更换和机床运行的情况，当工件被随机送入系统后，系统即辨认出每一零件并将其送至该去的机床。一般来说，FMS 系统具有生产周期短、在制品库存低、机床利用率高、间接和直接劳动少等特点。材料处理系统必须能把任何零件以任何次序送至任何机床，并能为每一台机床准备一组待加工的"库存零件"，以便使机床达到最大利用率。便于零件装卸，与控制系统相兼容及易于机床加工等是材料处理系统的其他必要特点。FMS 系统具有三级计算机控制。主控机监测整个系统的刀具和机床故障，安排工艺流程并编排传送路线将零件送至相应机床。

一个 FMS 系统在加工每根轴时需要三四个工人来装卸零件、更换刀具和进行日常性维护，FMS 系统的工人通常都是经过数控和计算机数控培训的高技术人员。

2 机 器 人

你每天看到机器人在您家中干活，虽然您可能并没有想到过它们是机器人；但是根据定义，洗衣机、电热炉等全部属于机器人。机器人也能够设计成在实验室和外层太空研究中做危险性的工作。

所有发射到外层太空的卫星上都安装有机器人，这些机器人通过无线电把有关宇宙的一些重要资料如温度、辐射等发回给地球上的主人。从太空很高的位置上它们甚至能够拍摄到地球和其他行星的相片。

当第一架太空船在火星和金星上着陆时，它上面很可能带的是机器人而不是人类。机器人能够描绘出这些星体的表面，做必要的地理研究，开发未知的地方，并为将来的太空船建造着陆地。

在我们今天使用的所有机器人中，装有电脑即计算机的机器人在彻底改革我们的生活方式方面正起着极其奇妙的作用。计算机起初开发是用来帮助人们解决某种科学问题，现在已经证明它们具有普遍作用，它们可以应用于很多不同类型的工作当中，它们已经把人类从繁重的工作中解脱出来，为人类提供更多的空闲时间。

在过去的20年里，工业界认识到：为了提高在世界市场的竞争力，必须提高生产率，降低生产成本。因为熟练技术工人的数量逐渐减少，以及越来越少的人员愿意从事单调、繁重、环境恶劣的工作，工业界发现很有必要对大部分生产过程实现自动化。计算机的发展使工业界生产可靠的机床和机器人成为可能。这些机床和机器人能使制造过程生产力更高、可靠性更好，从而提高产品在世界市场上的竞争力。

目前的工业机器人主要是单臂装置，该装置能根据计算机程序的设定，按操作或运行顺序来操作部件或工具。这些操作或顺序可以是重复的也可以不是，因为机器人能通过计算机做出逻辑性的决策。机器人能被应用到工业生产的不同生产过程中，而且可以"教"它们从一种生产过程转到另一生产过程。这种能力是基于灵活（可调）自动化的概念，即一台机器能经济地、经过最少量的设计和调试而执行不同的生产操作。

工业机器人的用途很广泛，其中最普遍的机器人应用包括：
- 安装和拆卸机床；
- 焊接；
- 移动重的零部件；
- 喷漆；
- 装配；
- 机械加工。

参考答案

第8章 机械通用技术

第1课

Keys to the Exercises

I.
1. B 2. C 3. A 4. D 5. A 6. A 7. B 8. C 9. B 10. C

II.
1. 在球面机构中，当连杆机构运动时，每一连杆都有某个保持静止的点，而且所有连杆的静止点都在同一位置上。
2. 平面副却不能加以约束，因此只相当于开式运动链。

3. 另一方面，在空间机构中质点的相对运动没有约束。
Ⅲ.
1. Mechanisms can be divided into planar, spherical, and spatial structure.
2. Theoretically, a planar pair might be included in this complex structure, there is no constraint in the structure.
3. The motion transformation is not necessary coplanar, nor must it be concentric.

第 2 课

Keys to Exercises

Ⅰ
1. 零件（元件或组件），链连接，零件可靠性，整机寿命，坚固件，连杆
2. 一些零件具有成对的关系，如：螺母与螺钉，花键与轴。
3. 机械零件最常见的例子是齿轮。它基本上是由轮子和轴组合而形成的。

Ⅱ
1. as   2. bolts   3. subassembly   4. which   5. number   6. shaft   7. expectancy
8. dimensions   9. all   10. standardized.

Ⅲ.
1. Sometimes certain elements are associated in pairs, such as nuts and bolts.
2. The wheel is fastened to the shaft with a key, and the shaft is joined to other shafts with couplings.
3. The individual reliability of machine elements becomes the basis for estimating the overall life expectancy of a complete machine.

第 3 课

Keys to the Exercises

Ⅰ.
1. heavier   2. hydraulic   3. driven   4. servo loop   5. for   6. of 7. with   8. to
9. than   10. though

Ⅱ.
为越野行驶的一些运输车辆设计的液压系统有所不同，因为这种液压系统不用转向杆和转向箱，方向盘和转向车轮只用液压管或液压软管连接。

动力转向系统包括一个盛油的储油箱，在发动机工作时，始终保持油压不变。但当转向系统不工作时，即转向盘不转动时，传动装置油缸中活塞两侧的压力相等，因此活塞不动。

Ⅲ.
1. To make cars easier to steer, the gear ratio in the steering box at the end of the steering column is changed so that turning the wheel requires less torque.

2. During World War II power steering was fitted to military vehicles.

3. Many cars would be nearly impossible to steer at parking speed without power steering.

4. If the hydraulics fails, the car can still be steered, though with greater effort made by driver.

5. The cars today are larger and heavier than earlier ones.

第 4 课

Keys to the Exercises

I.
1. A 2. B 3. D 4. A 5. C 6. B 7. C 8. D 9. C 10. D

II.
1. brake, parking brake, block brake, drum brake, disk brake, brake shoe, brake pedal.

2. Brake is a device used to slow or stop the motion of a vehicle or machine.

3. Braking is an energy-wasting process. Friction serves to convert the mechanical energy of moving wheel into heat.

4. One of the simplest types of brakes is the block brake, which consists of a wooden or metal block that serves as the brake shoe.

5. The disk brake used on motor vehicles and on many airplane wheels is the caliper type, instead of a drum.

III.

带式制动器是一种简单而有效的制动器，通常用于起重机、提升机等建设装备，它在自动变速中用于控制齿轮的转速。用于轿车、卡车、摩托车及绝大多数机动车辆的制动器通常是鼓形或盘形制动器，很多轿车这两种形式都采用，前轮用盘形，后轮用鼓形。

参考译文

第 8 章 机械通用技术

8.1 精读

第 1 课 机构

机构可用几个不同的方式进行归类，以证明原理之间的相同和差异之处。其中一种归类法是将机构分成平面、球面和空间三类。尽管这三类机构都有许多共同点，然而，可依据连杆运动的特性来建立分类标准。

在平面机构中，所有的点在空间绘出的是平面曲线，且所有这些曲线都在平行平面上，也就是说，所有点的轨迹都是与一个单一公共平面相平行的平面曲线。有了这一特点，就能够在单个图形或图形上，以实际的尺寸和形状来绘出平面机构的任意选择点的轨迹。这种机构的运动变换称为"共面"。平面四连杆机构、平面盘形凸轮、从动件及曲柄滑块机构等都是平面机构的常见例子。目前机构应用的绝大部分都是平面机构。

仅采用低副的平面机构叫做"平面连杆"机构，可以只包括转动副和菱形副，尽管理论上还可以包括平面副，但平面副却不能加以约束。因此，只相当于开式运动链。平面运动需要所有的菱形副的轴和转动副的轴都垂直于运动平面。

在球面机构中，当连杆机构运动时，每一连杆都有某个保持静止的点，而且所有连杆的静止点都在同一位置上，即每一点的轨迹都是包含在一个球面内的曲线。由几个任意确定的点画出的球面都是同心面。因此，在一个球面上以某个选点为中心作径向投影，就能完全绘出所有的质点运动。

球面连杆完全是由转动副组成。一个回转副不会产生额外的约束。因而，就相当于开式链，而所有其他的低副都有非球形运动。在球面连杆机构中，所有回转副的轴都必须相交于一点。

另一方面，质点的相对运动在空间机构中没有约束。运动的变换既不需要共面，也不需要同心面。空间机构可以有双曲率轨迹的质点。凡带有如螺旋副之类的连杆都是一个空间机构，因为螺旋副的相对运动是螺旋运动。

第 2 课　机械零件

任何机器无论多简单都是由单个零件组成的，这些零件通常被称为机械零件或部件。如果把一台机器全部拆散开来，这台机器便成为一堆如螺母、螺钉、弹簧、齿轮、凸轮、轴等简单部件，即构成所有机械的单元。因此，机械零件是通过设计来完成某个特定功能并与其他零件相结合的一个单元。有时，一些零件具有成对的关系，如螺母与螺钉，花键与轴等。还有些是由一组零件结合成为组件，如轴承、联结器、离合器等。

机械零件最常见的例子是齿轮。它基本上是由轮子和轴的组合而形成的一个齿轮。安装在轮毂或轴上的齿轮的旋转带动其他齿轮转动，并根据基轮的齿数来实现加速或减速。

其他的基本机械零件是在轮子和轴的基础上发展而成的。轮子必须要装在一根轴上才能转动；将轮子用花键固定在轴上；轴与轴之间用联轴器联结；轴必须套装在轴承上，并可由离合器来启动或由制动器来制动；一根轴可联结另一根轴的传动轮的皮带轮或链条轮来带动旋转；支撑结构的组装可用螺栓、铆钉或焊接。要正确应用这些机械零件，必须掌握结构的力和所用的材料强度。

单个机械零件的可靠性是估计整机全寿命的根据。许多机械零件已完全标准化了。通过测试和实践经验，已为常用的结构和机械部件的尺寸作了最恰当的规定。标准化带来了操作的统一和成本的降低。然而，并非所有的机械零件已经标准化。在汽车工业领域，只有紧固件、轴承、轴套、传动链和传动带为标准件，而曲轴和连接杆却未标准化。

第 3 课　动力转向系统

现今的汽车比早期的汽车大得多也重得多。为了降低压力，加宽了轮胎，也加大了轮胎间距，并给轮胎充了气。此外，汽车的发展趋势主要是把一多半的重量，特别是发动机的重量，由前轮承受，发动机本身也比早期的既大又重。

为使汽车容易转向，改变了转向柱末端转向箱的传动比，结果只需较小的扭矩转动方向盘。然而，这与1940年以前制造的汽车需要两周半或三周的转数相比，现代无动力转向装置的转向盘所需的转数增加了，而有动力转向装置的现代汽车其转数只需三周左右。

动力转向装置早在20世纪20年代首次研制出来；最初的装置之一是由皮尔斯·埃罗汽车厂的一位工程师、美国豪华汽车制造商研制出来的。在20世纪30年代初期，美国通用汽车公司卡迪莱克汽车分部打算提供动力转向装置作为某些型号汽车的备选装置，但是经济萧条妨碍了其发展。在第二次世界大战期间，动力转向装置曾装在军用车辆上。1952年克莱斯勒公司开始提供这种装置。现在这种动力转向装置是美国许多大型汽车的一种标准配置。

虽然曾试过电动装置，但现在用的动力转向装置常是液压的，由汽车发动机驱动一台泵，该泵使油压维持在1000磅/平方英寸（700千克/平方厘米）。该系统叫做伺服机构或伺服回路，其作用是进行调整以补偿驾驶员施加于转向盘的扭矩。伺服回路系统由一传动装置和一控制阀组成。该传动装置即是一个装有活塞或柱塞的油缸，此油缸的活塞可以从油缸中央向两个方向自由移动。控制阀的作用是通过开动油缸两端处的小阀对方向盘的扭矩做出反应，设计这一伺服系有助于转向联动装置，而不是代替转向装置。该系统不能完成全部转向动作，其余动作则由司机完成。这样如果液压系统一旦失灵，尽管司机费些力，汽车仍可开动，而且对路面的感觉始终可由汽车前轮机械地传到驾驶员握着方向盘的双手。而这是能安全驾驶的一个重要因素。动力转向装置对安全驾驶作出的另一个有益贡献在于：如果驾驶员碰到路面上的一个小障碍物或快速行驶中轮胎泄气，该动力转向装置使汽车更容易保持控制。许多安装了宽而坚固的径向网层轮胎的大型汽车，如果没有动力转向装置，当汽车以停车时速度慢行时，几乎不能对汽车进行转向操作。

为越野行驶的一些运输车辆设计的液压系统有所不同，因为这种液压系统不用转向柱和转向箱，而方向盘和转向车轮只用液压管或液压软管连接。

动力转向系统包括一个盛油的储油箱，在发动机工作时，始终保持油压不变。但当转向系统不工作时，即转向盘不转动时，传动装置油缸中活塞两侧的压力相等，因此活塞不动。

动力转向机构，有两种基本类型：一种是在转向箱内安装有控制阀，这里的控制阀通常是一种螺旋阀，另一种是当控制阀用作轴向柱塞阀时，该阀门与传动装置构成一个整体。

第4课 制动系统

制动器是一种用于车辆或机器降低运行速度或使其停止的装置。制动器最常用来控制或者停止机动车辆、火车、内行车以及像转轴和马达之类的旋转装置。有些制动器也起到锁定装置的作用，比如像汽车的停车制动器。多数制动器的制动是将相对静止的制动蹄紧压于运动轮或者其他旋转体上，以此产生摩擦来减缓或者停止旋转运动。制动蹄被制成多种不同的型号和形状，由于它们必须能够抗热耐磨损，所以制动蹄通常含有石棉或类似石棉的材料。

制动是一个浪费能量的过程。当一个制动蹄被压紧到旋转轮上时，摩擦作用将运动轮的机械能转化成热能，热能释放到周围的空中气中就造成了能量浪费。

最简单的一种制动器型式是含有木制或金属块作为制动蹄的块式制动器。块式制动蹄通常加工有与旋转轮外缘相配合的曲面。当制动器动作时，制动块靠压在旋转轮上产生制动效果。双块式制动器使用的两个制动块安装在旋转轮上相对的两边。块式制动器通常用火车头及车厢上。

带式制动器简单而有效。通常用于起重机、提升机等建设装备，在自动变速中控制齿轮的转速。常用的带式制动器有一条由金属或者其他材料制成的柔性配合缠绕旋转装置以便它能够拉紧旋转装置使其减速或停止运行。

用于轿车、卡车、摩托车及绝大多数机动车辆的制动器通常是鼓形或盘形制动器，很多轿车这两种形式都采用，前轮用盘形，后轮用鼓形。

在鼓形或内膨胀制动器中，制动机构封装在与运动轮固连笨重的金属鼓筒内。鼓筒内（而不与其连接）是两个有曲面的制动蹄及其操纵机构。当驾驶员踩下制动踏板时，制动蹄就被迫向外移动并且紧压在鼓筒内壁上。鼓形制动器的封装设计使制动机构免于灰尘和沙土的污染影响，然而这样的设计却不能够使快速或反复制动时产生的热很快地释放，因而会使制动蹄老化损伤制动能力。鼓形制动器也会受到潮湿空气的影响。

用于机动车辆和很多飞机轮子上的盘形制动器是一种钳盘制动式，而不是轮鼓式，它采用厚重的金属盘，并安装于轮子上面。用一个夹子式的卡钳组件安装在金属盘边缘但不随盘转动。当卡钳中的小制动蹄从金属盘两面抵触（抓住）盘面时，就产生制动作用。盘形制动器通常不会出现制动蹄老化，因为金属盘暴露在空气中能够使摩擦热很快消散。灰尘和水也很少产生问题，因为当制动蹄每次压紧旋转的金属盘时，灰尘和水就会被擦去。

8.2 泛读

第 1 课　液压传动

对于两点之间较远的传动，不适合用传动带和传动链传动的机械系统，可优先考虑采用液压传动。液压传动的优点是：低速大力矩、紧密结构、平稳传动且无振动，速度和方向能灵活控制，输出速度可实现无级快速变化。

由电力驱动的油泵提供有传递能量作用的油，并可供给液压马达或油缸，从而将液压能转化成机械能。液压油流动是通过控制阀进行控制的，压力油的作用产生线性的或螺旋性的机械运动，此时的油液产生的动能相对低，因此，有时候使用静压传动。液压马达与液压泵的结构几乎是相同的，任何液压泵都可当成马达应用，一定时间的流量可由调节阀或使用变量泵来控制。

一般来说液压传动可分为直线式的和螺旋式的，螺旋式传动产生螺旋运动，而由活塞及缸体部件产生往返的运动是线性运动。

所有液压马达的功能基于同一个原理，压力油被交替地挤入、挤出到油腔中，灌油循环由最小的腔体注油开始，当油腔达到最大容量时，使腔和进油隔开，就可停止进油，然后通过回油线路被返回到油箱中，同时另一个腔体开始灌油。

第 2 课　柴　油　机

柴油机是靠热力循环运转的一种内燃机。在热力循环中，吸入空气的压缩比要高到足以能点燃随后喷入燃烧室的燃料。这种发动机与普通的燃烧混合气的发动机有本质的区别。在后一种发动机中，空气与燃气在气缸外混合成一种易爆的混合气。该混合气被压缩，由电火花点火。柴油机使用多种燃料，其热效率较高，在许多方面的应用中显示出经济上的优越性。由 R·狄塞尔设计的，以多数低速发动机（约 300 转/分）为代表的理想柴油机采用一种燃料喷射系统，其喷射速度滞后并受控以保持在燃烧过程中的恒压。要使这个喷射原理适应高速（如 1 000～2 000 转/分）柴油机，而这种柴油机用于燃料喷射的时间却是如此之短（千分之几秒），就要在喷射时不考虑恒压的技术要求。但不考虑恒压条件燃烧下去就可能出现压力高峰。这些发动机使用非挥发性燃料是有利的。然而，这些发动机严格说来则不能认作是真正意义上的柴油机，而应叫做工业用柴油机更合适。一般地说，所有这样的发动机都归类为柴油机。

识别柴油机型号的可供选择的特征有：1. 二冲程或四冲程工作循环；2. 活塞水平运动或垂直运动；3. 单缸或多缸；4. 大功率（5000 马力）或小功率（50 马力）；5. 气缸：排列形式；直列式、对置式、V 形或星形；6. 单动式或双动式；7. 高速（1 000～2 000 转/分），低速（100～300 转/分）或中速；8. 恒速或变速；9. 可逆的或不可逆的；10. 气体燃料喷射或固体燃料喷射；11. 增压式或非增压式；12. 一种燃料或多种燃料。

柴油机的最大规格（5 000 千瓦）比汽轮机（1 000 000 千瓦）和水轮机（300 000 千瓦）要小得多：柴油机的原设计和实际热效率高达 20%—40%。发动机的输出功率是通过调整输入燃料的多少进行控制的，但并不随着空气的供给量而改变。对于给定的气缸容积和发动机速度来说，增压使气缸增加进气量，结果使功率输出增加。二冲程发动机的换气是靠曲轴箱内的压力和其前端的压力或靠独立工作的旋转增压器、往复增压器，或离心式增压器供给的。发动机气缸可不设阀门，而用完善的进排气双气孔控制机构，即用活塞开闭气道，对所换气体的进入及废气的排出进行控制。

参考答案

第 9 章　机械制造技术

9.1　精读

第 1 课

Keys to the Exercises

1. tolerance, fit, error, measuring instrument, extreme dimension, clearance fit, transitional fit, interference fit, hole-based system, shaft-based system

2. The designer must indicate the largest and smallest sizes that can be permitted.

3. Fits can be classified as follows: clearance fit, interference fit, and transitional fit.

II. 1. B　2. A　3. C　4. B　5. A

III.

配合是指两个零件之间的结合关系，考虑一下轴与孔的配合，如果轴比孔大，这种配合叫过盈配合，如果轴比孔小，这种配合叫间隙配合。

从理论上讲，为了减少加工刀具的数量，主要是采用基孔制，基孔制的孔是基准孔，可用于各种公称尺寸，可把轴加工比基准孔小或大，形成不同的配合，这就是所谓的基孔制。

第 2 课

Keys to the Exercises

I.
1. 热处理、临界温度、金属分子结构、退火、内应力、变形、淬火、回火、表面光洁度、成型加工。
2. 慢慢冷却的金属不如迅速冷却的金属容易产生这些内应力。
3. 它有助于消除内应力，使钢不像原先那样脆。
4. 因此，再把它加热到临界温度以下，然后使之慢慢冷却。
5. 这些热处理工序都是在各种成型加工过程中进行的。

II.
1. ways 2. which 3. as 4. above 5. cool 6. softer 7. machine 8. harder 9. critical 10. water

III.
1. We heat the steel above the critical temperature and permit it to cool very slowly.
2. This causes the metal to become softer than before, and much easier to machine.
3. High carbon steel is harder than tempered steel.

第 3 课

Keys to the Exercises

I.
1. on 2. than 3. as 4. At 5. dissolved 6. pressed 7. out 8. which 9. employed 10. welding.

II.
1. 把金属件连接在一起的方法很多，因金属的类型和所需接缝的强度不同而异。
2. 采用这种方法时，让电流通过两个电极，而金属面则置于两极之间。
3. 使用不同的方法把金属板焊接在一起，通常还采用称为点焊的方法。

III.
1. The simplest method of welding two pieces of metal together is known as pressure welding.
2. A number of different types of weld may be used, but for fairly a v-shaped weld should

normally be employed.

3. The heat for fusion welding is generated in several ways, depending on the sort of metal.

第4课

Keys to the Exercises

I.
1. with 2. called 3. from 4. that 5. father 6. planning 7. to 8. fed 9. of 10. with

II.
1. 钻床，刨床，磨床，刀口，公差，刀具
2. 铣削可根据所用的铣刀形状分别加工平面、槽口、缝、轮齿及其他的型面。
3. 粗磨是指切除精度不高的工件多余的金属。

III.
1. Most of the mechanical operations are commonly performed on five basic machine tools.
2. The lathe is commonly called the father of the entire machine tool family.
3. Grinding makes use of abrasive particles to do the cutting. Grinding operations may be classified as precision and non-precision.

参考译文

第9章 机械制造技术

9.1 精读

第1课 公差与配合

1. 极限尺寸与公差

人们普遍认为要制造一个没有误差的零件，实际上是不可能的，或者即使偶然制造一个没有误差的零件，但并不能表明该零件是绝对无误差的（因为测量仪器也存在误差）。因此，有必要注明最大允许误差。设计人员必须标注所允许的最大和最小尺寸，这种最大尺寸和最小尺寸称为极限尺寸，这两种极限尺寸之差叫公差。

在图纸上所标注的允许公差取决于所采用的加工类型，但还必须考虑到局部优先的原则。

2. 配合

配合是指两个零件之间的结合关系，考虑一下轴与孔的配合，如果轴比孔大，这种配合叫过盈配合，如果轴比孔小，这种配合叫间隙配合。

为了保证配合的正确性，必须把轴与孔的极限尺寸标准化。配合可分为如下三种：间隙配合，过盈配合和过渡配合。配合可采用基孔制和基轴制。为了获得一系列的过盈和间

隙等级，首先应规定各种轴与孔尺寸大小变量。例如，一个制造厂可以生产出许多公称直径为 25mm 的零件，但为了满足实际配合的需要，总会需要使用大量品种的钻头、铰刀和标准尺。

从理论上讲，为了减少加工刀具的数量，主要是采用基孔制，基孔制的孔是基准孔，可用于各种公称尺寸，可把轴加工比基准孔小或大，形成不同的配合，这就是所谓的基孔制。

第 2 课 钢的热处理

可以用各种方法来改变钢的特性。首先，含碳量极低的钢比含碳百分比较高的钢软，钢的含碳量最高不超过 2% 左右。其次，可以把钢加热到某一临界温度以上，然后再让它以不同的冷却速度冷却。在这个临界温度下，金属的分子结构开始发生变化。在通常所说的退火热处理过程中，我们把钢加热到临界温度以上，再让它慢慢冷却。这就使金属变得比热处理之前软，因而更易于机械加工。退火还有一个优点，即，它有助于消除存在于金属中的任何内应力。由于锻造或加工，或由于迅速冷却，金属中都很容易产生这些内应力。由于迅速冷却的金属其外部收缩比内部收缩得快，从而产生不均匀的收缩，就可能引起变形或破裂。故而慢慢冷却的金属不如迅速冷却的金属容易产生这些内应力。

另一方面，可以用速冷的方法使钢变硬。其方法是，把钢加热到临界温度以上，然后将其在水中或其他某种液体中淬火。温度的急促下降能使在临界温度上的钢的组织转变固定下来。于是，使钢变得非常硬。可是，这种经过淬火的钢材比一般钢容易断裂。因此，再把它加热到临界温度以下，然后使之慢慢冷却。这种处理方法叫做回火。它有助于消除内应力，使钢不像原先那样脆。由于回火钢具有这些性质，就使我们可以用它来制造那些需要用相当硬的钢制造的工具。高碳钢比回火钢硬，但加工高碳钢却困难得多。

这些热处理工序都是在各种成形加工过程中进行的。我们可以在轧钢厂里使用巨大轧机将钢轧制成型钢和板钢。冷轧时轧制压力必须比热轧时高得多，但是，冷轧可使操作者轧制出精确度和均匀性很高、表面光洁度较好的钢材。其他成型加工方法还有拉丝、铸造和锻造。

第 3 课 焊接

把金属件连接在一起的方法很多，因金属的类型和所需接缝的强度不同而异。软钎焊焊接薄钢件、薄铜件和薄黄铜件，其接缝合乎要求；但其强度比硬钎焊、铆接或焊接接缝要低得多。这三种连接金属的方法通常用于高强度的永久性接合。

把两块金属焊接在一起的最简单方法称为压焊。用火焰把每块金属的端部加热到白炽状态，铁的焊接温度应在 1300℃ 左右。在这种高温下，金属变成塑性体。然后，再把接头强压在一起或锤压在一起，最后把焊缝磨光。必须注意，首先保证焊件接头表面十分清洁，因为污物会减弱焊缝强度。此外，将铁或钢加热到高温时会引起氧化作用，从而在加热表面形成一层氧化膜。为此，要把某种助焊剂用在加热金属上，当达到焊接的高温时，助焊剂便熔化，并将氧化物同其他可能有的杂质一起溶解在其中。再将金属表面强压在一起，助焊剂即被从焊缝中挤压出来。焊缝的形式可有多种多样，但对于粗焊的金属件，通常应采用 V 形焊缝。它比普通对接焊缝强度高得多。

熔焊所需要的热量可用几种方法产生，选用时要根据待焊金属的品种及其形状而定。

氧乙炔火焰可产生炽热的火焰。对于某些焊接可使用电弧焊。采用这种方法时，让电流通过两个电极，而金属面则置于两极之间，电极有时可用碳制成，但较常见的是金属电极。工件本身构成其中一个电极，另一极则是绝缘的填允焊条。在两个电极间触发出电弧时，所产生的热量将焊接处的金属熔化。把金属板焊接在一起通常还采用称为点焊的方法。其做法是，先把两块金属板的板边搭接在一起，再在两个电极间通上电流。达到焊接温度时，对金属板施加强大的压力。氧化膜及被夹在两板之间的任何杂质就会被挤压出来，焊接便完成了。

第4课 机床

大多数的机械加工通常是在五种基本的机床上进行的：

钻床；

车床；

成型刨床或牛头刨床；

铣床；

磨床。

钻 削

钻孔是用一种称为"钻头"的旋转刀具进行的。大多数金属钻孔用的是麻花钻头。用于钻孔的机器叫做"钻床"。铰孔和攻丝也归类于钻孔。铰孔是在一个已钻好孔的基础上再切削少量的金属；攻丝是在一个孔中车出螺纹，以便装上螺钉或螺栓。

车削和镗削

车床通常被称为所有机床之父。在车削操作中，车床用一个单刃切削刀具在旋转的工件上进行金属切削。车削用来切削不同的圆柱形，如转轴、齿轮毛坯、滑轮、螺纹轴等。镗削用来扩大、精加工和加工中确定孔位。

铣 削

铣削用一个称为"铣刀"的旋转多刃刀具进行金属切削。铣刀制成不同的式样和尺寸。有些铣刀只有两个刃口，而有些铣刀有多达30个或更多的刃口。铣削可根据所用的铣刀形状分别加工平面或斜面、槽口、缝、齿轮的齿和其他的型面。

成型刨削和牛头刨削

成型刨削和牛头刨削用的是单刃刀具加工平面。在成型刨削的操作中，当工件被自动推向刀具时，成型刨床上的刀具作往复或前后移动。在牛头刨削操作中，工件被固定在一个沿着刀具作往复运动的工作台上。刀具切削一次后便自动向工件移进一点。

磨 削

磨削利用磨粒来进行切削。磨削可根据不同的目的分为精磨和粗磨。精磨应用于接近于公差限和非常光滑的磨削，粗磨是指切除精度不高的工件多余的金属。

9.2 泛读

第1课　材料性能

材料的性能可划分以下四种：物理性能、化学性能、机械性能和加工性能。

物理性能包括颜色、密度、熔点、凝固点、比热、热熔性、热扩张性、导电性和磁性等。

材料的化学性能中的抗腐蚀性能，通常包括抗化学或电化学腐蚀，在材料性能的选择中起着重要作用，同时抗腐蚀性能在生产过程中也很重要，由于在材料表面形成薄膜，而薄膜影响材料的摩擦与润滑及其导热和导电性能。

机械性能通常包括材料的承载能力。多数情况下工程人员在材料的选择中首先关心的是机械性能，因为只有了解材料的承载能力，才能对机械性能指标做出评价。

材料的加工性能，或工艺性，反映了对一个特定工艺过程材料的适应性，工艺性是十分复杂的且通常不能用单纯的数值来评价。

为了评价这些性能，产生了很多测试方法，用来描述材料的可加工性能、可成型性、可延伸性和可锻造性等。

第2课　钢铁

地球上蕴藏着大量对人类有用的金属，其中最重要的一种是铁。现代工业对这种金属（无论是铁的形态还是钢的形态）的需求量相当大。虽然某些有色金属，包括铝和锌，也很重要，但即使在今天，大多数工业产品仍是用铁或钢制造的。而且，铁具有磁性。因而使电力的发展成为可能。

我们在地下找到的铁矿石不是纯净的，其中含有某些杂质，必须通过冶炼加以去除。冶炼过程包括把铁矿石同焦炭和石灰石装到高炉里加热，并使它还原成金属。热风从高炉底部吹入高炉内，以供给铁矿石进行还原反应所需的氧气。铁矿石变成熔融状态后，其氧化物便与焦炭里的碳化合；矿石里的非金属成分便与石灰石结合生成液态炉渣。这种炉渣浮在铁水上面，经过出渣口流到炉外。留下的金属就是生铁。

我们还可以用另一种具有更多的焦炭和石灰石的炉子，即化铁炉，把生铁再次熔化，使它流进铁水包中或直接浇进铸模里。这就是铸铁。铸铁不具有钢那样的强度，质脆，而且在张力作用下容易破裂。但铸铁却具有若干性质，使它在制造机械设备方面非常有用。在熔融状态时，铸铁流动性很好，因此，容易浇铸成形状复杂的铸件。而且铸铁易于机械加工。铸铁含有少量其他非金属成分包括碳、硅和硫。这些成分的存在影响铸铁的性能。含碳量极少的铁，例如：熟铁，在性能上同含碳量高的生铁不同。

铸铁中的碳一部分呈自由石墨存在，一部分则以称之为渗碳体的铁碳化合物存在。渗碳体是一种非常硬的物质，故而也使铁变硬。然而，铁只能保持约1.5%的渗碳体。超过该百分比的任何碳成分，以片状石墨的形式存在。钢一点也不含游离石墨，其含碳量从几乎为零到1.5%。我们用含碳量极少的低碳钢制造钢丝和钢管，而用高碳钢制造钻头和切削刀具。

第10章 控制技术

10.1 精读

1 控制工程绪论

只要有目的地利用能量，都有必要采取某种控制形式。近年来，在自动控制领域取得了相当大的进步，其实这种技术历史悠久，可以追溯到1790年，当时瓦特就发明了离心式调速器来控制蒸汽发动机的转速。他发现在一些应用中有必要保持发动机转速不随负荷扭矩的变化而变化。但实际上，当加一个负载时速度就会下降或者去除负载后速度就会增加。

在一个简单的离心调速系统中，发动机转速的变化被探测并用来控制进入发动机的蒸汽压力。在稳定条件下，由于离心力的作用和蒸汽阀的开度足够维持发动机转速所要求的水平，瞬间与金属摆球的重量平衡。当额外的负荷扭矩加到发动机上，发动机的转速会下降，离心力减少，金属球将轻微下降，开口度控制蒸汽阀的开启，当开口度变大时将更多的蒸汽压力加到发动机上，这样转速就要上升，抵消了最初转速下降的倾向。如果额外的负载去除后，将发生相反的过程，金属球要轻微上升，蒸汽阀倾向于关闭，抵消了一些转速增加的倾向。

显然，没有这种调节器，速度就会降到底，然而，经过一个合适的调节系统，转速下降会很少。伴随高灵敏度的转速控制系统的出现，也会产生一些人们不希望出现的新问题，即控制量紧随被控制量（转速），从而在稳定的转速附近发生不规则的振荡和摆动。所有这种系统的真正问题是预防过度振荡的同时产生良好的调节作用。调节作用被定义为负载条件下被控制量的数值相对空载条件下被控量数值的变化百分比。各种调节器构成了一个重要的、完整的控制系统，他们通常能够保证各自所控对象（对应）的物理量（如速度、电压、液面高度、湿度等）在负载变化时保持恒定。一个好的调节器有很少的调节量。

1914—1918年战争促使军队工程师意识到为了赢得战争胜利需要准确而迅速地使重型装备（如船只和枪炮）机动。在20世纪20年代早期，美国的 N. Minorsky 从事了这项关于轮船的自动驾驶和在船甲板上自动配置枪的杰出工作。在1934年术语"随动系统"（来源于拉丁文）第一次出现是在 H. L. Hazen. 的文学作品中。他将伺服机构定义为一个能量放大装置，在该装置中，用以驱动输出量的放大元件由来源于伺服机构的输入和输出之间的偏差来控制。这种定义能广泛应用于多种多样的反馈控制系统。最近有人认为术语"随动系统"和"伺服系统"受反馈控制系统的机械位移变量限制。

在过去的30年里，控制工程通用领域中的一个极其重要的部分"自动控制"已经出现，并且被广泛应用于诸如化工、食品加工、金属加工等各种各样的大规模的工业过程控制当中。在发展的最初阶段，很难想象过程控制理论与随动系统和调节器理论密切相关。甚至在现在，过程控制系统的完善设计实际上不可能归功于我们对过程动力学的那些有限的理解。本书介绍的大部分理论中，以随动系统和调节器为例阐述分析方法，然而这种方法通常适用于过程控制系统，那些都是他们自己分批提出的。

Keys to the Exercises

I.
1. invented 2. increased 3. detected 4. at 5. decrease 6. removed 7. that 8. necessary 9. large-scale 10. stages

II.
1. 蒸汽机，伺服机构，离心力，力矩，反馈控制系统，动力学
2. 他将伺服机构定义为一个能量放大装置，在该装置中，用以驱动输出量的放大元件由来源于伺服机构的输入和输出之间的偏差来控制。
3. 如果额外的载荷去掉后，过程相反，金属球有点上升的趋势。

III.
1. Due to the centrifugal force, the metal spheres are just sufficient to maintain the engine speed at the required level.
2. It is obviously that while unloading, the speed of engine would rise considerably.
3. In the initial stages of research, it was scarcely realized that the theory of control is of importance.

2　自动控制的应用

虽然自动控制的应用范围实际上是无限的，但是我们的讨论仅限于现代工业中常见的几个例子。

伺 服 机 构

虽然伺服机构本身并不是一种控制的应用，但是这种装置在自动控制中却是常用的。伺服机构，或简称"伺服"，是一种闭环控制系统，其中的被控变量是机械位置或机械运动。该机构的设计使得输出能迅速而精确地响应输入信号的变化。因此，我们能把伺服机构想像为一种随动装置。

另一种控制输出变化率或输出速度的伺服机构称为速率或速度伺服机构。

过 程 控 制

过程控制是用来表示制造过程中多变量控制的一个术语。化工厂、炼油厂、食品加工厂、鼓风炉、轧钢机都是自动控制用于生产过程的例子。过程控制就是把有关诸如温度、压力、流量、液位、黏度、密度、成分等这样一些过程变量控制为预期值。

现在过程控制方面的许多工作都包含推广使用数字计算机，以实现过程变量的直接数字控制（DDC）。在直接数字控制中，计算机是根据设定点的数值和过程变量的测量值算出操纵变量值的。计算机的判定结果直接送给过程中的数字启动器。由于计算机兼有了模拟控制器的作用，所以就不再需要这些常规的控制器了。

发 电

电力工业首先关系到能量的转换与分配。发电量可能超过几十万千瓦的现代化大型电厂需要复杂的控制系统来表明许多变量的相互关系,并提供最佳的发电量。发电厂的控制一般被认为是一种过程控制的应用,而且通常有多达 100 个操纵变量受计算机控制。

自动控制已广泛地用于电力分配。电力系统通常由几个发电厂组成。当负载波动时,电力的生产与传输要受到控制,使该系统达到运行的最低要求。此外,大多数的大型电力系统都是相互联系的,而且两系统之间的电力流动也受到控制。

数 字 控 制

有许多种加工工序,如镗孔、钻孔、铣削和焊接都必须以很高的精度重复进行。数字控制是一个系统,该系统使用的是称为程序的预定指令来控制一系列运行。完成这些预期工序的指令被编成代码,并且存储在如穿孔纸带、磁带或穿孔卡片等某个介质上。这些指令通常以数字形式存储,故称为数字控制。指令辨认要用工具、加工方法(如切削速度)及工具运动的轨迹(位置、方向、速度等)等参数。

运 输

为了向现代化城市的各地区提供大量的运输系统,需要大型、复杂的控制系统。目前正在运行的几条自动运输系统中有每隔几分钟的高速火车。要保持稳定的火车流量及提供舒适的加速和停站时的制动,就需要自动控制。

飞机的飞行控制是在运输领域中的另一项重要应用。由于系统参数的范围广泛以及控制之间的相互影响,飞行控制已被证明为最复杂的控制应用之一。飞机控制系统实质上常常是自适应的,即其操纵本身要适应于周围环境。例如,一架飞机的性能在低空和高空可能是根本不同的,所以控制系统就必须作为飞行高度的函数进行修正。

船舶转向和颠簸稳定控制与飞行控制相似,但是一般需要更大的功率和较低的响应速度。

Keys to the Exercises

I.
1. B 2. A 3. B 4. C 5. D 6. C 7. D 8. A 9. D 10. B

II.
1. 虽然自动控制的应用范围实际上是无限的,但是我们的讨论仅限于现代工业中常见的几个例子。
2. 自动控制已广泛用于电能的传输。
3. 要保持稳定的火车流量及提供舒适的加速性能和停站时稳定的制动,就需要自动控制。

III.
1. A servomechanism is a closed-loop control system in which the controlled variable is

mechanical position or motion.
2. Ship-steering controls are similar to flight control.
3. Power systems are commonly made up of a number of generating plants.

3 可编程控制器

20世纪60年代，在控制器受到关注以前，机电装置一直是这个年代的流行产品。这些通常被称为继电器的装置被数以千计的系统用来控制许多制造过程和单独的机器。许多这样的继电器被应用于运输工业，更明确地说，应用于汽车工业。这些继电器使用成百上千的金属导线，他们的相互联系将影响控制的解决方案。至少作为一个单个的装置，继电器的性能是基本稳定的。但是，继电器盒通常需要安装三百到五百甚至更多的继电器，于是可靠性及维修和保养问题就不可避免地摆到了我们面前。成本问题成为另一问题，尽管继电器本身成本很低；但是继电器盒的安装成本很高，每个继电器总的成本，其中包括购买零件、配线和安装工作的成本，大体在30美元到50美元之间不等。更糟糕的事情是，控制面板需要经常不断地更改。对于继电器来说，这是一个昂贵的事实。因为这一更改过程需要大量的劳动在控制面板上重新接线。此外，这些变化有时很少备有证明文件的。这就使得以后的再次维护成为很头痛的事。按照这样考虑，丢弃整个旧的控制面板，同意使用一个适合的新的控制过程方式的相匹配的接线元件的控制面板，也是很常见的事情。这就给这些系统的维护成本增加了不可预知的、潜在的高成本。正如在昂贵的电动车辆生产线上一样。越来越清楚地认识到要使系统更可靠，更容易排除故障，更适合不断变化的控制过程需要，就必须改进控制过程。

在20世纪60年代，出现了第一个可编程控制器。这是第一个"革命性"的系统，这个系统是按照美国汽车制造工业的特定要求开发研制出来的。这些早期的控制器，即可编程逻辑控制器（PLC）是能应用于工厂车间的最早系统。这些控制器在不需要大量重新接线或改变元件的情况下能够作"逻辑"变化，一旦出现问题，它能够很轻易地诊断和修补。观察可编程控制器在最近15年取得的进步是很有趣的事情，在20世纪60年代末期早期的产品或许会使很多人感到惊恐和迷惑不解，例如，维修人员习惯了手动工具，那么对于电子仪器的部件和机电设备将会发生什么呢？改装过的计算机代替这些设备，正如电子器件代替继电器，甚至设计出了工具来作为继电器的替代品。我们现在有机会来审视一下前景，回顾过去，可编程控制器带给制造业是什么？

可编程控制器都包含了基本的功能模块，参见图10.1。为了理解控制系统的关系，我们将检查一下每一个模块。首先，我们看一下中心，它是系统的心脏。中心包括微处理器、存储当前控制逻辑的逻辑存储器、存储常变量数据的变量存储器，中心部分具有控制程序执行和为微处理器与存储器提供电力的功能。接着是I/O模块，它的功能是为CPU提供控制水平信号，并把它们转化为适合连接工厂级别的传感器和调节器的标准电压和电流。I/O类型可以是数字信号、模拟信号或是应用于某一特定应用的"智能"I/O。程序员通常仅需编写程序，而不需要考虑程序在系统中的运行。它也可以用来发现并修理系统故障，在检查系统故障的确切原因方面是个很有用的设备。在这里提到的设备代表了与I/O连接的各种传感器和调节器，它们是系统的手臂、腿、眼睛和耳朵，其中包括按钮、限制开关、行程开关、光敏元件、热电偶、位置传感器，作为输入的读卡机、标灯、显示设备、发动机、DC和AD驱动器、螺线管和作为输出的打印机。

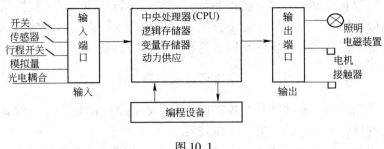

图 10.1

Keys to the Exercises

I.
1. as 2. for 3. supporting 4. issue 5. from 6. addition 7. of 8. in 9. programmable 10. manufacturers

II.
许多这样的继电器应用于运输工业，更明确地说，应用于汽车工业。这些继电器使用了成千上万的金属导线，他们的相互联系将影响控制过程的解决方案。

可编程控制器都包含了基本的功能模块，为了了解控制系统的关系，我们将检查一下每一个模块。首先，我们看一下中心，它是系统的心脏，中心包括微处理器。

III.
1. programmable controller，CPU，microprocessor，relay，Programmable Logic Controllers （PLC），thermocouple，sensor.

2. The first programmable controller was invented, in the late 1960s; this is the first "revolutionary" in control field in automotive industry.

3. The pioneer products of the late 1960s must have been confusing and frightening to a great number of people.

4 适应性控制系统

适应性控制系统是一种自动调整其参数以补偿过程特性的相应变化的系统。简而言之，该系统可以"适应"过程的需要。当然，必须有一些作为适应程序依据的准则。为被调量规定一个数值（即设定值）是不够的，因为要满足这一指标，不仅需要适应性控制。还必须另外规定被调量的某种"目标函数"。这是一个决定需要何种特殊形式的适应性控制的函数。

一个给定过程的目标函数可能是被调量的衰减度。因而，实质上有两个回路，一个回路靠被调量操作，另一个则依赖其衰减度。由于衰减度标志着回路动态增益，因此这种系统被称为动态适应性系统。

也有可能为一个过程规定一个静态增益的目标函数。为这种指标而设计的控制系统就是静态适应性系统。

实际上，这两种系统之间几乎不存在相似，以致它们在同一名称"适应性"之下，它们的分类已经引起了许多混淆。

要指出的是，第二个区别并非是目标函数，而是关于如何实现适应性控制的机理问题。如果对于过程有充分的了解，使得参数的调整能够与那些引起过程性质变化的变量有关系，那么适应性控制就可以程序化了。然而，如果必须根据目标函数的测量值来调整参数，则要利用反馈回路实现适应性控制。这种系统称为自适应系统。

动态适应性系统

动态适应性系统的主要功能是给控制回路一个始终如一的稳定度。因此，动态回路增益就是被调量的目标函数，其数值要予以规定。

最容易变化的过程特性是增益。在某些情况下，静态增益会发生变化，这种情况通常称为非线性。另外，一些过程表现出可变的周期，这就对动态增益产生了影响。但是不论回路的稳定性受到哪种机理的影响，都能通过适当调整调节器的增益来恢复稳定性（这里假定：首先，所希望的衰减度是可以达到的，这就排除了极限环的情况）。

有关可变过程增益的许多情况已经叙述过了。通常，为了补偿这些变化，采取的办法是在控制系统中引入一个经过选择的非线性函数。例如，调节阀的特性通常是考虑到为这个目的进行的选择；但是用这种方法所作的补偿可能由于下列原因而不能满足。

（1）引起增益变化的根源位于回路以外，从而不能从调节器的输入或输出识别这些变化。

（2）所需要的补偿是几个变量的综合函数。

（3）过程增益随时间而变化。

静态适应性问题

凡动态适应性系统都是控制回路的动态增益，那么，与它相对应的静态适应系统就寻求不变的静态过程增益。当然，这意味着静态过程增益是变化的，而且有一个特定值是所期望的。

以控制燃烧系统为例，要获得最高燃烧效率，应调节其燃油、空气比。过量燃油或过量空气都会降低燃烧效率。真正的被调量是燃烧效率，而真正的控制量是燃油-空气比。本例中，期望的静态增益是 $dc/dm = 0$。该系统应在这样的控制点上运行，即在这一点上燃油-空气比无论是增大或减小，都会降低燃烧效率。这是静态适应性控制的一种特殊情况，称为"最佳化"。然而，也可以合理地规定一个非零增益。

凡是能满足目标函数的被调量数值是针对该过程的一些主要情况，那么就能够容易地为适应性控制编制出程序。例如，在各种空气流量和温度情况下的最佳燃油-空气比可以是已知的。因此，用改变控制器设定值的方法来设计控制系统，使燃油-空气比适应于空气流量与温度的变化，作为动态适应系统例子中的一个流量函数。

Keys to the Exercises

I.

1. whose 2. meet 3. that 4. so 5. self adaptive system 6. control loop 7. with 8. set 9. which 10. to

II.

一个给定过程的目标函数可能是被调量的衰减度。因而，实质上有两个控制回路，一个回路靠被调量操作，另一个则依赖其衰减度。由于衰减度标志着回路动态增益，因此这种系统被称为动态适应性系统。

III.

It is also possible to stipulate an objective function of the steady-state gain of the process. A control system designed to this specification is then steady-state adaptive.

There is, in practice, so little resemblance between these two systems that their classification under a single title—adaptive- has led to, much confusion.

10.2 泛读

1 闭环控制系统

众所周知，闭环控制系统有如下三种基本组成。

1. 误差探测器。这是一个能接受低功率输入信号和输出信号的装置，这些信号可能具有不同的物理性质。为了降低误差，将他们转换成普通的物理量，该设备能减少误差，输出能改正其物理性质的低功率误差信号来驱动控制器。误差信号的探测器通常包括传感器，它们是能把一种实物形态的信号转换成另外一种装置。

2. 控制器。它是一个放大装置，接收低功率放大信号和从外部输入的能量，一个控制功率值（正确的物理性质）被提供给输出元件。

3. 输出元件。提供与控制器输出信号一致的正确物理性质能量加载。

另外一些装置，如齿轮箱和"补偿"装置有控制系统的特征，但是这些通常被认为构成一个或其他元件的一部分。

2 数字控制系统

在数字控制系统中，中央处理机对许多控制回路顺序能进行必要的计算。计算的结果可以被用来直接驱动调节阀或设置模拟调节器的设定值。前一种方案称为直接数字控制（DDC），后者称为设定值控制（SPC）。用计算机求解的控制算法在这两种情况下都是一样的。但是究竟利用计算机进行直接数字控制，还是进行设定值控制，这一抉择对于我们比较详细研究每种方案的优缺点是很重要的。

直接数字控制或设定值控制（DDC 或 SPC）

图 10.2 中表示实现直接数字控制的两种方法。上半部回路配备了一个数字式手动设定器（HIC）作为手动备用。如果计算机出了故障，阀门就保持在最后位置上，而 HIC 放在手动模式，用指示灯表明该设定器正处于手动位置，以引起操作人员的注意。如果操作人员把设定器切换到手动，就有一个逻辑信号被送到计算机，报告其动作。当设定器又回到数字控制时，计算机就应"预置"储存在存储器内的数据，以便自动控制能无扰动地进行，而且在用手动时，在阀的最后位置上开始自动控制。在计算机出现故障的情况下，操作人员必须照料通常处于计算机控制下的所有回路。回路可能多达 100 个或更多，这要取决于装置。有些回路可能要求非常严格，不容许用手动控制。对于这些回路，可以选择模拟备用，如图 10.2 下半部回路所示。在计算机出现故障的情况下，模拟控制器承担回路调

节。然而，必须考虑模拟控制器的预定点，否则不希望的扰动可能影响切换到模拟状态。

一种作法是在计算机小故障时先切换到手动，然后由操作人员自己决定是否再切换到模拟控制。另一种作法是使模拟调节器的设定值跟踪它的测量值，以便在切换时不存在偏差。或者换个办法，由模拟设定值跟踪数字设定值，以免开始模拟调节时，其设定值可能成为过渡工况期间形成的一个不希望有的数值。

在模拟备用的情况下，安装了两个调节器（计算机加模拟调节），不过在任何给定的时刻只用一个调节器。因此，除了极为特殊的情况以外，采用模拟备用是过于昂贵的。要证明这种系统是合理的，计算机对过程的控制必须比模拟调节器的效果要好得多。在实际应用中，情况未必如此。

如果要求数字计算机简单地重复模拟控制的功能，那么根据方程式：$\Phi_\Delta = -180\Delta t/\tau_0$，由于采样动作要导致回路的相位滞后，所以计算机将不会很好地完成这种功能。如果采样周期比回路周期短得多，这个作用就可忽略。因此，对于一些反映较慢的回路，数字控制可能被证明是合理的。但是，像流量和液位那样快的回路，甚至一秒钟的采样周期也会使响应明显地恶化。而在典型的化工厂或炼油厂中，大多数回路都是这样的回路。要以一秒钟或更短的采样周期来控制许多回路，就使计算机的负担太重了，所以计算机最好是专门用来计算一些不太频繁的大量计算的复杂任务。

流量和液位最好是用模拟调节器来调节。流量调节器可以由计算机来指挥，采用设定值控制。除了计算机的输出是 FIC（流量指示调节器）的设定值，而不在阀位以外，SPC 的结构和图 10.2 下半部的回路是相同的，流量调节器总是在控制，计算机出故障只是停止更新设定值而已。可用反馈算法或者用生产计划、前馈控制等各种计算中的任一方法来产生设定值。操作人员可以把 FIC 放在手动位置或放在带有设定的自动位置和带有计算机驱动设定的自动位置。每当操作人员把回路切换到最末工况时，计算机总是预置其储存的数据，以免干扰操作人员已设置的设定值。

参考答案

第 11 章　计算机辅助设计与制造技术

11.1　精读

第 1 课

Keys to the Exercises

Ⅰ.

1. to 2. with 3. or 4. answer 5. drawing 6. with 7. that 8. early 9. modified 10. until

Ⅱ.

1. CAD（Computer-aided Design），visual display screen，keyboard，graph plotter，disk，graph，memory，VDU，finite element technique

2. In the broadest sense, Computer-aided Design (CAD) refers to any application of a computer to the solution of design problems.

3. An important change came with the introduction of CAD in the early 1960s.

4. In the past, the conventional tools of the engineer in his/her role as a designer have been drawing boards and instruments, calculators and technical data sheets.

5. the designer enables to test a design idea and to rapidly see its effects; the design idea can then be modified and reassessed.

Ⅲ.

计算机辅助设计在工程技术领域中有着重要的作用,例如:计算机系统生成工程图纸的应用;求解复杂构件的热应力问题的有限元技术的使用;机械装置和连接的分析以及大量的辅助工程应用。

第 2 课

Keys to the Exercises

Ⅰ.
1. D 2. B 3. A 4. B 5. C 6. A 7. C 8. D 9. D 10. B

Ⅱ.
1. CAPP has been recognized as playing a key role in ClMS.

2. For increasing the intelligence of CAPP systems, some new concepts, such as neural networks, fuzzy logic, and machine learning have been explored for the new generation of CAPP systems.

3. CAPP can be defined as the functions which use computers to assist the work of process planners.

4. This phenomenon is entitled concurrent or simultaneous engineering.

5. Automated process planning systems have been recognized as playing a key role in CIMS.

Ⅲ.

工程技术人员在 20 多年前首次提出了应用计算机帮助制定工艺流程。他们为发展 CAPP 系统付出了极大的努力。随着时间的推移,研发 CAPP 系统的意义集中于智能化和集成工艺流程系统。

第 3 课

Keys to the Exercises

Ⅰ.
1. with 2. related 3. on 4. machinery 5. by 6. simulation 7. unit 8. to 9. to 10. at

Ⅱ.

If traditional methods are adopted for meeting the requirements, development will cost more and need more time, but increased competition demands lower development cost and shorter project times.

This new simulation system has been proved to be more flexible, more accurate, and especially more efficient for the user, except for some pre-study engineers.

Ⅲ.

1. 在研究过程中企业的目的是在最短的时间内，利用最少的成本研制出高性能、高效率，高操作性能的产品。

2. 当转换齿轮的工作状态由后退变为前进时，装载机仍在后退。

3. 当发动机转速降低时，扭矩也会相应地变小，并且低速时发动机的响应变得迟缓，这主要是涡轮增压器的转动惯量造成的。

4. 在设计的早期阶段，人们已经汲取了一些有价值的经验，尤其在概念设计时期。

5. 可能所有的工程师都熟悉虚拟样机技术的应用目的。

第 4 课

Keys to the Exercises

Ⅰ.

1. computer simulated   2. virtual   3. immersed   4. models   5. in   6. sensations   7. prototype   8. of   9. similar   10. though

Ⅱ.

1. 虚拟现实，仿真，远程沉浸，视频会议，原型系统，头载监视器

2. 研究人员还戴着头式跟踪设备和偏振眼镜就像看三维电影一样。

3. 这种自然的交互方式能使参与者在虚拟世界中产生沉浸感。

Ⅲ.

Virtual reality simulations differ from other computer simulations in that they require special interface devices that transmit the sights, sounds, and sensations of the simulated world to the user. These devices also record and send the speech and movements of the participants to the simulation program.

参考译文

第 11 章　计算机辅助设计与制造技术

11.1　精读

第 1 章　计算机辅助设计技术

在广义上讲，计算机辅助设计（CAD）指的是计算机在解决设计问题中的应用。工程技术人员可以借助于直观显示屏幕、键盘、绘图仪和人机接口等诸多方式与计算机通

信。工程技术人员可以提出问题并能很快从计算机得到解答。更确切地说，CAD 是使工程技术人员和计算机协同工作，彼此发挥长处的技术。

过去，工程技术人员设计时所使用的传统工具是制图板、制图仪、计算器和技术数据图纸。后来，计算机的出现导致了工业中的巨大变化。随着数字控制、计算机数字控制、机床的相继引入，计算机在制造业中的应用在 20 世纪 50 年代末期首次有了实质性进展，通过磁带输送到机器中的数据控制着生产装配零件机器的运转。除制图和制表外，这一切对工程设计者并没有直接影响。

20 世纪 60 年代初随着计算机辅助设计的引入产生了一场重大变革。CAD 允许设计者以图形方式与计算机交互作用，工程技术人员能够检验一个设计思想，并很快地查看到设计效果，然后对其进行修改和重新评价。如此循环往复，直至形成一个合格的设计。每重复一次，设计方案都会得到进一步的改善。因此，在时间、材料和资金允许的条件下所执行的循环次数越多，设计效果就越好。

计算机能加快设计进程，提高设计的精确程度。它能够在短时间内完成大量的、复杂的计算并得出准确和可靠的结果。由于在有限的时间内某些设计所需要的大量计算不能简单地由人来完成，计算机的上述特征证明其作为一个设计工具的作用是无法估价的。

计算机可在诸如磁盘的永久性介质上保存大量的信息，或者临时存储在直接存储器上。因此，以数字形式描述一个工程图纸的细目或一个汽车车身的造型，并把信息存储在存储器中都是可以做到的。这些数据能从存储器中检索、快速转换并显示在 VDU（视频显示器）图形屏幕，或交替地利用绘图仪绘制在纸上。此外，设计者还可以迅速、容易地更新或修改图纸的任何部分。也能把修改后的图纸数据写回到存储器中。

计算机辅助设计在工程技术领域中有着重要的作用，例如：计算机系统生成工程图纸的应用；求解复杂构件的热应力问题的有限元技术的使用；机械装置和连接的分析以及大量的辅助工程应用。

第 2 课　计算机辅助工艺设计

计算机辅助工艺设计是计算机协助工艺员完成工艺流程的功能。辅助的程度水平依赖于执行系统不同的策略方法。低水平决策仅通过计算机完成存储和修复工艺过程的数据，用以构建手工的工艺流程；同时为工艺员提供新任务的数据补充。对比低水平决策，高水平决策是应用计算机自动生成具有简单几何形状工件的工艺流程。有时工艺员需要输入所需数据和调整那些不适合某些具体产品要求的工艺流程。最高水平决策是 CAPP 的最高追求，即当工艺知识、专门技术和工作经验被融合在计算机程序中时，用计算机代替工艺员制作生成工艺流程。最高水平决策的 CAPP 系统数据库将直接集成在相关系统中，如 CAD 和 CAM 系统中，CAPP 被认为在 CIMS（计算机集成制造系统）中起关键作用。

工程技术人员在 20 多年前首次提出了应用计算机帮助制定工艺流程。他们为发展 CAPP 系统付出了极大的努力。随着时间的推移，研发 CAPP 系统的意义集中于智能化和集成工艺流程系统。为提高 CAPP 系统的智能化程度，一些新概念，如神经网络，模糊逻辑学和学习机器在新生代 CAPP 系统中被探索开发。为增加 CAPP 系统的集成性，设计开发的焦点集中于设计中的典型特征、典型特征的功能、工艺过程和行程安排一体化，并集成了制造原料计划的工艺流程，该现象能够有资格说是并行工程。

由于工艺流程决定了在制造和装配零件时所需的方法、机器、顺序、工装和刀具，不难看出编制工艺流程是制造系统要执行的基本任务之一。传统上推行任务的困难和详细工艺过程制定由精通制造工艺的操作工人来解决。许多熟练的工人，现在被认为是工艺员，已经或接近退休，然而却没有年轻有资格的工艺员来接替他们的位置。工艺员的缺口逐渐增加。随着世界市场竞争压力的加大，追求合作化的集成产品将幸存下来并获得成功。自动化的工艺流程系统已经被认为是 CIMS 中至关重要的部分。这就是许多公司关注计算机辅助工艺设计的原因。

第 3 课　动态仿真技术在机械设计中的应用

1. 概述

可能所有的工程师都熟悉虚拟样机技术的应用目的。如今严格的法律法规（例如有关废气排放和噪声方面的）和苛刻的用户需求（例如有关设备性能和操作方面的）都需要更为先进、复杂系统的技术支持，用传统的方法很难优化。所以，如果我们采用传统的设计方法来满足这些要求，将会花费较多的研制费用和时间，但竞争日益激烈的市场则要求降低研制费用和缩短研制周期。

最近人们公布了一些对整台机器进行仿真的应用实例。这些仿真的目的是对仿真技术本身进行评估、对整台机器的子系统进行评估、对机器舒适度相关方面进行评估以及对整台机器的耐用性进行评估。本文将讨论整台机器的动态仿真问题，同时也将对整台机器的全部工作性能和与这些性能的相关方面进行分析和优化。本文所讨论的主要焦点是靠液压驱动的轮式装载机，所得到的结果也适用于其他越野机械。

2. 设计方法和可视化

目前所研究的课题目的是对现在通用的产品研制方法进行扩展，而不是借助于设计科学对其变革。因此，现在所研究的问题是如何发展目前具有动态仿真技术的设计方法。正如前文所述，本文研究的重点是对整台机器的所有工作性能及其相关方面进行分析和优化。

所改进的设计方法必须实现以下几个预定的目标，即，所设计的新产品与现代产品相比：所节约的资源（如时间、钱和人力）应当被用来优化前面所提到的有关整台机器的工作性能。

（1）应具有较高的工作性能、生产率和可操作性；
（2）耐用度提高；
（3）研制周期缩短；
（4）研制费用降低。

在越野汽车设计的早期阶段，人们已经汲取了一些有价值的经验，即在重复改进设计阶段，尤其在工程车辆的概念设计时期，设计和生产的速度都是非常重要的。当 Volvo 公司的旧装载计算程序被认为高级的程序替代后，上述工作就可以用独有的仿真系统完成，这些系统是在多种系统和现代数据库的基础上发展起来的。现在人们已经证明，这种新的仿真系统对用户来说，适应性、精度和效率都比较高，但对于那些进行预研工程师来说，其优越性并没有显现出来。由于这种系统得到结果的方式是借助于多体仿真技术，而不是求解难懂的数学方程，所以，每运行一次花费的时间均比旧程序长。在以往的旧程序中，对越野汽车复杂受力情形的优化往往非常耗时，但对于这种新的仿真系统，如果事先了解机器的受力情况，并在确定研制目标的时候就考虑到这些因素，人们是完全可以研制出一个专门简化的系统来解决上述问题的，但所算得的结果精度不高。

比如有这样一个例子：在一个所谓的"短装载机循环中"存在着一个临界阶段，就是让一个装满货物的机器改变其前往货物接收装置的方向，这时在主系统之间经常存在着密切的交互作用。

（1）为了机器转向，操作人员往往要降低其发动机的速度（否则会使齿轮换挡速度较快，最终导致传动联合器过早失效）。当发动机转速降低时，扭矩也会相应地变小，并且低速时发动机的响应变得迟缓。这主要是涡轮增压器的转动惯量造成的。

（2）当转换齿轮的工作状态由后退变为前进时，由于装载机仍在后退，这样就迫使该机器的变矩器的涡轮旋转方向发生突变，致使齿轮轮齿间产生滑动。这常常导致发动机运转所需要的扭矩急剧增大。

（3）有些操作人员在装载机转向的时候并不停止装载货物，这样就需要更多的油来提供动力。我们假定载荷传感泵与发动机的机轴直接相连，通常发动机的油量是和液压泵的排量及发动机的机轴转速成一定比例的，这样当发动机的转速降低、需油量增加时，该泵的排量趋于最大值。一般发动机油泵运转所需扭矩的大小与该泵的排量和其产生压力的数值成一定的比例，这是因为当装载机装满货物时（包括装载货物的几何尺寸），其泵的压力变高，排量趋于最大值，因而所需要的扭矩增大。

3. 结论

本文介绍的是 Volvo 装载机制造公司和 Linktoping 大学合作研究的科研项目。该项目是研究通过对整个装载机的仿真来分析和优化整机性能的。在研究过程中企业的目的是在最短的时间内，利用最少的成本研制出高性能、高效率，高操作性能的产品。目前我们已经研究出一些改进的方法，同时也提出了未来的研究计划。

第 4 课 虚 拟 现 实

虚拟现实系统是指能使一个或多个用户在计算机模拟环境中移动并能够与环境交互的系统。系统中各种各样的仪器能使参与者真实地感知和操纵虚拟的物体。这种自然的交互方式能使参与者在虚拟世界中产生沉浸感。这里的虚拟世界是由数学模型和计算机程序创造出来的。

虚拟现实仿真与其他计算机仿真的不同之处在于它需要特殊的接口设备，这种设备把虚拟世界的视觉、声音及感觉传递给用户。同时这些设备记录参与者的语言和动作并发送给计算机仿真程序。

在未来，你的办公室可能已不再像小卧室而更像星际旅行中的全息驾驶舱。计算机科学家已经在做远程沉浸技术的实验。这项技术使我们在几百英里外能看到同事的办公室，就像我们与他们正处于同一个物理空间一样。

从事"国家远程沉浸初步研究"项目的一些大学的计算机科学家已经展示出了一个原型样机系统，这个系统能使一个科学家在小山上通过安装在他办公桌右边的两个屏幕看到离他很远的同事。就好像从办公室的另一边透过玻璃朝里看一样。与视频会议不同，远程沉浸能提供与实物一样大小的三维图像。

在这个原型系统中，每个研究人员身边都有一排从不同角度监视他运动的数字照相机。研究人员还戴着头部跟踪设备和偏振眼镜，这种眼镜好像看三维电影的眼镜一样。当研究员头部移动时，他视野里的同事的位置也相应地变化。如果他向前倾，他的同事就会和他靠得更近，尽管实际上他们相隔几百英里。

为了使系统运行，高性能计算机把每个参与者的数字图像处理成数据，并在因特网上进行传输，然后重建图像并投影到屏幕上。目前为止，因为现在电脑传输数据的速度不够快，运动图像的显示还不连续。

科学家希望远程沉浸技术能开发出大量的其他应用，例如，地处乡村的病人能由遥远城市的医生来治疗。

11.2 泛读

第 1 课 软件开发的五个阶段

大型软件包的开发过程可以划分为五个主要阶段。

1. 确定要求

在软件开发的初始阶段，软件工程师和其客户要交换各种文件并举行一系列会议，以便开发一个完整的、一致的、没有歧义的程序设计规范。目的是使这些设计规范可作为开发程序的各方共同遵守协议的基础，在运行过程时作为软件产品开发必须完成的工作内容。

2. 设计子程序

在第二个阶段，程序员及其设计工程师要决定使用什么样的硬件设备，采用什么样的编程语言及专业人员如何来实现子任务。在这一阶段，在构造和列出整个软件包的各个组成部分内容时要使用程序流程图和其他可视化辅助工具。

3. 编写命令

设计阶段完成之后，就用适当的语言对命令进行编码。我们往往把编程阶段看作是专业程序员的基本任务，而事实上，编程工作大约只占程序员六分之一的时间和精力。

4. 测试程序

程序的最初几个版本往往错误百出。其中某些错误可以由计算机自动测试出来，其他的错误则必须进行一系列测试才能确定它们的位置并加以纠正。这种测试只是运行事先知道正确结果的程序。一般一次测试只能试验整个程序的一小部分；因此，如果人们想要肯定程序作为一个整体基本上是无错的话，就需要大量地进行这类测试。实际上，通常不可能证明某个具体的程序已经完全"调试"好，许多程序在发布运行之后很久还会发现包含有许多的错误。例如，第一个 FORTRAN 翻译程序在其正式发行 18 个月以后还发现有几个编程错误。

5. 运行和维护程序

程序调试通过后，就可以按常规的方式运行了。然而这还不是程序设计的终点。由于随后出现需求的变动及各种各样的差异，大多数程序必须按照某种连续的方式加以维护。当人们提到"维护"某个程序的时候，人们所指的是为了使程序满足这些重要的需求而对程序经常进行改动。程序维护经常被当作一种相当乏味的事情，而事实上，目前它给美国的全体专业编程人员提供了60%的就业机会。

第2课　数据库技术

许多计算机应用程序要求所处理的数据按顺序存放，然而如此简单地存放数据是不够的。一个普通的计算机系统，甚至只是一个小系统，可有几十个磁盘和磁带，每一个都为几十个不同的应用程序保存数据，对任意给定的应用程序，只用到一组数据。对一个给定的程序所需要的特殊数据，必须能存储、定位和检索，这就涉及到数据管理的问题。

传统的数据管理存在一些问题，许多问题是由于只考虑应用而引起的，例如，工资单问题，大多数组织机构都用计算机做职工的工资单，因为用计算机可代替一小批职员，节省了开支，所以公司开发了一个为处理工资文件的工资程序。存货清单、收入账、支出账和一般分类账分析的应用都与工资单相类似，于是，公司又开发了清单程序、清单文件、收入账程序、收入账文件等等。每个程序都是独立的，并且每个程序都只处理自己的独立的数据文件。

为什么这是问题呢？对某件事，不同的应用需要同样的数据，例如，学校要产生账单和学生成绩报告单，把它们看作独立的应用程序。账单程序读出一个账单数据文件，成绩报告程序读出一个成绩数据的独立文件。两个程序的输出都要邮递到每个学生家中，因此学生的姓名和地址必须重复地记录在两个文件中。当学生搬家时，会发生什么情况呢？除非两个文件都被修改，否则就有一个是错的。重复的数据是很难维护的。

较错综复杂的问题是数据的依赖性。为了存贮和检索数据，每种存取方法都有自己的规律，某些数据管理技巧能够极大地改善一个给定程序的效率。因为用计算机的动机是为了节省钱，所以程序员总想利用这些效率来节省更多的钱。因此，程序的逻辑结构变得依赖于数据的物理结构、当程序的逻辑结构受到它的物理数据结构的约束时，改变数据结构肯定需要改变程序，结果是采用传统存取方法的程序很难维护。

解决以上两个问题的方法经常是把数据组成一体化的数据库，这样就能把控制存取所有数据的任务集中在一个中心的数据库管理系统中。

使用集中式数据库是如何解决数据冗余的问题呢？把所有的数据都收集和存放在一个地方，因此任意给定的数据元素只有一个拷贝。当一个元素的值，例如地址改变时，只修正惟一的数据库，要求存取这些数据元素的任何一个程序都能得到同样的值＋原因是只存在一个值。

数据库又是如何协助解决数据依赖性问题呢？由于数据库管理系统负责存取物理数据，因此，程序员就可不考虑物理数据结构。导致了程序更少地依赖于它的数据，一般是更容易维护。可以预料，数据库管理会继续向前发展。

参考答案

第12章 信息和网络技术

12.1 精读

第1课

Keys to the Exercises

I.
1. 全球定位系统，无线电导航系统，原子钟，接收机，三维空间位置，纬度，经度，海拔高度
2. 全球定位系统是一种以太空为基础的无线电导航系统，由24颗卫星和地面机站组成。
3. 由于GPS突破了许多现有导航系统的局限性，因而，受到广大用户的关注。
4. 时间信息以代码的形式由卫星传播，便于接收机不断地确定传播信号发送的时间。
5. 但是，如果使用第四颗卫星定位和测量，接收机就可以不要原子钟。

II.
1. satellites 2. navigation systems 3. of 4. difference 5. that 6. from 7. locations 8. for 9. sent 10. longitude

III.
1. Global Positioning System (GPS) consists of 24 satellites and ground support.
2. GPS provides users with accurate information about their position.
3. GPS became attractive to a wide range of users.
4. The receiver uses the difference between the time of signal reception and the time of broadcast to compute the distance.
5. The receiver uses four satellites to compute latitude, longitude, altitude, and time.

第2课

Keys to the Exercises

I.
1. E-mail, Usenet, internet, World-Wide-Web (WWW), intranet, website, database, server, client
2. E-mail is often used to send messages between individuals or groups of individuals separated by long distances.

3. The networking of these servers makes such discussions available worldwide.

II

1. A 2. C 3. B 4. B 5. D

III

服务器一收到信息，就把该信息传送到邮件应到达的特定计算机上去，发送电子邮件的过程刚好相反。作为一种既非常方便又廉价的传送信息的途径，电子邮件已经大大地影响到科学、个人和商务通信。

第3课

Keys to the Exercises

Ⅰ.

1. 美国国家计算机安全局、美国国防部信息系统局、美国联邦调查局、信息技术、信箱（邮箱）、黑客、防火墙、万维（环球）网服务器

2. 美国国家计算机安全机构引用美国联邦调查局数据，在调查的计算机犯罪中，有80%以上是未被授权访问互联网进行的。

3. 文章的焦点完全集中在通信的隐私上，而忽略了来自于互联网攻击的可能性。

4. 将来不会由于对安全的忧虑而阻止许多组织去发掘利用互联网所提供的潜在商机。

5. 很难从文献给出的全球防火墙市场的统计数字中区分出欧洲或英国所占比例。

Ⅱ.

1. that 2. which 3. than 4. unauthorized 5. from 6. As 7. and 8. Intranets 9. Web 10. units

Ⅲ.

1. It is difficult that Putting a value on the damage done by hacker attacks is hardly determined.

2. Given that approximately 40% of the fortune 500 companies using the Internet have still to install a firewall.

3. It is little surprise that the security auditing business is booming.

4. The annual growth rate of the Internet firewall market is expected to hit 174%.

5. It is difficult to assess the potential risks of Internet security.

第4课

Keys to the Exercises

Ⅰ.

1. digital television, flat television, LCD, signal transmission, stereo speaker, tube (kinescope), semiconductor, video audio

2. There have been only two major changes in the way that TV sets work.

3. Digital set is already on sale in Europe and planned to be introduced to the United States this fall.

4. Semiconductor company may hasten the development of large size flat TV.

5. Flat TV weighs only a few pounds and could be hung on a wall like a painting.

II.

1. A 2. B 3. A 4. C 5. D 6. C 7. D 8. B 9. B 10. D

III.

电视机的工作方式发生了两个重大的变化：一是，1954年引入了彩色；二是，70年代由电子管改为晶体管，现在即将发生一个深刻的变革。

称为4500型平板印刷机能够生产厚度为1英寸的18英寸的彩色液晶显示屏，数字电视有希望为电视观众提供比目前市场出售的电视更清晰更稳定的画面。

参考译文

第12章 信息和网络技术

第1课 全球定位系统

1. 介绍

全球定位系统是一种以太空为基础的无线电导航系统，由24颗卫星和地面机站组成。在地球上任何一个角落，在各种气候下，它能为用户提供其精确的位置，速度和时间信息。

2. 历史与发展

全球定位系统创建于1973年，由于它突破了许多现有导航系统的局限性，因而受到广大用户的关注，在传统的导航应用中GPS一直很成功，由于它小巧灵便和廉价，因此，有了很多新的应用。

3. 工作原理

GPS的工作原理是通过计算信号发送与接收的时间差来定位，GPS上安装有原子钟可以提供很精确的时间，时间信息以代码的形式由卫星传播，便于接收机不断地确定传播信号发送的时间。这种信息包含有多种数据，接收机用它们来计算卫星的位置，为满足精确定位需要，需要进行一些其他方面的调整，接收机通过信号接收与信号传播的时间差计算得出接收机到卫星的距离或范围，同时接收机还应考虑电离层和对流层造成传输延迟或信号传播速度衰减的影响。当信号发送时，接收机利用三颗卫星的范围和位置信息计算出自己的三维方位信息。

通过三种不同卫星信号的来定位，原子钟必须与GPS同步，但是，如果使用第四颗卫星定位和测量，接收机就可以不要原子钟。这样可以计算出经度、纬度、海拔高度以及时间。

第2课 电子邮件

因特网上使用最广泛的工具是电子邮件，或称E-mail。电子邮件用于地理位置很远的个人之间或团体之间发送信息。E-mail 信息一般通过邮件服务器发送和接收——该服务器由专门处理和传送 E-mail 的计算机来承担。服务器一收到信息，就把该信息传送到邮件应到达的特定计算机上去。发送电子邮件的过程刚好相反。作为一种既非常方便又廉价的传送信息的途径，电子邮件已经大大地影响到科学、个人和商务通信。

电子邮件是集团与个人之间组织交往的基础。例如，数据服务器使寻找订户清单成为可能，既可以用单向通信，以保持人们对最新产品的感兴趣，也可以在线讨论小组中进行双向通信。

电子邮件的另一个用途是 Usenet（世界性的新闻组网络系统），可进行分组专题讨论，形成许多新闻组。共有数千个新闻组，主题覆盖的范围非常广泛。新闻组的信息并不直接发送给用户，而是以有序列表的形式存放在当地专用的新闻服务器上以供访问。这些服务器的联网使全世界范围内的用户均可参与这种讨论。相关软件不仅使用户可以选择他们想读的信息，而且可以通过将信息发送到新闻组的方式加以回复。

第3课　网络安全问题

当把一个可信赖的网络与一个不可信赖的网络连接在一起时，将牵涉到对可信赖网络的安全负责的问题。关注与互联网的连接，可能大部分基于从广泛的媒体报道安全突破口收集的轶事类的证据。然而，进一步接近检查事实及媒体报道背后的统计，将会深化这种关注。例如，美国国家计算机安全机构声称，许多对计算机系统的攻击未被发现并报告，美国国防信息系统机构称，美国国防部 9 000 台计算机遭到攻击。这些攻击有 88% 获得成功，有 95% 未被目标机构检测到。只有 5% 的察觉了攻击，只有 22 个网站对攻击进行了反抗。

值得注意的是，这些网站属于美国国防部，而不是商业网站，商业网站的安全级别低于美国国防部的网站。

美国国家计算机安全机构引用美国联邦调查局数据，在调查的计算机犯罪中，有 80% 以上是未被授权访问互联网进行的。

这些攻击造成的损失是难以估量的，Ernst&Young 1995 年的调查显示，一个纽约的会计公司，由于公司外计算机用户的恶意操作，三分之一的交易连接在互联网上，两年内财政损失超过 100 000 美元。互联网上多于 2% 的公司声称损失了一百万美元。

在计算机安全行业对这一问题的无知简直是令人吃惊的。理解其中的风险需要很多的知识，现实生活中也找不到相似的例子，例如，没有人会担忧一个夜贼能通过在信箱里投放一些神秘的消息从而骗开他们的前门。当有一个好的"黑客"故事可做报道时，出版社都快疯了，但是一般人的警觉水平确实出奇地低。例如，以准确报道 IT 主题而自诩的《星期日时报》最近发表一篇文章声称，大多数商家并不太担忧互联网的安全问题。文章进一步解释说加密对于安全来说已足够了。文章的焦点完全集中在通信的隐私上，而忽略了来自于互联网攻击的可能性。

尽管对安全问题有所恐惧，但还是有许多组织把进入互联网作为它们战略计划的一个重要组成部分，将来不会由于对安全的忧虑而阻止许多组织去发掘利用互联网所提供的潜在商机。最终，公司将不得不找出办法来管理安全问题。这使得互联网安全市场的成长直接与互联网的成长绑在一起。受互联网和内部网发展的带动，1995 年到 2000 年，互联网防火墙市场的年混合增长率计划达到174%。驱动这种增长的最主要的动力来自WWW服务器在互联网和内部网上的快速而广泛的配置。Web服务器软件的单位出货量预计将从1995年的12 700份增加到2 000年的超过五百万份。尽管IT业一向以高速成长而自豪，这样的增长水平还是前所未有的。

很难从文献给出的全球防火墙市场的统计数字中区分出欧洲或英国所占比例。1996年欧洲和英国防火墙市场的活跃程度大概和1995年的美国差不多。1995年，计算机安全协会对政府机构和财富500强公司所做的一份调查显示，大约有78%的被调查者使用互联网，而与此同时，39%却没有防火墙。与此相似的是，在1996年2月的美国国家计算机安全局防火墙与互联网安全专题会议上，40%的听众没有使用防火墙。假设财富500强中使用互联网的公司中约40%将不得不安装防火墙，而且互联网将持续每年翻番增长的话，因此，人们对安全检查的业务将会快速发展感到不足为奇了。商家们发现现在他们缺乏必要的内部技术和知识来评估目前所处的状态或潜在的风险，对于它们所需要的安全级别也在不断地探索中。

第4课 数字电视与平板电视

自从菲罗·特·法斯沃茨1927年在其印第安纳的车库里组装出第一台电视机以来，把电子图像带进家庭的基本工艺技术原理一直没有改变。电视机的工作方式只发生了两个重大的变化：一是，1954年引入了彩色；二是，70年代由电子管改为晶体管。现在即将发生一个深刻的变革，这就是数字电视。数字电视利用不同方式进行信号传输，将会大大改变未来电视机的画面及工作方式。

这种数字电视机是介于电子计算机终端设备与现用电视机之间的一种混合品种。在欧洲已上市。并计划于今年秋季引入美国。虽然它产生的差异也许不是惊人的，但随着其质量的改进将会使现场直播的变焦效果、立体声以及定格景观等成为平常的事。数字电视有希望为电视观众提供比目前市场出售的电视更清晰更稳定的画面。

自从50年代以来，几乎所有电子产品的体积都已经逐步变小。现在，计算器可以放进支票簿内，比砖块还小的立体声扬声器能产生出巨大的音响效果，唱片工业能够生产高密度的唱片。在整个变革过程中，人们心爱的电视机却依然很庞大，这主要是由于缩小电视机的主要部件的显像管的体积比较困难，而且也不经济。但是，最近美国一家小型半导体公司在技术上的突破，可能会加快大尺寸平板电视、计算机和其他影视屏幕的研制步伐，这是电子厂商多年来一直追求的目标。

MRS技术股份有限公司研制出了一种平板印刷系统，专门用于大量制造平板有源矩阵液晶显示器。称为4500型平板印刷机能够生产厚度为1英寸的18英寸彩色液晶显示屏。它们的重量只有几英磅，可以像油画一样挂在墙壁上。MRS公司声称，这是同类加工过程中经济实惠上首屈一指的。并且断言，由于有了它，普通尺寸的有源矩阵显示屏可在最近将来在市场上出售。MRS公司销售副总经理威廉·施奈德解释说："变化不会在一夜之间发生。"但是，你可以指望在大约一年的时间内开始见到它们，而且，我预计它们将在10年内：占领市场。为了实现这一目标，许多人已经花费了大量的钱财。

12.2 泛读

第1课 数据总线技术的应用

近年来，我国在大吨位起重机上已开始应用数据总线技术，该技术是计算机技术、网络通信技术、控制技术和转换技术的综合与集成。使用数据总线技术可以将发动机、变速箱、车桥转向和 ABS 等系统进行总线数据传输，也可以将力矩限制器系统、单缸伸缩系统、上车发动机系统和液压系统及各传动部件之间依靠总线进行数据传输和管理，借助检测装置和显示装置可以对整个行驶和作业过程进行监控，实时显示各种状态和信息。

数据总线的应用大大简化了电气线路连接，提高了数据传输效率和精度，同时具有极高的拓展功能。

第2课 多媒体技术

你知道有很好的理由在家里拥有一台具有事务处理能力的 PC 机，它帮助你完成繁重的工作任务，否则这些任务将迫使你留在办公室里开夜车。但是，当你不工作时，你在这些强大的家用 PC 机上能干些什么呢？这正好引入多媒体。在今天的家用 PC 机上增加立体声、CDROM 光盘机和 Windows 操作系统相对而言是便宜的。你最终得到的收获远比一台仅能说话、能播放光盘和能显示美丽图像的计算机更具有革命性。你的多媒体 PC 机（为简单起见，称之为 MPC）成了完成以下各项活动的关键：它是一本通过图像和话音将思想带入实际生活的书籍或百科全书；发现最好的娱乐质量和趣味相媲美的游戏；发现能发挥你音乐、动画和视频图形方面的个人创造力的软件。

多媒体是一种计算机技术，其应用包括声音、图像、全景录像、图形等各种数据的集成处理。目前，许多传统的计算机应用领域如顾客服务、办公自动化及计算机辅助教学等都在进行多媒体应用开发。在多媒体环境中，我们可以同时得到图形和文本，也可以增加图片、动画、高质量的音响和全景录像，这些技术使得计算机的能力更强并且更容易使用。

关于 MPC 机的要求在 Microsoft 公司的《多媒体 PC 机规范第 10 版》一书中有详细的描述。下面是规范中的两个重要术语。

全动图像：全动图像是数字记录的视频图像，以 30 帧的电视广播标准或者以非常接近于 30 帧的速度重现图像，因而这些视频图像看上去很自然，没有跳跃感。

MIDI：MIDI 是乐器数字接口的缩写，它是由音乐合成器制造商开发的标准规范。一个键盘能控制几个乐器的概念已发展成一种方法，客观上讲，它能把乐器、磁带录音机、录像机、混响器、甚至舞台灯光都置于单台计算机的控制之下。

参 考 文 献

［1］ 沈宏. 自动控制专业英语. 北京：电子工业出版社，2003.
［2］ 严俊仁. 机电专业英语翻译技巧. 北京：国防工业出版社，2000.
［3］ 卜艳萍. 计算机专业英语. 北京：电子工业出版社，2002.
［4］ 孙建中，周龙. 计算机专业英语. 北京：中国水利水电出版社，2001.
［5］ 司爱侠，张强华. 计算机英语教程. 北京：电子工业出版社，2002.
［6］ 孙萍. 电子技术专业英语. 北京：机械工业出版社，2001.
［7］ 杨春生，陆荣明，袁琦睦. 机电专业英语. 北京：电子工业出版社，2002.
［8］ 陆国强. 现代英语词汇学. 上海：上海外语教育出版社，1983.
［9］ 胡庚申. 文献阅读与翻译. 北京：高等教育出版社，2000.
［10］ 胡庚申. 英语论文写作与发表. 北京：高等教育出版社，2000.
［11］ 贾杰，金郁. 电子技术专业英语. 成都：电子科技大学出版社，1999.
［12］ 王贵堂，陈纬. 自动化、自动控制专业英语文选. 北京：机械工业出版社，1989.